E. S. S Rouse

The Bugle Blast; or, Spirit of the Conflict

Comprising Naval and Military Exploits, Dashing Raids, Heroic Deeds....

E. S. S Rouse

The Bugle Blast; or, Spirit of the Conflict
Comprising Naval and Military Exploits, Dashing Raids, Heroic Deeds....

ISBN/EAN: 9783337113179

Printed in Europe, USA, Canada, Australia, Japan

Cover: Foto ©ninafisch / pixelio.de

More available books at **www.hansebooks.com**

THE BUGLE BLAST;

OR,

SPIRIT OF THE CONFLICT.

COMPRISING

NAVAL AND MILITARY EXPLOITS, DASHING RAIDS, HEROIC DEEDS, THRILLING INCIDENTS, SKETCHES, ANECDOTES, ETC., ETC.

When Northerner with Southron meets,
    Except the Southron fly,
I tell you then is bloody strife,
    For one or both must die.

E. S. S. ROUSE.

PHILADELPHIA:
JAMES CHALLEN & SON.
1864.

CONTENTS.

THE BUGLE BLAST;

OR,

SPIRIT OF THE CONFLICT.

COMPRISING

Naval and Military Exploits,

DASHING RAIDS, HEROIC DEEDS,
DESPERATE CONFLICTS, CAPTURES AND ESCAPES
SKETCHES, POEMS, INCIDENTS,
ANECDOTES, &c.

(9)

PREFACE.

When flashing eyes and clashing arms
In direful fury meet,—
I tell you, then, 'tis life or death,
Or victory, or defeat!

While the moderate dimensions of this work, and
consequent cheapness, place it within the reach of all,
it is hoped that its contents will be found adapted to
the tastes, and habits of reading, of that numerous class
who have neither time nor inclination to peruse a
prolix, consecutive history of the war: and that it will
also be found to contain much interesting matter, not
included in any hitherto published history; thus rendering it a conservatory of valuable materials, for his use,
who shall, in the future, aspire to the high honor of
giving to the world *the* history of the greatest of all
modern wars.

Believing it too early to write the history of the war,
while it is yet in progress, and while many facts,
destined to impart new phases to many of the acts and
motives of prominent actors, are yet perdue, in the
inaccessible portfolios of officers and others, and may,
when disclosed, require essential modifications of *prema-
ture history*, it was deemed best to make the present
offering but a conservatory of materials—a depository
of known facts, of intense interest, and worthy of pre-
servation.

Impartial history requires *abiding the time* and waiting for the facts, lest men and their motives should

(11)

frequently be misjudged, their conduct misunderstood, and praise or censure improperly bestowed.

Like all works of historical character, this has been, to a considerable extent, derived from the writings of others, and consequently, has but small claim to originality—if, indeed, such a condition of mental action as exclusive originality of thought be recognized, when it is perfectly logical, that to minds exactly similarly constituted, and under precisely similar circumstances, identical thoughts *may* be suggested, or, to put the case stronger—*should* be suggested; and, consequently, all our thoughts may have been thought ten thousand times before.

In conclusion, it is incumbent on the compiler to state, that aside from personal observation and private correspondence, he is chiefly indebted for the facts of this work to Southern debates, official reports, and the army correspondence of the loyal press: and in no instance has any published history of the war been consulted. When, on comparison of accounts, the facts of one have been found correctly stated, in proper terms, both the facts and the language, in some instances, have been adopted. Under other circumstances, modifications, more or less extensive, have prevailed. The poems introduced are, unless otherwise credited, what the world calls original, at least in composition.

As the materials for a work of this kind are by no means exhausted, and will continue to accumulate as long as the war shall last, it is quite probable that a second volume may follow should this meet an encouraging reception. Awaiting the decision of an intelligent reading public, the present volume is hopefully submitted by the

COMPILER.

PROLOGOMENA.

"The tragedy has now been played, which was to overthrow the Government of Washington, and Hancock, and Adams, and Jefferson: and let those who have sought to aid a crusade so causeless and infernal, look upon it and receive instruction. For such unalloyed villany and baseness, I assert that the records of depravity and infamy, from the fall of man to the present moment, may be ransacked in vain, and those who remain among us and merely take side politically with a wholesale murder, that they are too cowardly to help on, with arms in their hands, * * * will certainly occupy an important niche in the world's pillory hereafter. * * * * * * *

"The loyal mind is for an out and out, up and down, horizontal and diagonal overthrow of the rebellion, without any condition or compromise, of any name or kind, to the ninth part of a hair; and while it does not want to see the Government go out of its way to look after incidents, it will rejoice to see the alleged cause of the rebellion fall with it; that wicked men and devils, hereafter, may not be tempted to repeat, in the next century, the experiments of this."

Hon. D. S. DICKINSON.

B   (13)

> O for a tongue to curse the knave,
>   Whose treason, like a deadly blight,
> Comes o'er the councils of the brave,
>   And blasts them in their hour of might!
> May life's unblessed cup for him,
> Be drugged with treacheries to the brim.—MOORE.

When at length the rash and wicked attempt was made, had a man of Jacksonian stamp been at the helm of State, the rebellion would have been suppressed as was that of Calhoun in 1832, the particulars of which event must give place to the following poem, by F. D. H. Janvier, as more appropriate to this work.

THE STIGMA.

It is related that some thirty-two years ago, John C. Calhoun, a Senator of the United States from the State of South Carolina, and at that time employed in perfecting the great nullification scheme of which he was the author, was, one night at a late hour, seated in his room alone, and engaged in writing, when falling asleep, he had a dream, the incidents of which are here woven into verse.

> Between the acting of a dreadful thing
> And the first motion, all the interim is
> Like a phantasma, or a hideous dream.—SHAKSPEARE.

In a chamber grand and gloomy, in the shadow of the night,
Two wax tapers flaming faintly, burned with a sepulchral light—
On an oval oaken table, from their silver stands they shone,
Where, about them, in disorder, books and manuscripts were
        strewn;
Where, before them, sat a Statesman, silent, thoughtful and alone!

Suddenly a stranger entered,—entered with a serious air,
And with steady step advancing, near the table drew a chair!

Folded in an ample mantle, carefully concealed from sight,
There he sat, and his companion watched him through the wavering light,
Wondering at his bold intrusion, unannounced, and in the night!

Wondering at his staid demeanor, wondering that no word he
spoke,
Wondering that he veiled his visage in the volume of his cloak—
'Till as though unwilling longer, satisfaction to postpone,
"Senator from Carolina," said he in a solemn tone,
"What are you engaged in writing, here at midnight and alone?"

Then the Statesman answered promptly, "'Tis a plan which consummates,
When complete, the dissolution of the Union of the States."
Whereupon rejoined the stranger, in an accent of command,
"Senator from Carolina, let me look at your right hand."
And the Statesman had no power that calm dictate to withstand.

Slowly, then, uprose the stranger, and the startled Statesman saw
From the fallen cloak emerging, one from whom he shrunk with
awe!
Stern and stately stood before him, Freedom's first and favorite
son—
He whose patriotic valor universal homage won—
He who gave the world the Union—the immortal Washington!

And he thrilled with strange emotion, in the patriot's steadfast
gaze,
As he held the hand he proffered, held it near the taper's blaze—
As he thoughtfully proceeded—"Then you would with this right
hand,
Senator from Carolina, desolate your native land;
You would sign a declaration this fair Union to disband!"

And the Senator responded: "Yes, should chance such service
claim,
To an Act of Dissolution I would freely sign my name."
But the words were scarcely spoken, when amazed he saw expand
Dim at first, then deeper, darker, an unsightly blackened brand,
Like a loathsome, leprous plague-spot, on the back of his right
hand.

"What is that?" he cried with horror, as the dreadful stigma
    spread,
And the patriot's grasp relaxing, undisturbed he gravely said:
"That black blotch your hand o'erspreading is the mark by which
    they know
One who honored by his country, basely sought its overthrow—
That detested traitor, Arnold, in the dismal world below!"

Pausing then he from his mantle drew an object toward the light,
Placed it on the oaken table, in the shuddering statesman's sight,
Placed it on the very writing which that traitorous hand had done:
Still, and stark, and grim, and ghastly, 'twas a human skeleton!
There it lay, and then he added, calmly, as he had begun:

"Here behold the sacred relic of a man who long ago
Died at Charleston, on a gibbet, murdered by a ruthless foe—
Isaac Hayne, who fell a martyr, laying down his life with joy,
To confirm this noble Union, you so wantonly employ
Powers for virtuous ends intended, treacherously to destroy.

"When you sign a solemn compact, this blessed bond to disunite,
Lying here upon your table, you should have his bones in sight.
He was born in Carolina, so were you, but all in vain;
Will you look for treason's stigma, will you seek the slightest stain
On the hand of that pure patriot, the right hand of Isaac Hayne?"

Saying this, the stranger vanished, but the skeleton remained,
And the black and blasting stigma, still that traitorous hand re-
    tained!
Sinking in their silver sockets, fainter still the tapers gleamed;
Suddenly, athwart the chamber, morning's rosy radiance streamed,
And the Statesman, wan and weary, wondering woke—for he had
    dreamed!

He had dreamed—but pause and ponder, you who would the
    Union rend.—
Ponder at the bare beginning, on the foul and fatal end.
Ponder on dark desolation, sweeping through this cherished land,—
Heavy hearts, forsaken firesides, waste and woe with war's de-
    mand.—
Ponder on the Traitor's Stigma—pause and look at your right
    hand!

Gen. Jackson, as President of the United States, informed Calhoun that if he persisted in his treason. that "by the Eternal, he would hang him high as Haman:" and subsequenty regretted that he had not done it. It might have deterred Jeff. Davis & Co.

How striking the contrast between the loyal firmness of Jackson, in thus suppressing incipient rebellion, and the treacherous imbecility of Buchanan, which gave to treason its greatest encouragement.

On receipt of the news of Major Anderson's removal from Fort Moultrie to Fort Sumter, "the Cabinet was assembled directly, when Mr. Buchanan, explaining the embarrassment of the Secretary of War, remarked that "the act of Major Anderson would occasion exasperation in the South; he had told Mr. Floyd that as the government was strong, forbearance toward erring brethren might win them back to their allegiance, and that that officer might be ordered back!" After an ominous silence the President inquired how the suggestion struck his Cabinet. Mr. Stanton. then Attorney-General, answered; "That course, Mr. President, ought certainly to be regarded as most liberal toward 'erring brethren;' but while one member of your Cabinet has fraudulent acceptances for millions of dollars afloat, and while the confidential clerk of another—himself in Carolina teaching rebellion—has just stolen $900,000 from the Indian Trust Fund, the experiment of ordering Major Anderson back to Fort Moultrie would be dangerous. But if you intend to try it, before it is done, I beg that you will accept my resignation."

"And mine," added the Secretary of State, Mr. Black.

"And mine, also," said the Postmaster General, Mr. Holt.

"And mine, too," followed the Secretary of the Treasury, Gen. Dix.

This of course opened the bleared eyes of the President, and the meeting resulted in the acceptance of Mr. Floyd's resignation."—THURLOW WEED.

Jefferson Davis, in a speech made in Boston, a few years ago, said "there is none so infamous as he who should raise his hand against the Union." Albert Pike, the renegade Massachusetts school teacher, who led a brigade of savages at the battle of Pea Ridge, had some time previously thus hymned the unutterable wickedness of Disunion, and the remorseless doom of traitors:—

> Good God! what a title—what name
>   Will history give to your crime!
> In the deep abyss of dishonor and shame,
>   You will writhe till the last hour of time,
> As braggarts who forged their own chains,
>   Pulled down what their brave fathers built,
> And tainted the blood in their children's young veins,
>   With the poison of slavery and guilt:
> And Freedom's bright heart be hereafter tenfold,
> For your folly and fall, more dishonored and cold.

Alexander H. Stephens, the Vice President of the bogus Confederacy, in a speech in Milledgeville, December, 1860, paid the following eloquent tribute to the Government he subsequently sought to overthrow:—

"That the Government of our fathers, with all its defects, comes nearer the objects of all good governments than any other on the face of the earth, is my settled conviction.   *   *   *   *   *   *

"Where will you go, following the sun in its circuit

round our globe, to find a government that better pro-
tects the liberties of the people, and secures to them the
blessings we enjoy? I think that one of the evils that
beset us is a surfeit of liberty; an exuberance of the
priceless blessings for which we are ungrateful."

*   *   *   *   *   *   *   *   *   *

"What right has the North assailed? What interest
of the South has been invaded? What justice has been
denied? and what claim founded in justice and right
has been withheld? Can either of you to-day name one
governmental act of wrong, deliberately and purposely
done by the Government of Washington, of which the
South has a right to complain? I challenge the
answer.   *   *   *   *   *   *

"Now for you to attempt to overthrow such a Government as this, under which we have lived more than
three-quarters of a century, in which we have gained
our wealth, our standing as a nation, our domestic
safety, while the elements of peril are around us, with
peace and tranquility, accompanied with unbounded
prosperity, and no rights assailed—is the height of
madness, folly and wickedness to which I can neither
lend my sanction nor my vote."

It would be well, at times, for those who are seeking
to find, and eager to proclaim excuses for the Southern
rebellion, to ponder these truthful sayings. Yet alas
for human frailty! this same Alexander II. Stephens,
sinning against light and knowledge, accepted the Vice
Presidency of the Rebel Confederacy; thus, lending his
sanction to that madness, folly and wickedness, against
which he had so vehemently protested.

The Rebels hastened to open fire on Sumter, fearing
the fort would be evacuated, and the opportunity to

"strike a blow," and precipitate Virginia and the other border States, lost. Such was the commencement of the war, and from that moment there was no possibility of making peace with the Rebels, save by acknowledging their independence.

As was concisely stated, by Daniel S. Dickinson, in one of his speeches, "South Carolina began to scrape lint before the Presidential votes were counted;" and yet the Federal Government stands accused by secessionists with inaugurating the war.

The supremacy in the Government, which they had enjoyed so long, and had so ruthlessly perverted, was about to decline. They had seen the handwriting upon the wall, and could interpret it without the aid of a political Daniel. They knew that unless they could divide and conquer the free North, or frighten her from her propriety, as they had so often done, and extort from her some suicidal concessions, their power in the Union was about to depart forever. They therefore tried the old disunion dodge once more, with great ferocity, and it proved for once of no avail. The old boneless-back compromisers with iniquity were many of them gone, and truer men to liberty and right were in their places. They raved and threatened as madly as ever, and, as many supposed, expecting somebody to hold them as formerly. But nobody held them, and they went too far: they had crossed the Rubicon. Their friends of the border States proposed various compromises, but they were all pseudo, and faithless to right. They were altogether unequal. They were but a new series of exactions in behalf of the South, demanding to be met by impossible and absurd concessions on the part of the North. Some of them demanded the right of transit and sojourn, with their slaves, in States whose constitutions, aye, whose laws and public sentiment would not tolerate the same in their own citizens for a moment; a demand which, if granted, would enable Senator Toombs to realize his hope, sooner than he expected, of living to see the day when he should call over his roll of slaves at the foot of Bunker Hill Monument.

The "Crittenden Resolutions" were then offered under the guise of a mild and pleasant panacea, like those sugar-coated pills that children are said to cry for, and by those Union-savers, whose motto is "Union for the sake of the Union," regardless of principle, the free North was denounced as contumacious, and responsible for the rupture for not surrendering principle, honor, manhood, and right, and taking it at once, and asking for more of the same sort!

But what were they? An insult to Northern principle and sentiment. Compromise, forsooth! demanding of the free North the unholy concession to the South of the right to the extension of slavery into and over all the vast Governmental domain now owned, or ever to be acquired, either by purchase, fraud or plunder; and to guarantee its protection and defence there, virtually, for all coming time! And what was the quid pro quo that she was to receive for this humiliation?—what concession was the South to make in return?—for that is no compromise in which there is not something yielded on both sides. Hear it! O, ye of the North! Hear it! O, ye of the East! Hear it! O, ye of the West! the South was to agree to abide in connection with you during your good behavior and her good pleasure, and defer, for the present, ruining herself and tearing the Union into infinitesimal fragments! Astonishing condescension!

O, East! O, West! O, North! Why were ye such stubborn asses as not to receive, at once, the proffered bit, and, crouching low, suffer your Southern would-be masters, booted and spurred, to mount your super-serviceable backs and ride you to the devil?

＊　　＊　　＊　　＊　　＊　　＊　　＊　　＊

But, *cui bono?* South Carolina had already plunged into the turbid cesspool of secession, and others of King Cotton's domain had followed; their drivers (not leaders) boldly avowing that were a *carte blanche* given them to write their own terms of adhesion to the Union, they would decline. They were but executing a long contemplated plan. As long as they were in power they could afford to stay in the Union, but no longer; out of power, out of the Union. Their practical motto—

"Better to reign in hell, than serve in heaven!"

Their policy—rule *or* ruin; their practice—rule *and* ruin!

That they had long premeditated a disruption of the Union, is a matter of undeniable history; though that purpose is quite generally supposed by people of the free States, to have originated in recent events. This erroneous supposition has arisen from a non-observance of the state of public sentiment at the South, especially that of South Carolina, as betrayed for several years, through their speeches and public prints, which, however, it must be admitted, have had but limited circulation among ordinary readers in the free States.

Thirteen years ago, at least, without reference to any earlier period, hostility to the Federal Government, as expressed by the leaders of public opinion in South Carolina, was as vehement as it was during the year immediately preceding the late rebellion, called by them secession. It was well known, and by many of them had been openly avowed, that they had been engaged for years in treasonable designs, founded, as many believed, with some show of reason, on an abstract enmity to the Union.

The *Charleston Courier's* report of a debate in the Legislature of South Carolina, in 1850, on a proposition to convene a "Southern Congress," ostensibly for devising measures for the defence of the South, will give the reader an insight into the spirit which prevailed in that body:

"Mr. W. S. Lyles said he would not recapitulate the series of wrongs inflicted upon us; [for the very good reason there were none,] the only question he would consider was the *remedy*. The remedy is the union of the South, and *the formation of a Southern Confederacy*. The friends of the Southern movement in the other States look to the action of South Carolina, and he would make the issue in a reasonable time, and the only way to do so is by *secession*. There would be no concert among the Southern States *until a blow is struck*.

"Mr. Sullivan proceeded to discuss the sovereignty of the States and the right of secession, and denied the right or power of the General Government to coerce the State in the case of secession. He thought there never would be a union of the South until this State (South Carolina) strikes the blow and makes the issue.

"Mr. W. F. Richardson would not recapitulate the evils which had been perpetrated upon the South. (Still harping upon my daughter.) Great as they have been, they are comparatively unimportant, when compared with the evils to which they would inevitably lead. We must not consider what we have *borne*, but what we must bear *hereafter*. There is no remedy for these evils in the Government; we have no alternative left us, then, but to *come out of the Government.*

"Mr. PRESTON said he was opposed to calling a convention, because he thought it would impede the action of *this State* (South Carolina) on the questions now before the country. *He thought it would impede our progress toward disunion.* All his objections to a convention of the people applied only to the proposition to call it *now*. He thought conventions dangerous things, except when the necessities of the country absolutely demand them. He said he had adopted the course he had taken on these weighty matters simply and entirely *with the view of hastening the dissolution of this Union.*"

"Mr. KEITT said he would sustain the bill for electing delegates to a Southern Congress, because he thought *it would bring about a more speedy dissolution of this Union.*"

The following extracts from the debates had on the passage of the secession ordinance, in the late South Carolina convention, sufficiently prove our assertion:

Mr. PARKER. "Mr. President: it appears to me, with great deference to the opinions that have been expressed, that the public mind is fully made up to the great occasion that now awaits us. *It is no spasmodic effort that has come suddenly upon us, but it has been gradually culminating for a long series of years, until at last it has come to that point when we may say the matter is entirely right.*"

Mr. INGLIS. "Mr. President: If there is any gentlemen present who wishes to debate this matter, of course this body will hear him; but as to delay for the purpose of discussion, I, for one, am opposed to it. As my friend (Mr. Parker) has said, most of us have had this matter under consideration *for the last twenty years ;* and I presume we have, by this time, arrived at a decision-upon the subject."

Mr. KEITT. "Sir, we are performing a great act, which involves not only the stirring present, but embraces the whole great future of ages to come. *I have been engaged in this movement ever since I entered political life.* I am content with what has been done to-day, and content with what will take place to-morrow. We have carried the body of this Union to its last resting place, and now we will drop the flag over its grave. After that is done, I am ready to adjourn, and leave the remaining ceremonies for to-morrow."

Mr. RHETT. "*The secession of South Carolina is not the event of a day. It is not anything produced by Mr. Lincoln's election, or by non-execution of the Fugitive Slave Law. It has been a matter which has been gathering head for thirty years.* * * * Now, in regard to the Fugitive Slave Law, *I myself doubt its constitutionality,* and I doubted it on the floor of the Senate, when I was a member of that body. The *States,* acting in their sovereign capacity, should be responsible for the rendition of fugitive slaves. That was our best security."

Thus, it will be seen that it was in furtherance of this long cherished scheme of South Carolina, that her secession convention was held in December, 1860; and in accordance with the conviction that *a blow must be*

c

struck before there would be any concert of action among the Southern States, that South Carolina, after trembling awhile on the brink of the awful secession gulf, in a vain effort to induce Georgia to take the lead, by her treasonable ordinance of the 20th December, plunged headlong, without her leaders being able to agree among themselves on any justifiable pretext or cause, into irretrievable ruin! And thus the blow was struck! The die was cast! The fatal step was taken! The Rubicon was crossed!

SKETCH BOOK OF THE WAR.

STORY I.

OF THE STAR OF THE WEST.

An impression having been quite extensively made that the first Rebel outrage upon our national flag was the reduction of Fort Sumter, and political stump orators, impelled by a zeal not according to knowledge, having frequently conduced to the rendering of that impression more indelible, by heedlessly ignoring the precedent historic fact of the outrage upon the steamer "Star of the West," a correction of that error seems called for.

The story of the "Star of the West," though perhaps of less thrilling interest than that of Fort Sumter, yet is too intimately connected with it to be excluded from this work, and its priority, as a matter of history, entitles it to precedence.

Major Anderson, while in the faithful discharge of his duties, as commandant of the Charleston forts, not being privy to the truckling compliances, pledges, and assurances made by the President, in complaisance to avowed treason-plotters, and believing Fort Moultrie untenable, in the event of the Rebels seizing Fort Sumter, of which there were sufficient indications of their intention, either found authority in the last orders he

(27)

had received from the War Department, for shifting his little force, of about seventy men, from Moultrie to Sumter, or assumed the responsibility of so doing. Under the circumstances, his course would have been justifiable, in absence of such orders. Accordingly, on the night of the 26th of December, 1860, having spiked the guns, burnt the gun-carriages, and destroyed the buildings, he abandoned the fort, and transferred the garrison and stores over to Fort Sumter, which was a much stronger Fort, commanding the harbor, and, to a great extent, Fort Moultrie itself.

The people of Charleston were thereupon thrown into great excitement, and Governor Pickens sent one of his aids to ascertain by what authority the commandant had acted, and to desire his return to Fort Moultrie.

Major Anderson replied that he had acted on his own responsibility, and declined to return. Castle Pinckney and Sullivan's Island, as also Fort Moultrie, were seized on the 27th by order of Governor Pickens. The revenue cutter William Aiken was also surrendered by her commander to the South Carolina authorities. Those authorities were very indignant at Major Anderson's change of position, and Mr. Buchanan censured him for it, while General Scott approved his action by letter, proffering to stand by him to the last; and the House of Representatives, on the 7th of January, 1861, passed a resolution approving "the bold and patriotic act of Major Anderson in withdrawing from Fort Moultrie to Fort Sumter."

It having been decided, by a majority of one, in Cabinet Council at Washington, on the evening of the 29th of December, not to withdraw Major Anderson's force from Fort Sumter, it became necessary to reinforce it; accordingly, at a Cabinet session, held on the 2d of January, 1861, that measure was determined on, and in pursuance of that determination, the "Star of the West," an unarmed steamer, was dispatched with a reinforcement of 200 men.

The original design was to send the reinforcement by the Brooklyn, but on reflection, the days of conciliation having not yet passed, the "Star of the West" was substituted for the purpose of avoiding the appearance of a hostile demonstration.

The "Star of the West" left New York at 5 P. M., on the 5th of January, 1861, with four officers and 200 soldiers, with proper equipments, designed to reinforce Sumter, and arrived off Charleston bar at 1½ o'clock A. M. on the 9th, and, finding the buoys removed and lights out, was obliged to proceed with great caution, running slowly, and frequently sounding in quest of the main channel, with lights out to prevent being seen. After 4 o'clock she was hove to, to await daylight.

At daybreak the soldiers were all ordered below to prevent being seen, and none but the ship's crew allowed on deck. As soon as it was light enough to see she crossed the bar and proceeded up the channel to about two miles from Fort Moultrie—Fort Sumter being about the same distance—when a fire was opened on her from a masked battery on Morris Island, less than a mile distant.

She continued on, with the national flag displayed, under fire of the battery for ten minutes, Fort Moultrie also saluting her in the same manner, some of the shot passing over her, and others taking effect, till her position becoming critical from the circumstances that she would have to approach within easy range of Fort

Moultrie before she could bear away for Fort Sumter,
and a supposed armed schooner was approaching from
Fort Moultrie, in tow of a steamer, and the "Star of
the West" being defenceless, her commander, Captain
McGowan, deemed it proper, in order to avoid certain
capture or destruction, to reverse her course, and, if
possible, get to sea. She wore round, and steamed
down the channel, the battery still firing upon her till
the shot fell short. She cautiously proceeded, crossed
the bar at 8:50 A. M., and continued on her return
course to New York, where she arrived on the 12th of
January.

Thus it is manifest, from the foregoing account, that
it was the boom of the Rebel cannon, fired upon the
"Star of the West," instead of the outrage upon Sumter, as the stump orators commonly have it, that was
the death-knell of slavery.

The authorities at Charleston had been apprised of
the sailing of the "Star of the West" for Fort Sumter
by a telegram from Secretary Thompson, at Washington; in fact, there was but very little transpired at
Washington, that could be of any interest to the Rebels,
that they were not immediately apprized of. In truth,
not only Senators and Representatives, but high Government officials, were in complicity with them.

The Government dispatches to Major Anderson had
been intercepted by the rebels, so that he was ignorant
of the approach of reinforcements, and of the character
of the "Star of the West," if not also of the secession
of South Carolina. He only knew that the steamer
which had been attacked carried the United States flag,
and supposed the assault some unauthorized mistake
which would be disapproved and corrected by the proper

authorities. His communication to Governor Pickens explained why he did not open fire on the assailants.

In that letter, he said to the Governor, "Two of your batteries fired, this morning, upon an unarmed vessel bearing the flag of my Government. As I have not been notified that war has been declared by South Carolina against the Government of the United States, I cannot but think that this hostile act was committed without your sanction or authority. Under that hope, and that alone, did I refrain from opening fire upon your batteries."

In reply, the Governor informed him that his letter had been received, and that "certain statements in it very plainly showed that he, (the Major), had not been fully informed, by his Government, of the precise relations which then existed between it and the State of South Carolina; that the political connection formerly existing between them had ceased; that the Government of the *late United States* had been officially notified of that fact," and though it still retained possession of Fort Sumter, he plainly intimated that it had been obtained dishonorably.

STORY II.

TREASON OF GENERAL TWIGGS.

The annexation of Texas had cost the United States, through the Mexican war, a hundred millions of dollars, beside many valuable lives. In addition to all that, the Government undertook to pay the debts of Texas, amounting to some ten millions more. All the indemnity the Government had, for so vast an outlay, was, that the public lands of Texas were ceded to it. Being thus out of debt and in the Union, with an enlarged boundary, acquired by the United States' arms, she caught the secession fever, claiming that by secession she would re-acquire all the domain she had formerly ceded to the United States. General Houston resisted to the last the call for a convention, and yielded only, when it was clear that it would be called without his authority, if he would not concur. The convention met on the first day of February, 1861, and passed a secession ordinance with but little opposition.

General Twiggs, who had been in command of the Texas department for several years, was suspected of disaffection to the Government; and Colonel Waite, who was then at Camp Verde, in Texas, was ordered to relieve General Twiggs of his command, immediately on his arrival at San Antonia. Before his arrival, however, General Twiggs, who it appears had been treating for the purpose with the secessionists as early as the 7th of February, surrendered, on the 18th, all the Government property and troops in his command to Texas, comprising nearly one-fourth of the whole effective military force of the United States, at that time. Thus, by a perfidy that might well astonish the nation, was an army of 3,000 men and 121 officers, composing a regiment of cavalry, thirty-three companies of infantry, and five companies of artillery, stationed in thirteen forts and ten camps, fully provisioned and equipped, together with 35,000 stands of arms, 26 pieces of mounted artillery and 44 pieces unmounted, 1,800 mules, 950 horses, 500 wagons, 500 sets harness, $250,000 in tools, wagon materials, nails, iron and horse-shoes, $7,000 in corn,

$75,000 in commissary stores, $150,000 in clothing, $400,000 in ordnance stores, and $55,000 Government funds, worth in the aggregate from two to three millions of dollars; all turned over to insurgents and Rebels, to be used against the Government (except the men), and all, including the glorious flag of our Union, surrendered without a shot being fired. By the perfidious surrender of that important department, the Government lost and the Rebel cause gained advantages, naval, military and commercial, beyond the power of money to estimate, or of language to express.

The officers and men were not surrendered as prisoners of war, for the very good reason that there was no war: the object being to get them out of the State, that the State might be forced out of the Union, while the Government would be powerless to prevent it. It was, therefore, stipulated by the joint commission of Twiggs* and the rebels, that the officers and men, who were mostly stationed at and around San Antonia, and on the line of the Rio Grande, should be marched to the coast unmolested, with their side arms, and thence shipped to the North; but hundreds of them, on nearing the coast, were captured as prisoners of war, disarmed and discharged on parole. Why Colonel Waite, (who, by order of Government, superseded Twiggs on the 19th, being the next day after the stipulated treason.) carried out that stupendous iniquity on his arrival, instead of countermanding it, when as yet nothing had been given up and no movement made, is another cause for astonishment, not satisfactorily explained. All the opposing force was Ben McCulloch's five or six hundred mounted

---

* Major Vinton, Major Macklin, and Captain Whitely, on the part of Twiggs.

3

ragamuffin rangers—a force not at all adequate to the
enforcement of the treachery of Gen. Twiggs.   The pretence that "they were betrayed into the hands of the
enemy," has but little plausibility, unless it be admitted
that there was a general conspiracy among the officers
for that purpose.

This was a heavier dose of treason than Mr. Buchanan's non-coercion philosophy could ignore, or bear,
without making some sign.   He had hoped to be able
to pass the few remaining days of his official term in
letting things in general fortuitously slide, and things
in particular go with the general drift.   But this was a
case of such flagitious enormity, that something must be
done.   Not merely the horse, but the whole caravan
was stolen.   As it was too late to lock the stable-door,
and the thief, if not *non est inventus*, was probably *non
est come-at-ibus*, the thing remaining to be done was to
give him a bad name.   So, thereupon, on the 1st day
of March, 1861, by orders emanating from the War
Department, "Brigadier-General David E. Twiggs was
dismissed from the army of the United States, for
treachery to the flag of his country."

STORY III.

LIEUTENANT SLEMMER SAVES FORT PICKENS.

On the 12th of January, 1861, Commodore Armstrong. being in command at the Pensacola Navy Yard,
basely surrendered it, without resistance, to the demand
of Major Chase (in behalf of Florida), who also seized

Fort Barrancas, and a large amount of cannon, shells, powder, coal, &c.

The intention of the Rebels was to have seized Fort Pickens also, but Lieutenant Slemmer, who had been in command of Fort McRae, aware of their purpose, adopted the same course that Major Anderson had done at Charleston by abandoning Fort McRae and occupying Fort Pickens, two days previously; much to the chagrin of the Rebels, as it commanded the Navy Yard and Fort McRae also; besides being a stronger work, and mounting 240 guns, while Fort McRae had but 161. Failing in their designs on Fort Pickens, the Rebels immediately seized this latter fort.

Though with a force of but 80 men, Lieutenant Slemmer was now secure from any attack; and might have destroyed the Navy Yard, yet he forbore, and carefully avoided collision, acting strictly on the defensive, in conformity to the orders of an imbecile Executive, whose anxious purpose evidently was, at whatever expense of fidelity and duty, to defer the bursting of the impending storm, till the advent of the in-coming administration.

Commodore Armstrong's excuse for his dereliction, was, that three-fourths of the 60 officers and men in his command were secessionists, and would have revolted, had he attempted resistance to the demand of Major Chase, who had over 400 hundred men. But the Commodore did not put his men to the test. It was more in accordance with his secession proclivities to speak for them. He did so; but who knows how truthfully? It certainly would not have been difficult for him to have influenced them to be true to the flag under which they had enlisted, and which they had sworn to defend. They had no interest in slavery, nor in any other secession object. But that was not his wish.

THE INAUGURATION.

President Lincoln's Inauguration took place on the 4th day of March, 1861, at the Capitol in the city of Washington, according to law and established usage. The day, after an inclement morning, became favorable. The loyal multitude of spectators was immense. The hireling assassins, awed by the military, kept at a respectful distance, or feared to make any treacherous demonstration.

The President elect appeared, and in full view of the vast audience, took the oath of office, and read his inaugural address, which occupied about one hour, and gave very general satisfaction.

Though grave apprehensions for the President's safety had pervaded the minds of his numerous friends, yet the day and the ceremony passed off without any occurrence to darken the one or mar the other.

The President, in conclusion, retired to the White House, and received numerous friends there presented: on which occasion the following lines were presented to him, by the author, with a request that he would read them at his leisure, and hand them to Mrs. Lincoln, to which he assented:—

Awake! arise! thou mighty chief; and gird thine armor on!
Base Treason raves, while Justice sleeps, with sword as yet un-
Resolve, and firmly dare to do,—and execute the laws. |drawn!
And millions wait to back thy hand, in Freedom's injured cause!
Heaven hath no attribute that can with traitors coincide;
And retribution will not sleep for aye, nor long abide :—
Men may not Freedom's fame subvert, in recklessness and pride.

Long life to him—the people's choice, may God his heart incline
In Wisdom's ways of Perfectness, and Truth, and Right divine;
Nor traitor's schemes, nor madmen's deeds, his equal rule impair;
Corruption's miscreants all avaunt, nor e'er his presence dare!
O may prosperity and peace, disperse all wants and pains!
Life, liberty, and joy increase, and fire the poet's strains!
Nor vile Secession hold its head, while Lincoln holds the reins!

STORY IV.

BOMBARDMENT OF FORT SUMTER.

On receipt of the notice from Washington of the
purpose of the Government to provision Sumter—
peaceably if it could, forcibly if it must—General Beauregard telegraphed the purport to Montgomery, and
received in reply from Secretary Walker, on the 10th
of April, an order to demand at once the evacuation of
the fort, and, in case of refusal, to proceed to reduce it.
The demand was not made, however, till two o'clock,
P. M., of the 11th, when time was allowed Major Anderson till six o'clock to answer.   Major Anderson replied
that "his sense of honor and his obligations to his
Government prevented his compliance."

At one o'clock on the morning of the 12th, Major
D

Anderson received another communication from Beauregard, stating that, as he understood the garrison was
short of provisions and would soon have to evacuate, he
wished him to set a day when he would do so. Major
Anderson, on consultation with his officers, replied,
" Provided Fort Sumter or the flag it bore was not
fired on, he would be obliged to evacuate by Monday,
the 15th." But it did not suit the purpose of the Rebels
to wait. They had made great preparations to bombard
the fort; "a blow must be struck to fire the Southern
heart," as Pryor had said; and they were too eager for
the fray, not to prefer force to evacuation. After a few
moments consideration, Beauregard's deputies informed
Major Anderson that the batteries would open their fires
in one hour. Thereupon, they immediately left the fort,
it being then 3:30 A. M., and in one hour, it commenced.

After the deputation had left, the sentinels were
immediately removed from the parapets of the fort, the
posterns closed, the flag drawn up, and the troops
ordered not to leave the bomb-proofs, on any account,
till summoned by the drum.

At 4:30 A. M., one bomb-shell was thrown, bursting
directly over the fort. After a short pause, the firing
became general on the part of the Rebel batteries, doing
the greatest credit to the artillerists. The command did
not return a single shot until the men had their break-
fasts. As the number of men was small, and the garrison so nearly exhausted by the several months siege
they had endured, it was necessary to husband their
strength: the command was therefore divided into three
relief, or equal parties, who were to work the different
batteries by turns, each four hours.

The first relief opened upon the iron batteries at Cumming's Point, at a distance of 1,600 yards; the iron floating battery, distant 1,800 or 2,000 yards, at the end of Sullivan's Island; the enfilading battery on Sullivan's Island, and Fort Moultrie. This was at 7 o'clock A. M., Captain Doubleday firing the first gun; all the points named being opened upon simultaneously. For the first four hours, the firing was kept up with great rapidity; the enthusiasm of the men, indeed, was so great, that the second and third reliefs could not be kept from the guns.

Shells burst with the greatest rapidity, in every portion of the work, hurling the loose brick and stone in all directions, breaking the windows and setting fire to whatever wood-work they burst against. The solid shot firing of the enemy's batteries—particularly Fort Moultrie—was directed at the barbette guns of Sumter, disabling four and tearing away a large portion of the parapet.

The explosion of shells, and the quantity of deadly missiles that were hurled in every direction, constantly, rendered it almost certain death to go out of the lower tier of casements; and also made the working of the barbette, or upper, uncovered guns, which contained all the heaviest metals, and by which alone shells could be thrown, quite impossible. During the first day there was hardly an instant of time that there was a cessation of the whizzing of balls, which were sometimes coming half a dozen at once. Before dinner, several vessels of the fleet, beyond the bar, were seen through the port-holes; they dipped their flags, but it was impracticable to pass the bar; Sumter's flag was dipped in return, while the shells were bursting in every direction.

About noon the cartridges were exhausted, and a party was sent to the magazine to make more out of blankets and shirts, the sleeves of the latter readily answering the purpose. The great misfortune was, nothing for weighing powder.

When it became so dark as to render it impossible to see the effect of their shot, the port-holes were closed for the night; while the Rebels continued to fire all night.

During Friday, seventeen mortars, firing ten-inch shell, and thirty-three heavy guns, mostly columbiads, were engaged in the assault. The iron battery was of immense strength, and most of our shot struck and glanced off. We succeeded in dismounting two of the guns on Cummings' Point battery; but the full effect of our firing could not be ascertained.

During the day the officers' barracks were three times set on fire by the shells, and three times put out, under the most destructive firing.

The firing of the rifled guns from the iron battery on Cummings' Point, became very accurate on Friday afternoon: cutting out large quantities of masonry about the embrasures at every shot, throwing concrete among the cannoniers, slightly wounding some, and stunning others. One piece struck Sergeant Kearnan on the head and knocked him down. On reviving and being asked if he was badly hurt, he replied: "No; I was only knocked down temporarily;" and went to work again.

Meals were served at the guns of the cannoniers, while the guns were being pointed and fired.

For the fourth time, the barracks were set on fire, early on Saturday morning, and attempts were made to put out the fire; but, on account of the rapidity with which hot shot were being thrown into the fort, it was found impossible to check the conflagration.

As many of the garrison as could be spared were set to work to remove the powder from the magazines. This was desperate work, as they had to roll the barrels of powder through the fire. Ninety barrels were thus got out, when the heat became so great as to make it impossible to get out any more.

The doors were then closed and locked, and the fire spread and became general. The wind so directed the smoke as to fill the fort so full that the men could not see each other, and were nearly suffocated with hot air. Soon they were obliged to cover their faces with wet cloths, in order to get along at all, so dense was the smoke and so scorching the heat.

After the barracks were well on fire, the Rebel batteries increased the rapidity of their cannonading upon Fort Sumter. About this time, the shells and ammunition in the upper service magazines exploded, scattering the towers and upper portions of the building in every direction.

The crash of the beams, the roar of the flames, the rapid explosion of the shells, and the shower of fragments of the fort, with the blackness of the smoke, made the scene indescribably terrific and grand.

This continued for several hours. Meanwhile, the main gates were burned down, the chassis of the barbette guns were burned away on the gorge, and the upper portions of the towers had been demolished by shells.

The fire spread to the men's quarters. on the right hand and on the left, and endangered the powder which had been taken out of the magazines. The men went through the fire and covered the barrels with wet cloths; but the danger of the fort's blowing up became so imminent, that they were obliged to throw the barrels out through the embrasures. All but four barrels were thus disposed of, and those four remaining were wrapped in wet blankets. But three cartridges were left, and those were in the guns. While this was being done, all the guns of Moultrie and the batteries were worked with increased vigor.

The flag-staff of Fort Sumter was now shot down, some fifty feet from the truck, being the ninth time it had been struck by shot. The men cried out "The flag is down! it has been shot away!" and in an instant Lieutenant Hall rushed forward and brought the flag away. It was then nailed to the staff and planted upon the ramparts, while batteries in every direction were playing upon them.

Ex-Senator Wigfall now appeared at an embrasure, with a white handkerchief upon the end of a sword, and begged admittance. He asked to see Major Anderson, and was told that he was at the main gate; but he crawled in through the embrasure, paying no attention to what had been told him.

He was met by Captain Foster, Lieutenant Mead and Lieutenant Davis, to whom he said: "I wish to see Major Anderson. I am General Wigfall, and come from General Beauregard;" adding in an excited manner, "Let us stop this firing. You are on fire and your flag is down. Let us quit."

Lieutenant Davis replied: "No, sir, our flag is not down. Step out here and you will see it waving over the ramparts."

"Let us quit this," said Wigfall. "Here's a white flag; will anybody wave it out of the embrasure?"

One of the officers replied: "That is for you to do, if you choose."

Wigfall responded: "If there is no one else to do it, I will," and jumping into the embrasure, waved it toward Moultrie.

The firing still continued from Moultrie and the batteries of Sullivan's Island. In answer to Wigfall's request that one of our men might hold the flag, Corporal Binghurst jumped into the embrasure; but, the shot continuing to strike all around him, after waving the flag a few moments, he jumped down again, saying: "Damn it, they don't respect this flag; they are firing at it."

Wigfall replied: "They fired at me two or three times, and I should think that you might stand it once."

Wigfall then said: "If you will show a white flag from your ramparts, they will cease firing."

Lieutenant Davis replied: "If you request that a flag shall be shown there, while you hold a conference with Major Anderson, and for that purpose only, it may be done."

At this point, the Major came up. Wigfall said: "I am General Wigfall, and come from General Beauregard, who wishes to stop this."

Major Anderson replied: "Well, sir?"

"Major Anderson," said Wigfall, "you have defended your flag nobly, sir. You have done all that it was possible for men to do; and General Beauregard wishes to stop the fight. On what terms, Major Anderson, will you *evacuate* this fort?"

Major Anderson replied: "General Beauregard knows my only terms."

"Do I understand that you will evacuate upon the terms proposed the other day?"

"Yes, sir, and on those conditions only;" was the reply of the Major.

"Then, sir," said Wigfall, "I understand, Major, that the fort is to be ours?"

"On those conditions only, I repeat."

"Very well," said Wigfall, and retired.

Shortly after his departure, the Staff of General Beauregard approached the fort with a white flag, saying that they came from General Beauregard, who had observed that the flag had been down and raised again soon afterward, and had sent over, desiring to know if he could render any assistance, as he had observed that the fort was on fire.

Major Anderson, in replying, requested them to thank General Beauregard, on his behalf, for his offer, but it was too late, as he had just agreed with General Beauregard for an evacuation. The gentlemen were surprised, and asked with whom? Major Anderson, observing that something was wrong, remarked that General Wigfall, who had just left, had represented himself as the aid of General Beauregard, and that he had come to make the proposition. They replied that Wigfall had not been with General Beauregard for two days. Major Anderson then stated that General Wigfall's offer, and its acceptance, had placed him in a peculiar position. They then requested him to put in writing what Wigfall had said to him, and they would lay it before Beauregard.

Before this reached Beauregard, he sent his Adjutant-

The evacuation took place on Sunday afternoon, April 14th, after the burial, with military honors, of private Hough, who had been killed by the bursting of a gun.

It was a painful sight to all, to see the stars and stripes finally hauled down; but we felt that we had done our duty and must submit. The fort was not surrendered, but *evacuated*, almost on our own terms, with colors flying and drums beating, bringing away company and private property, and saluting our flag with fifty guns.

Major Anderson and his brave band shipped on board the Baltic, Captain Fletcher, for New York, where they arrived on the Thursday following. Thus ended the second act in the Great Rebellion Drama.

> O star-spangled banner, the flag of our pride!
> Though tempted by traitors, and basely defied,
> Fling out to the glad winds your red, white and blue,
> For the heart of the North-land is beating for you!

mighty West, ere they were drowned in the shouts of indignant freemen, demanding to be led against the traitors, who, having plotted to divide and destroy the country, had commenced, without provocation, the fratricidal war: the vast North and the populous East reverberated the shout, and the great, united heart pulsated with one intense fire of indignation, demanding retribution.

Party lines were obliterated—party ties hushed—men forgetting that they were Democrats or Republicans, in the newly aroused anxiousness that they were Americans. Seeing their country—their Government—their Capitol threatened and endangered by traitors, all baser passions were subdued, and amor patria ruled supreme.

There could be no use in looking away from the fact. Civil war was upon the country and must be met. The American people must demonstrate that they still had a Government, and that there was a difference between freedom and anarchy.

President Lincoln issued his Proclamation on the fifteenth day of April, setting forth the fact, "that the laws of the United States had been for some time, and then were opposed; and the execution obstructed in the States of South Carolina, Georgia, Alabama, Florida, Mississippi, Louisiana, and Texas, by combinations too powerful to be suppressed, by the ordinary course of judicial proceedings, or by the power vested in the Marshals by law;" and "calling forth the militia of the several States of the Union to the aggregate number of seventy-five thousand, in order to suppress said combinations, and to cause the laws to be duly executed."

The Free States responded enthusiastically to the President's call for men; but the Governors of the border Slave States, generally, treated the requisition with contumacious refusal of compliance.

Promptly respondent to the call,
Instanter move the Free States all.

The border States the call defy,
With rude and insolent reply.

Yet still there is no lack of men,
From hill and valley, glade and glen.

Seventy-five thousand men were called,
And thrice that number are enrolled.

Still the shrill fife and spirit-stirring drum
Proclaim the tramping legions come.

The capitol must never be
Despoiled by the base rebelry.

Forbid it Justice! strike the blow!
And lay the Rebel rascals low!

From Maine to the Lakes, from Pittsburg to St. Louis, from Cleveland to Cincinnati, every where, the starry flag in its proud undulations greeted the glad eyes of patriotic beholders; and the all-absorbing, predominant business was preparation to march beneath its folds.

From prairie, O plowman, speed boldly away!
There's seed to be sown in God's furrows to-day!
Row landward, lone fisher! stout woodman come home!
Let smith leave his anvil, and weaver his loom,
And hamlet and city ring loud with the cry,
"For God and our country we'll fight till we die!"
Invincible banner! the flag of the free!
O, where treads the foot that would falter for thee?
Or the hands to be folded till triumph is won,
And the eagle looks proud, as of old, to the sun?

EDNA DEAN PROCTOR.

SKETCH OF GENERAL LYON.

GENERAL NATHANIEL LYON, of Connecticut, was eleventh in the West Point class of 1841, which numbered fifty-two. He was brevetted for gallantry at the battles of Contreras and Cherubusco. He was wounded in the attack on Belen Gate, city of Mexico.

The following brief sketch of General Lyon is from a description written by a Lieutenant of an Iowa regiment on duty in Missouri in 1861:

"General Lyon is a man of thirty-five or forty years, some five feet eight inches high, and weighs, perhaps, one hundred and forty to fifty pounds. He is wiry in build and tough-looking in appearance. His hair is long and thick, his whiskers bushy and heavy—both are indescribably sandy in hue. His eyes are his most remarkable feature—either blue or grey, perhaps at times both: a sort of stormy expression dwells constantly in them, which is heightened by the wave-like wrinkles around them. * * * His forehead is high, and of even width, giving him, when uncovered, the appearance of great intellectual force, which is aided by the firm outlines of his mouth. He smiles little or none; is a strict disciplinarian; has the full confidence of his men, among whom or at least among the regulars, he is known as 'Daddy.' He is the sort of man that one will stop to take a good look at as he passes. I don't think he has any thing like physical fear. He is all through a soldier, and *will make his mark high* in the military world."

STORY V.

CAPTURE OF CAMP JACKSON, (ST. LOUIS,) BY LYON.

A COUP DE GUERRE.

As a preparatory measure for carrying Missouri out
of the Union, Governor Jackson called out the State
Militia, ostensibly for instruction. A considerable body
of them, composed chiefly of rabid Secessionists, occupied a regular encampment near St. Louis. They did
not hesitate to avow their hostility to the Government,
treated the President's order to disperse with defiant
contempt, and their purpose of seizing the St. Louis
Arsenal was too evident to admit of a doubt.

Governor Jackson had arranged with the Southern
Confederates for a supply of war munitions, and a
steamboat, bearing the secession flag, arrived with a
large amount of cannon, bombs, balls, rifles, muskets,
powder. &c., which were taken to Camp Jackson, as the
Rebel camp was called.

The main avenues of this camp were marked with
the names of Davis and Beauregard; and the occupants
openly wore the dress and badge distinguishing the
army of the Southern Confederacy. The seizure of the
Arsenal was part of the Secession programme. *per se;*
the successful accomplishment of which would probably have resulted in the forcible Secession of the State.
The first move in the seceding States had invariably
been to seize the Government arms and other property.

To prevent this, and for general security against
Secession outrages, and in answer to the President's

E   4

requisition, four regiments of volunteers were organized at St. Louis.

General Harney, who had been in command at St. Louis, having been ordered to Washington, Captain Lyon, of the 2d United States Infantry, succeeded to the command.

From the formidable preparations and threatening attitude of Camp Jackson, Captain Lyon did not esteem it prudent to wait, as had been the practice of others, for the *overt act*. He preferred the initiative.

On the 10th of May, 1861, with the 1st, 2d, 3d, and 4th Regiments of Volunteers, under Colonels Blair, Boernstein, Sigel, and Shuttner, and the 3d and 4th Regiments United States Reserve Corps, under Colonels McNeil and Brown, he marched, in double quick time, up Market street, and on arriving at Camp Jackson, rapidly surrounded it, planting batteries on all the heights overlooking the camp, and posting picket guards, with orders to let no one pass the lines.

Captain Lyon then sent a note to General Frost, commandant of camp Jackson, informing him that his command was regarded as evidently hostile to the United States, and demanding the surrender of the same; intimating, at the same time his ability to enforce the demand, and allowing the general half an hour's time for compliance. Within the time specified, General Frost sent a note to Captain Lyon, announcing his compliance with the demand.

Thereupon, the surrender having been made, the rebel brigade was formed in column, preparatory to marching as prisoners under escort of the Arsenal troops. In the meantime an immense crowd of people had assembled in the vicinity; some from motives of curiosity, others having seized rifles, shot-guns, or whatever weapons they could lay their hands upon, rushed to the assistance of the State troops, as the Secessionists called themselves, but on arriving, found their designs impracticable.

The column marched through the wood to an opening made in the fence adjoining the turnpike; General Frost and his staff at the head of the column on horseback, the United States troops enclosing them by a single file on each side, with colors flying and drums beating, Colonel Blair leading the column.

Having entered upon the road a halt was ordered, when a large crowd of excited citizens drew near and cheered the Secession officers and grossly insulted and abused the guards, especially the German troops, till at length, forbearance ceasing to be a virtue, several sharp reports of fire-arms were heard at the head of the column, and the spectators, who lined the adjacent hill, alarmed for their safety, precitately fled.

Fortunately, no one was hurt, and the soldiers who had fired were placed under arrest. Tranquillity had scarcely been restored when a succession of rifle reports were heard in the rear of the column; and men, *women*, and *children*, strange to say, whose curiosity or disloyalty had surpassed their prudence, were seen running frantically from the scene.

Many, of various ages and different sexes were shot down; the sufferers being, as usual in such cases, mostly innocent persons. Twenty-two were killed and a great number wounded. Of the latter class were several German soldiers: several shots having been returned by the mob, and some, even, were fired at the troops before they commenced firing. One man discharged three barrels of a revolver at Lieutenant Faxon, and was thrust through with a bayonet. The mob had treated them with the most vehement defiance and vituperation; and their efforts to press back the excited crowd, by presenting bayonets, served only to increase their frenzied exasperation.

The prisoners, being about eight hundred in number, (many being absent in the city,) were marched to the Arsenal, after which, they were tendered a release on parole, provided that they would take an oath not to take up arms against the United States Government; this they at first declined to do; but subsequently, with but few exceptions, they complied and were released.

OUR BROTHER.

Call him not " brother," whose unhallowed hand
    Hacks down the roof-tree of our common home !
Call him not " brother," who, with sword and brand,
    Lays waste the heritage of our fatherland !
Call him not " brother," who, 'mid cannon's boom,
Beats down old landmarks, shrouds in endless gloom
    The hapless ones his greed hath barred and banned !
He is a Cain ! Cainlike must be his doom.
The prodigal, repentant, may return !
    Repentant ? Yes ! Recusant, never ! No !
The renegade from freedom all men spurn.
    Who strikes for slavery makes the world his foe :
Who draws the sword, shall by the sword be slain :
And whoso ' raises Cain,' must reap the hurricane."—Anon.

        Though lately drifting on the reef,
        Our gallant ship and faithless chief,
        She now the helm begins to feel,
        There's a new pilot at the wheel.

STORY VI.

DEATH OF COLONEL ELLSWORTH.

On the morning of the 24th of May, 1861, General Scott moved 13,000 troops across the Potomac to Alexandria and Arlington Heights, under the immediate commands of Major-Generals Mansfield and Sandford.

Colonel Ellsworth's regiment of Zouaves constituted a part of the force, and, embarking on steamers at the navy yard, reached the wharf at Alexandria about five o'clock A. M. Though several shots were fired at the boats (by Secessionists) as they came to the wharf, yet the men landed in good order, in double quick time, forming on the street by companies, facing the river.

After detailing Company E, Captain Leveridge, to destroy the railroad track leading to Richmond, Colonel Ellsworth directed the Adjutant to form the regiment, and then, with his aid, Lieutenant Winser, and a file of men, proceeded, in double quick time, up the street for the telegraph office for the purpose of cutting the wires.

Having proceeded for the space of three blocks, Colonel Ellsworth's attention was attracted by a large Secession flag flying from the roof of the Marshall House, kept by J. W. Jackson. He entered the hotel, and inquired of a man there, "Who put that flag up?" The man answered, "I don't know; I'm a boarder here."

Colonel Ellsworth, Lieutenant Winser, the Chaplain of the regiment, Mr. House, a volunteer aid, and the four privates, went up to the roof, and Colonel Ellsworth cut down the obnoxious flag. As the party were returning down the stairs, Francis E. Brownell, a private of Company A, being foremost, they met the man in the hall who had said he was a boarder, but who proved to be the landlord, Jackson, having a double-barrel gun, which he levelled at Brownell. Brownell struck up the gun with his musket, and Jackson at the same instant pulling both triggers of the gun, lodged the contents of both barrels in the body of Colonel Ellsworth, who was descending next to Brownell.

Colonel Ellsworth, who was at the time rolling up the flag, received the fatal charge between the second and third ribs, and immediately fell forward upon the hall floor, and exclaiming "my God," instantly expired.

Brownell instantly levelled his musket at Jackson's head and fired. The ball struck on the bridge of his nose, and, crashing through his skull, killing him on the spot. As he fell forward, Brownell followed the shot by a bayonet thrust through his body, pinning him to the floor. Jackson's wife, hearing the reports of the guns, entered the hall, and, perceiving her husband's dead body, uttered the most piercing cries, and though treated with the greatest sympathy, remained for a long time in a state of the wildest frenzy. The house was in the utmost confusion. The lodgers hurried from their rooms, but were held in control by the zouaves of the Colonel's party, who at once established and maintained order until the arrival of reinforcements.

Their protracted absence having alarmed Adjutant Leaser, he ordered Company A, Captain Coyle, to search for them. The company found their Colonel dead, and their comrades in possession of the hotel. A surgeon was then sent for, but Colonel Ellsworth being already dead, it was a useless measure. The company then made a litter of their muskets and, placing the body of the Colonel on it, returned to the boat, leaving, however, a detachment to guard the hotel and make prisoners of all its occupants.

The following beautiful poem, which appeared anonymously in the newspapers, is deemed worthy of a place in this connection:

Don't shed a tear for him!
  Lay him to rest,
The bright cross of honor
  Ablaze on his breast.
The shouts of a Nation
  Shall cheer him to God:
The hopes of a people
  Spring fresh from his blood.

Don't shed a tear for him!
  Heroes must die,
In gladness, in triumph,
  Like suns from the sky:
Battle-red banners,
  And war-tramp above;
They only break camp up,
  Forward to move.

Don't shed a tear for him!
  Mourn him in blood!
Quick-dropping bullets
  Shall work him most good.
Fight for him, fall with him,
  Die as he died—
Living or dying,
  Our hope and our pride.

Don't shed a tear from him!
  Better to go
Eager for victory,
  Facing the foe.
For one life like this life
  A thousand shall pay,
And the fury it kindles
  Shall carry the day.

STORY VII.

BRILLIANT EXPLOIT OF LIEUTENANT TOMPKINS.

On Saturday morning, June 1, 1861, just at break of day, Lieutenant Tompkins and Second Lieutenant Gordon, with fifty-two men of Company B, United States cavalry, and two men of the New York 5th, and three officers, Adjutant Frank, Quartermaster Fearing, and Assistant Quartermaster Carey, having surprised the picket four miles from Fairfax Court House, dashed into the town, sounded the charge, and galloped through the principal streets, under a heavy fire from the city hall, post office, private houses, fences, streets, and sidewalks, from soldiers, some of whom were mounted; there being from 1,000 to 1,500 in the town—infantry, cavalry and artillery.

Five mounted men were captured in this charge, being seized by the neck and swept on with the troops. At the end of the street they turned, and, holding their prisoners with a firm grasp, charged again the whole length of the street; then, wheeling, charged through the third time, cutting, slashing and firing right and left upon all assailants.

The most of those they shot were in the streets, but wherever they saw a gun flash, in door or window, five or six shots answered it. One man cried "Halt!" "Wait a bit," said Lieutenant Tompkins, and shot him instantly. A squadron of cavalry was drawn up across the street. A charge was sounded, and the line was broken, our men sweeping on. A company of infantry next appeared, drawn up on a cross street. This was also charged and broken. A brass six-pounder now appearing at the end of a street, and the dragoons apparently surrounded, as a company of mounted riflemen was discovered guarding the only other exit from the street, they opened a fence and escaped across the fields to the road leading to Vienna, twenty-two miles distant, and thence home, having their prisoners strapped on behind them.

Lieutenant Tompkins had two horses shot under him in the affair, and Lieutenant Gordon one. Our loss in men was one killed, three wounded, and two taken prisoners. Of the rebels, twenty-seven were killed, including Captain Mar, and many wounded—number not ascertained. Our loss in horses, six.

Of the prisoners captured, Captain John B. Washington, of the Rebel infantry, was prominent in resisting our cavalry, until a trooper rode up, caught him by the hair, lifted him bodily upon the pommel of his saddle, and, thus holding him, charged twice through the town to the utter astonishment of the captain.

Altogether, the sally was a daring and brilliant affair. But successes, as well as reverses, do not always come single. Having got word during the night that the two dragoons, taken prisoners on Saturday, were to be hung the next morning, Company B was immediately summoned from their quarters, and mounting, rode to the scene of their late exploit, ascertained by some means the location of their imprisoned comrades, made a dash into the village, recovered the two men, and brought them back in triumph to the camp at daybreak.

STORY VIII.

GOVERNOR JOHNSON AND THE REBEL CHAPLAINS.

AMONG the secesh clergymen of Nashville sent to "safe quarters" by Governor Johnson, for refusing to take the oath of allegiance to the Union, was the Rev. W. H. Wharton, chaplain of the penitentiary.

Wharton, before our occupation of the city, had made a written report in favor of liberating certain convicts from prison, to join the Rebel army. When summoned before Johnson, he equivocated, and tried to shelter himself under his clerical garb, calling himself "a citizen of Heaven." His claim of a higher citizenship than of earth was rather damaged when the governor, producing his jail-delivery recommendation, sternly said: "Is that your report, sir, and your name? Do you call that the language of 'a citizen of Heaven,' to advise the turning loose of felons from the cells where justice has placed them, that they may join in the work of killing loyal men, and destroying the best Government in the world? I don't believe the Almighty approves of such teaching as that."

> Avaunt! base hypocrite! hug your damning sin,
> And don 'heaven's livery to serve the devil in.'
>
> PLAGIARISM.

Others of the Rebel clergymen, among whom were Rev. Mr. Sehon and Mr. Elliott, being brought before Governor Johnson, the following dialogue ensued:

Gov. JOHNSON. "Well, gentlemen, what is your desire?"

Mr. SEHON. "I speak but for myself. I do not know what the other gentlemen wish. My request is that I may have a few days to consider on the subject of signing this paper. I wish to gather my family together and talk over the subject: for this purpose, I desire about fourteen days."

Gov. JOHNSON. "It seems to me there should be but little hesitation about the matter. All that is required of you is to sign the oath of allegiance. If you are loyal citizens, you can have no reason to refuse to do so. If you are disloyal, and working to obstruct the operations of the Government, it is my duty, as the representative of that Government, to see that you are placed in a position so that the least possible harm shall result from your proceedings. You certainly cannot reasonably refuse to renew your allegiance to the Government that is now protecting you and your families and property."

Mr. ELLIOTT. "As a non-combatant, Governor, I considered that under the stipulations of the surrender of the city, I should be no further annoyed. As a non-combatant, I do not know that I have committed an act, since the Federals occupied the city, that would require me to take the oath required."

Gov. JOHNSON. "I believe, Mr. Elliott, you have two brothers in Ohio."

Mr. ELLIOTT. "Yes, Governor, I have two noble brothers there. They did not agree with me in the course I pursued in regard to Secession. But I have lived in Tennessee so many years, that I have considered the State my home, and am willing to follow her fortunes. Tennessee is a good State."

Gov. JOHNSON. "I know Tennessee is a good State:

and I believe the best way to improve her fortunes is to remove those from her borders who prove disloyal and traitors to her interests, as they are traitors to the interest of that Government which has fostered and protected them. By your inflammatory remarks and conversation, and by your disloyal behavior. in weaning the young under your charge from their allegiance to the Government, you have won a name that will never be placed on the roll of patriots. A visit to the North may be of benefit to you."

CAVALIER SONG.

Merrily. merrily off we go,
　　Slumber all forsaking,
Cheerily dashing on the foe,
　　Ere the day is breaking.

Consternation seize them all—
　　Shrieking, groaning, dying!
Such as neither stand nor fall,
　　Helter-skelter flying!

Swift, again. we face the breeze,
　　Nought of danger fearing—
Moonlight glittering through the trees—
　　O, but it is cheering!

Our bonnie steeds are sure and fast,
　　Eagerly advancing—
Snorting at the bugle's blast,
　　Cheerily, cheerily prancing.

Verily foiled—the rebel foe,
　　Haste away is making;
Merrily, merrily home we go,
　　Ere the day is breaking.

STORY IX.

DESPERATE FIGHT OF CORPORAL HAYES'S PARTY WITH REBEL CAVALRY.

On the 26th of June, 1861, Colonel Wallace, of the 11th Indiana Volunteers, dispatched his mounted pickets, thirteen in all, Corporal Hayes commanding, to Frankford, midway between Cumberland and Romney (West Virginia), to ascertain if there were any Rebel troops there.

They went within a quarter of a mile of the place, and found it full of cavalry. In returning they overtook forty horsemen, and at once charged on them, routing and driving them back more than a mile, killing eight of them and securing seven horses.

Corporal Hayes was severely wounded, with sabre cuts and bullets. Taking him back, they halted about an hour, and were then attacked by the enemy, who were reinforced to about seventy-five men. The attack was so sudden that our soldiers abandoned the horses and crossed to a small island at the mouth of Patterson's creek.

The charge of the Rebels was bold and confident, yet under the fire of our brave pickets, no less than twenty-three of them, two of whom were officers, fell close about and on the island.

> When flashing eyes and clashing arms,
> In direful fury meet—
> I tell you, then, 'tis life or death,
> Or victory or defeat!

The pickets so greatly outnumbered, being unable to

F

continue the desperate conflict. retired from it, scattering, each man for himself, and all arrived safe in camp the same evening, excepting John C. Holdingbrook, who was taken prisoner in the fight, and afterwards brutally murdered.

Three companies went to the ground the next morning and recovered everything belonging to the pickets except a few horses. The enemy had been all night boxing up their dead. The report of the skirmish, says Colonel Wallace, sounds like fiction, but it is not exaggerated. The fight was really one of the most desperate on record, and abounds with instances of wonderful daring and courage.

STORY X.

HOW THE REBEL FLAG WAS TAKEN AT DE SOTO.

Having been informed of the existence of a rebel organization at Potosi, Mo., General Lyon dispatched two companies of soldiers, under command of Captain Cole, to arrest the parties. The soldiers surrounded the town before daybreak, and captured one hundred and fifty Rebels, most of whom took the oath of allegiance and were released. Those who refused to take the oath were taken to St. Louis.

The expedition also captured at Potosi and De Soto, forty horses, one thousand dollars worth of lead, some uniforms, &c., and at the latter place a Confederate flag, which was to have been raised at a Secession love-feast held on that day.

Apprehensive of the safety of their flag, in the presence of the troops, they had secreted it, as they supposed, in a place least likely to be searched. The guard surrounded the house supposed to contain it, and Dr. Franklin and Sergeant Walker entered.

After searching in vain for some time the doctor thought he observed the lady of the house sitting in an uneasy position, and very politely asked her to rise. She at first hesitated to do so, but the doctor persisting, she slowly arose, and lo! the blood-red ensign appeared below the lady's hoops!

The doctor bowing a graceful "beg pardon, madam," stooped, and quietly catching hold of the gaudy color, carefully delivered the lady of a Secession flag thirty feet long by nine feet wide! The doctor bore off his prize in triumph to the camp.

The stars and stripes, being in better favor with the expedition. were soon run up on the pole prepared by the Secessionists for their pitiful imitation, and a guard left to protect it. The Union people were wild with delight for their deliverance, and manifested their gratification by providing breakfast and dinner for the troops, and bestowing bouquets and flags on the officers, and inviting them and their men to stay a month at the expense of the inhabitants. This the nature of the service compelled them to decline, and they returned to St. Louis by six P. M., greeted with shouts for Lyon, Blair, and the flag of our Union.

STORY XI.

MATTHIAS' POINT SKIRMISH. DEATH OF CAPTAIN WARD.

ON the 27th of June, 1861, Captain James H. Ward, with the steamers Freeborn, Pawnee, Resolute and Reliance, made an expedition against the Rebels at Matthias' Point, who had for a long time been in the habit of firing upon vessels in the Potomac, from the concealment of brushwood thickets.

Landing about forty men, under cover of the guns of the squadron, for the purpose of cutting and burning the brushwood and erecting batteries, they were suddenly fired upon by some twelve or fourteen hundred Rebels, concealed in the thick wood. The Federal party were compelled to make a hasty retreat, several of the men jumping into the water and swimming to the Freeborn.

Lieutenant Chaplin, of the Pawnee, who commanded the party on shore, remained steady and cool, amidst a perfect hail of musketry, collected his men and made good his retreat, without leaving the enemy a trophy, beyond a few sand-bags and some axes and the muskets of the wounded men.

The last man left the shore with him, and not being able to swim to the boat with his musket, the lieutenant took him on his back, musket and all, and reached the boat in safety, without a scratch, save a bullet-hole through the top of his cap.

While protecting his men, as far as possible, with his guns, having fired from twelve to fifteen shots among the Rebels, Captain Ward was struck in the breast by a bullet, while. in the act of firing a gun, (the gunner being wounded,) and, in the course of an hour thereafter, died from internal hæmorrhage.

Captain Ward was a gentleman of excellent education. He entered the navy at the age of seventeen years. He had seen much active service, and had been a professor in the Naval School at Annapolis; also, for four years commander of the Receiving-ship North Carolina. He was fifty-five years of age, having been born at Hartford, Connecticut. in 1806.

STORY XII.

. ESCAPE OF THE SUMTER, AND SOME OF HER DEEDS.

On the 30th of June. 1861, the piratical. armed steamer Sumter, which it was well known had been long lying at the head of the Pass-à-l'Outre. waiting for an opportunity of escaping the blockade, effected her purpose in the following manner:

At day-break. the look-out discovered a vessel in the offing acting so suspiciously as to induce the belief of her intention, if possible, to run the blockade. The blockading ship, the Brooklyn, immediately went in pursuit of her.

As the vessel kept standing off, the Brooklyn was led a chase of some fifteen miles from her anchorage, when, overhauling her and finding her to be an English bark. in ballast, from some Spanish West India port, bound for New Orleans, she was warned not to attempt to enter.

During this chase, it was reported to Captain Poor
that, taking advantage of the absence of the Brooklyn
from the Pass, a steamer was making its way down the
river with all possible speed; instead of instantly
putting about and hastening back to the river, Captain
Poor kept steaming on until, overtaking the bark, he
simply warned her off. as above stated.

When the Brooklyn returned, finding that the
Sumter had succeeded is crossing the bar, Captain
Poor, as if just appreciating the importance of the case,
ordered all possible steam and sail on, and started in
pursuit of the fugitive.

This order had hardly been carried into effect when
a terrible squall came up, and continued with such
severity as rendered it necessary, to avoid the danger
of grounding. to slacken the speed, and finally, to stop
altogether, till the squall had passed, when the Sumter
was discovered far ahead, going at a rapid rate.

The Brooklyn then made all sail, the wind coming
around fair, and freshening every moment, and it was
soon evident that she was fast gaining on the Sumter,
when, to the surprise of all hands on board, Captain
Poor ordered the ship to be put about, to abandon the
chase, and to return to her anchorage.

Thus was suffered to escape a very fast ship, carrying five guns of large calibre, (one sixty-four and four
thirty-two pounders,) and some one hundred and
twenty men: being a Jeff. Davis letter-of-marque of
five hundred tons burden: and in all respects well
appointed and well calculated to do our commerce
incalculable injury.

Having thus escaped from her pursuers, the Sumter

proceeded to business. Her first prize, being the Golden Rocket, of Bangor, was taken on the 3d of July, and burnt. She next captured the brigs Machias and Cuba, off Cienfuegos, on the 4th of July. A prize crew of four men were put on board the Cuba, and Midshipman Hodgson acting as prize master.

The Sumter towed her prizes all night, and at four o'clock on the morning of th 5th, the hawser parted, and the Cuba was ordered to steer in for the land. She then left the Sumter with the Machias is tow.

On Monday, the 8th, P. M., the prize crew having carelessly laid their arms about the deck, and some of them gone to sleep, Captain J. D. Strout, of the Cuba, having secured the weapons, recaptured his vessel. He then ordered the pirates aft, put two of them in irons, and secured the other three with ropes, not having a sufficient supply of manacles.

Two of them, Spencer and Davison, were soon after transferred to the brig Costa Rica, Captain Peel, from Aspinwall; the other three, Hodgson, Donnelly and O'Brien, remained on the Cuba, and both ships arrived in due time at New York, when the prisoners were delivered to the officers of the Harbor Police, at Quarantine, by whom they were taken to the United States Marshal's office. The Sumter went on her way, plundering and to plunder, and on the 16th of July, entered the harbor of Cienfuegos, Cuba, with seven prizes, and having procured a supply of coal, left on the next day. The prizes were laden with sugar and molasses, and were mostly owned at New England ports. They were subsequently released, by order of the Spanish Government.

STORY XIII.

PIRATICAL SEIZURE OF THE STEAMER ST. NICHOLAS.

On Friday, the 28th of June, 1861, at four o'clock P. M., the steamer St. Nicholas left Baltimore with freight and passengers for different points on the Potomac, including Alexandria, Washington, and Georgetown.

Among her passengers were about fifty Secessionists, disguised as mechanics going to points on the Maryland shore of the Potomac. Of this number, however, was Captain Thomas, of St. Mary's County, who was disguised as a French lady, and retired to a state-room immediately after going on board.

After the steamer left Point Lookout, Captain Thomas threw off his disguise, and appeared in full military costume, armed with revolvers, and with a cutlass by his side, and, with the aid of the passengers, seized the boat, which was immediately put across to Cony river, on the Virginia side.

There those passengers who were not parties to the plot were landed, including the captain of the boat, who was placed under guard. A company of 100 Tennesseeans, who were there in readiness, were taken on board.

Two passengers, who came on board at Point Lookout, proved to be retired naval officers, took charge of the boat, and headed up the river in search of the Pawnee, it being part of the programme of the pirates (it being late at night) to run into the Pawnee, and in the surprise to leap on board and take possession of her.

Not finding the Pawnee, the St. Nicholas turned

round, and steamed for the bay.   Between Smith's
Point and the Rappahannock they captured three vessels, laden with ice, coal and coffee, respectively, with
which they steamed up the Rappahannock to Fredericksburg.

On Monday, the 8th of July, Lieutenant Carmichael,
of Provost Marshal Kenly's police, went down the bay
in a brig, and boarded the Mary Washington, to arrest
one of the Baltimore 19th-of-April-rioters, who was
expected to come on board at the Patuxent.

On coming up the bay he found that Captain Thomas,
alias the French lady, who headed the pirates in the
seizure of the steamer St. Nicholas, was on board with
seven of his confederates, their object supposed to be
the seizure of another steamer in the same manner.   On
arriving abreast of Fort McHenry, Lieutenant Carmichael ordered the captain to stop at the wharf, where he
communicated with General Banks, who ordered a company of Massachusetts troops to arrest all on board.
Seven of the pirates were found, but Captain Thomas
had concealed himself, and, after an hour's search, was
found hid in a large bureau drawer in the ladies' cabin.
Not having even letters of marque from Jeff. Davis for
their protection, they could be regarded in no other
light than as pirates, and were consequently detained at
the fort, as were also several witnesses who were on
board the St. Nicholas at the time of seizure.

An old maid, who has her eye a little sideways on
matrimony, says: "The curse of the war is, that it will
make so many widows, who will be fierce to get married, and who know how to do it, that modest girls will
stand no chance at all."

STORY XIV.

WHY BUCKNER FAILED TO TAKE LOUISVILLE.

THE fact that General Buckner did not take the city of Louisville, instead of stopping at Green river, when he invaded Kentucky, on the line of the Louisville and Nashville Railroad, was due not to any foresight or force of the United States authorities, or of the Union men of Kentucky, but to the loyalty, courage and tact of one obscure individual.

The Secessionists had laid their plans to appear suddenly in Louisville with a powerful force. They had provided for transportation four hundred cars and fifteen locomotives, and had eight thousand men with artillery and camp equipage on board. They had secured the services of the telegraph operators, one of whom forwarded to Louisville a dispatch explaining the detention of trains on the road, and were moving forward at a grand rate. Everything was going well with them, and Louisville, with, perhaps, the exception of a few Secessionists, was unsuspecting and unguarded. General Anderson having no knowledge of the movement, James Guthrie, President of the road, totally in the dark, and General Rousseau lingering in camp on the Indiana shore.

But, at a station just beyond Green River, there was a young man in the service of the road who was a warm friend of the Union, and who, comprehending the meaning of the monster train when it came up, seized a crowbar used for taking up rails to make repairs, and, while the locomotives were being wooded and watered, ran across a curve, and in a deep narrow cut wrenched the spikes from four rails.

The train came along at good speed, the rails spread, the locomotive plunged into the ground, the cars crashed on top of it, and it was twenty-four hours before the train could go ahead. In the meantime Louisville was saved. The hero of the occasion had not had time to get out of the cut before the crash came, and was taken, but in the confusion and excitement managed to escape to a place of safety.

SKEDADDLE.

The shades of night were falling fast,
As through a Southern village passed
A youth, who bore, not over-nice,
A banner with the gay device,
                    Skedaddle!

His hair was red, his toes beneath,
Peeped like an acorn from its sheath.
While with a frightful voice he sung
A burden strange to Yankee tongue,
                    Skedaddle!

He saw no household fire where he
Might warm his tod or hominy;
Beyond the Cordilleras alone,
And from his lips escaped a groan,
                    Skedaddle!

"O stay," a colored person said,
"An' on dis bosom res' your hed!"
The octoroon she winked her eye,
But still he answered with a sigh,
                    Skedaddle!

" Beware McClellan, Buell and Banks,
Beware of Halleck's deadly ranks !"
This was the planter's last Good Night.
The chap replied, far out of sight,
                    Skedaddle !

At break of day, as several boys
From Maine, New York and Illinois,
Were moving Southward, in the air,
They heard these accents of despair,
                    Skedaddle !

A chap was found, and at his side
A bottle, showing how he died,
Still grasping in his hand of ice
That banner with the strange device,
                    Skedaddle !

There, in the twilight, thick and gray,
Considerably played out he lay ;
And through the vapor gray and thick,
A voice fell like a rocket stick,
                    Skedaddle !—VANITY FAIR.

STORY XV.

MASTERLY RETREAT OF SIGEL.

GENERAL LYON, having posted troops at the principal
places where needed throughout Northern Missouri,
leaving Colonel Schaeffer with about five hundred men
at Boonsville, took his departure with 2,000 men, on
the morning of the 3d of July, 1861, for the southwest.
Colonel Sigel had preceded him ·from Rolla, and occupied a position to the west of Springfield.

Governor Jackson was collecting his forces on Clear

creek, eight miles south of Osceola, where he had some 1,500 men, 300 horses and 6,000 muskets. General Rains was encamped a little further south, with 4,000 men and 6 cannon. General Price had 250 men on the north fork of Spring river.

On the 5th of July, Generals Rains and Parsons, with a force of 5,000 men, 1,500 being cavalry, took position on a ridge or elevation in the prairie, seven miles east of Carthage, which being known to Colonel Sigel's troops, though the force of the enemy was unknown by them, they were impatient for a brush; and Colonel Sigel determined to give them battle. Starting at three o'clock in the morning he came upon them with his command of only about 1,100 men, at about half-past eight o'clock. He found the Rebels strongly posted, having five pieces of artillery,—one 12-pounder in front, and two 6-pounders on each flank. The infantry were in rear of the artillery, and the cavalry on each flank.

Colonel Sigel arrayed his forces to the best advantage, having four pieces of artillery in the centre, and one on each flank, the infantry in columns on the right, and left, and in the rear. Before opening fire the Colonel briefly addressed his troops, reminding them of former victories, and asking them to stand by him now. He then commenced firing with shrapnell from the piece of artillery on his left, and soon the engagement became general. The Rebels had no grape-shot, nothing but balls, and proved themselves poor artillerists, as most of their balls flew high, plowing up the prairie behind our troops. They had Confederate flags flying on their extreme right and left divisions, and the Missouri State flag in the centre. Twice were the Confederate flags shot down by Sigel's troops, their first shots being especially aimed at those objects, the men saying they had no desire to fire on the State flag.

In three-quarters of an hour the 12-pounder in the Rebels' central front was dismounted, and their centre column completely broken. In two hours more their artillery was entirely silenced. After a short interval they renewed their fire, but were again silenced. They then commenced flank movements with their cavalry, threatening an attack in the rear, and the capture of Colonel Sigel's baggage train, three miles behind.

To prevent such a calamity, the colonel hurried back one piece of artillery and a detachment of infantry to guard a ferry, with a view to secure his retreat from being cut off; and then adroitly commenced a retrograde movement with his entire command, dispatching at the same time an order for the advance of the baggage train.

In this movement he preserved the order of his columns, the artillery continuing to do admirable service, and fighting deliberately over every inch of ground till the baggage wagons were reached; when they were immediately formed in solid columns of eight, with the infantry and artillery posted on all sides, presenting an impregnable array.

Thus, with perfect order, with Colonel Solomon's battalion in front, the column continued alternately fighting and retreating, in the face of greatly superior numbers. At the crossing of Dry fork, our lines were very near being broken, when by the timely arrival of 200 men from Shoal creek, they effected a crossing, with a loss of five killed and two mortally wounded.

The retrograde toward Carthage continued, till at last, at five o'clock, they came to a place where the road passed directly through a high bluff, after passing a small creek. On the two sides of this divided bluff, 800 of the Rebel cavalry took position, prepared to resist the passage of the creek and the road. The position was one of difficulty, and would have seriously perplexed any less skillful officer than Colonel Sigel.

With the utmost coolness he instantly conceived and adopted a splendid stratagem, which placed his foes entirely at his mercy, and eventually secured the unimpeded movements of his command. He ordered an oblique movement on the right and left of his forces, as if to pass around the sides of the bluff, at the same time advancing the two pieces of artillery on the sides, to a position in front, giving Colonel Solomon's battalion the strength of two pieces on his right, and two on his left.

The oblique movements of the infantry were accompanied by a feint of the artillery in the same direction. The Rebel cavalry construing these manoeuvres very much in their favor, rushed down into the road from both sides of the bluff, evidently intending to make a grand charge upon Colonel Sigel's centre.

With the quickness of thought the movements to the right and left were reversed, and a terribly destructive cross-fire was opened upon the Rebels, the distance being about 300 yards, and the guns heavily charged with grape-shot. In ten minutes the route of the cavalry was complete. They fled in great disorder ; and the the prairie was full of flying and riderless horses, of which our men captured 85. They also picked up 65 double-barrel shot guns, which the flying Rebels had cast away. Two officers were also here captured, who stated that up to this time they had lost 250 men.

Colonel Sigel was now anxious to reach Carthage, three miles distant, and to take a position in the woods north of that place, on the Sarcoxie road, so as to prevent the annoyance of the Rebel cavalry. This movement took from half-past six to half-past eight o'clock in the evening, and here was the hottest fighting of the day; the enemy appreciating the colonel's desire to get under cover of the woods, stubbornly resisted his progress. Finally, against great disparity of numbers, he gained the timber, when the enemy retired to Carthage.

Ascertaining soon that the Rebels had given up the day, Sigel then immediately took up his line of march, and pressed on twelve or fourteen miles to Sarcoxie, where they arrived, without further trouble, at three o'clock in the morning, after a most arduous and heroic struggle of twenty-four consecutive hours. Here they partook of refreshments and rest till the next evening, when they marched to Mt. Vernon, in Lawrence county, where they were heartily welcomed and hospitably entertained.

The loss of the Rebels in the affair above narrated, according to their own acknowledgment, was 500, while the loss of the Government troops was only 10 killed, 43 wounded, of whom 11 died, and 4 missing; making a total of 57.

The assault, on the part of Colonel Sigel, was very bold and dreadfully destructive to the enemy. The retreat was one of the most skillfully conducted, brave, orderly, and successful on record; partaking more of the nature of victory than of defeat. In fact it was a retrogradely fought battle, in which the enemy was held completely in check and foiled at every point; and had Colonel Sigel's expected reinforcements from Neosho and Sarcoxie met him at Carthage, his victory would have been complete.

The object of Colonel Sigel in giving battle as he did was probably to intercept the Rebels' march on Carthage, and cut up their forces in detail, if possible, and and thus prevent their junction, and keep them in check till the arrival of General Lyon and Major Sturgis, both of whom, though yet north of the Osage, might possibly reach Springfield in six or eight days. The guard of 120 men left by Sigel at Neosho, were subsequently captured by Ben McCulloch's Arkansas troops, and released on taking oath not to bear arms against the Southern Confederacy.

"I FIGHTS MIT SIGEL."

I met him one morn, he was trudging along,
 His knapsack with chickens was swelling,
He'd "blenkered" those dainties, and thought it no wrong,
 From some Secessionist's dwelling.
"What regiment's yours? and under whose flag
 Do you fight?" said I, touching his shoulder,—
Turning slowly around he smilingly said,
 (For the thought made him stronger and bolder,)
      "*I fights mit Sigel.*"

The next time I saw him his knapsack was gone,
 His cap and his canteen were missing;
Shell, shrapnell and grape, and the swift rifle ball,
 Around him and o'er him were hissing:
"How are you my friend, and where have you been,
 And for what and for whom are you fighting?"
He said, as a shell from the enemy's gun
 Sent his arm and his musket a "kiting,"
      "*I fights mit Sigel.*"

And once more I saw him and knelt by his side,—
  His life blood was rapidly flowing :
I whispered of home, wife, children and friends,
  And the bright land to which he was going.
" And have you no word for the dear ones at home,
  The ' wee one,' the father or mother ?"
"Yaw ! yaw !" said he. " tell them, oh tell them,"—(quite done,
  Poor fellow ! he thought of no other)—
            " *I fights mit Sigel.*"

We scooped out a grave, and he dreamlessly sleeps
  On the banks of the Shenando' river ;
His home and his kindred alike are unknown,
  His reward in the hands of the Giver.
We placed a rough board at the head of his grave,
  " And we left him alone in his glory,"
But on it we marked, ere we turned from the spot,
  The little we knew of his story—
            " *I fights mit Sigel.*"

                      GRANT P. ROBINSON.

STORY XVI.

AN AFFECTING INCIDENT OF THE WAR.

THE following incident affords a striking but sad
illustration of the effects of civil war : In the fall of
1860, a young gentleman of Richmond was introduced,
by a mutual friend, to a young lady belonging to a
family in Alexandria. The young people soon became
intimately acquainted, and, quite naturally, fell in love.
The parents on both sides consenting, the parties were
betrothed, and the marriage day was fixed for the 4th
of July ensuing.

In the meantime, however, Virginians were called

upon to decide on which side they would stand. The
lady declared herself on the side of the Government,
but the gentleman joined the Rebel forces. No opportunity was afforded for the interchange of sentiments
between the young folks, or anything settled as to their
future movements.

Matters remained thus till the 4th of July, 1861,
when, exactly within an hour of the time originally
fixed for the marriage, intelligence was conveyed to the
residence of the lady that the young man had been shot
by a sentry, two days before, while attempting to desert
and join his bride. His betrothed did not shed a tear,
but, standing erect, smiled, and then remarking to her
mother, "I am going to desert, too," fell to the floor,
while the life-blood bubbled from her lips, and the next
morning she was carried to her last resting place.

[N. Y. EXPRESS.

DAVE TOD, otherwise "Tod and Victory," spent
about ten thousand dollars in getting up a regiment
for the war, and his son belonged to it and carried a
musket. Of course, as Mr. Tod was a man of distinction and wealth, his son could have had a commission,
whether he was of any account or not. But that was
not old Dave's way. His son must go into the ranks.
The boy is a good one, too—one of the best shots in the
regiment—and has the reputation of killing two of the
prowling Secession assassins. Honor to whom honor is
due; and who deserves it better than the efficient Governor Tod, of Ohio?

STORY XVII.

TRAGEDY OF THE SCHOONER S. J. WARING.

THE schooner S. J. Waring, Captain Francis Smith, the third day out from New York, on the 7th of July, 1861, being 150 miles from Sandy Hook. in latitude 38° 55′, and longitude 69° 4′, was brought to by the Rebel privateer brig Jeff. Davis. A boat full of men was sent alongside, who ordered the captain to haul down the United States flag, and declared the Waring a prize.

They took from her a quantity of provisions, and then, taking away Captain Smith. the two mates and two seamen. leaving the steward, two seamen and a passenger on board, they placed on her. as a prize crew, Montague Amiel, a Charleston pilot, in command, —— Stevens, mate. Malcom Sidney. second mate, and two men.

Of the tragedy which subsequently ensued, the fol-lowing is a narrative of the steward, William Tillman, a colored man, and the hero of it. He is described as being "of medium height. rather strongly built, crisp hair. nearly unmixed negro blood. bearing in his pock-marked countenance an expression of honesty and strong common sense, with some touches of humor." He says he was born of free colored parents, in Milford, Delaware, and was twenty-seven years old, and had fol-lowed the sea ten years.

"The schooner S. J. Waring had started on a voyage to Montevideo, with an assorted cargo, which, with the vessel, was valued at $100,000.

"There were on board—the captain and mate; W. Tillman, steward; William Stedding, seaman, a German, twenty-three years of age; Daniel McLeod, seaman, of Cape Breton, Nova Scotia, thirty years of age, and Bryce McKinnon, a passenger.

"On the 7th of July we fell in with the Jeff. Davis, and a prize crew of five were put on board, who were unarmed. We run ten days, and didn't find Charleston; we were, however, only 50 miles south of Charleston, and 100 miles eastward. On the voyage they treated me the best kind of way, and talked the best kind of talk.

"One day the first lieutenant of the pirates was sitting in the cabin, cross-legged, smoking, and he said to me, 'When you go down to Savannah, I want you to go to my house, and I will take care of you.' I thought, yes, you will take care of me when you get me there. I raised my hat, and said, 'Yes, sir; thank you.' But afterward, I said to Billy, (the German,) 'I am not going to Charleston a live man; they may take me there dead.'

"He had been told by the prize-master that he would get well rewarded in Charleston for performing his duty so well, in bringing the schooner in. He also overheard conversation not intended for his ears, in regard to the price he would probably bring: and he had heard the prize-master say to one of his men: 'You talk to that steward, and keep him in good heart. By God,' said he, 'he will never see the North again.'

"Tillman conferred with two of the seamen about taking possession of the schooner; but they declined adopting any plan, saying that none of them knew how

6

to navigate her back, should they succeed in getting control.

Tillman thought the matter for three days, and then made an appeal to the German, and said, "If you are a man and stick to your word, we can take this vessel easy. Then (in Tillman's words) we made a plan that I should go to my berth, and when most of them were asleep, he was to give me some sign or awake me.

"We tried this for two nights, but no good chance offered. But last Tuesday night we caught them asleep, and we went to work. The mate comes to my berth and touches me. He says, 'now is your time.' I went into my room and got my hatchet. The first man I struck was the captain. He was lying in a state-room on the starboard side.

"I aimed at his temple, as near as I could, and hit him just below the ear, with the edge of the hatchet. With that he made a very loud shriek. The passenger jumped up, very much in a fright. I told him, 'do you be still; I shall not hurt a hair of your head.' The passenger knew what I was up to; he never said a word more. I walked right across the cabin to the second mate's room, and gave him one severe blow in the mole of the head—that is right across the middle of his head.

"I didn't stop to see whether he was dead or not, but I jumped on deck, and as I did so, the mate, who had been sleeping on the companion-way, started from the noise he had heard in the cabin. Just as he rose upon his feet, I struck him in the back of the head. Then the German chap jumped over, and we 'mittened' on to him and flung him over the starboard quarter."

Marshal Murray. "What did you do then?"

Tillman. "Then we went down straight into the

cabin. The second mate was not quite dead. He was sitting, leaning against his berth. I catched him by the hair of the head with my left hand, and struck him with the hatchet, which I had in my right hand. I told this young German—'Well, let's get him overboard as soon as we can.' So we hauled him over onto the cabin."

The Marshal. "Was he quite dead?"

Tillman. "No; he was not quite dead, but he would not have lived long. We flung him over the starboard quarter. Then I told this German to go and call the man Jim, the Southern chap, (one of the pirates,) here. He called him aft. Says I, 'Jim, come down here in the cabin. Do you know that I have taken charge of this vessel to-night? I am going to put you in irons.' 'Well,' says he, 'I am willing.' He gave right up. I kept him in irons till eight o'clock next morning. I then sent the German for him, and I said, 'Smith,' (the name Milnor went by on board,) 'I wan't you to join us, and help take this vessel back. But mind, the least crook, or the least turn, and overboard you go with the rest.' 'Well,' said he, 'I will do the best I can.' And he worked well all the way back. He couldn't do otherwise. It was pump or sink."

Marshal. Did they beg, any of them?"

Tillman. "They didn't have any chance to beg. It was all done in five minutes. In seven minutes and a half after I struck the first blow the vessel was squared away before the wind, and all sail on. We were fifty miles south of Charleston, and one hundred to the eastward."

Tillman said, that at first he had thought of securing all the men, and bringing them all to New York alive, in irons, but found this was impracticable. To use his own language, "There were too many for that; there were five of them and only three of us. After this I said, well, I will get all I can back alive, and the rest I will kill."

The testimony of Mr. McKinnon, though giving further particulars, does not contradict or invalidate, but confirms, Tillman's statement, which may, therefore, be deemed reliable. Mr. McKinnon concludes the narrative as follows:

"The steward now took command, and the schooner was headed for the North, with a fair wind. None of us knew any thing of navigation; but we trusted to good fortune and the land, to enable us to make out our course. Of course, we had to be vigilant. Two of our hands might turn upon us at any moment, and McLeod was not faithful. Stedding, Tillman, and I, managed so that two of us were on deck all the while, and always aft of the other three. The men on watch carried the two pistols, and the one that slept always kept one eye open, lest we might be attacked.

"On Friday the 19th, we made the land at eight o'clock in the morning, which became quite distinct by noon; and we kept on our way, with good weather, sounding as we went. On Sunday morning, at nine o'clock, we got a pilot off Sandy Hook, and soon after hired a tug for $60, to tow us up to New York, where we arrived about four, P. M., truly thankful for our great deliverance."

TERRIBLE FATE OF THE REBEL PRIVATEER PETREL.

THE United States frigate St. Lawrence had cruised for a month along the Atlantic coast, between Cape Henry and Savannah, and on the morning of the 1st of August, 1861, while just outside the harbor of Charleston, espied a long rakish schooner, filled with men, and mounting three or four guns, sailing rapidly down upon her.

The port-holes were still shut, but the flag was at the peak, and the St. Lawrence looked not unlike a great lumberly merchantman, becalmed in a strange latitude, and too unwieldy for any purpose save the holding of a large cargo for the avarice of an enemy to court, and a daring privateer to secure.

As the stranger came down, the St. Lawrence hoisted all sail, and affected to be anxious to get out to sea. In reality, however, she was edging in closer to shore, and making arrangements below to receive the reckless visitors with appropriate largess.

Directly, a shot came skipping over the water, falling into the sea a few rods ahead of the frigate, and a number followed it in quick succession, but nearly all either falling short or passing over. The final discharge consisted of grape and canister, which made some little dalliance with the frigate's rigging, admonished the commander that the play was growing serious.

At this time the vessels were within speaking distance, and a man in uniform was seen mounted upon the pirate's deck, who shouted to the St. Lawrence to lay-to

H

and send over a boat. The crew were distinctly seen flourishing their cutlasses, and the gunners ramming and pointing their guns. She carried three guns, supposed to be rifled cannon.

Then the St. Lawrence threw up her ports, and disclosed a whole broadside of cannon, with the gunners at the breech of the guns. holding lighted fuses, and directly the broad decks were filled with seamen in blue jackets, armed with muskets, who sprung into the shrouds, and ran out on the yards, laying prone in the maintop, on the bowsprit, in the forecastle, and at every point where aim could be taken with advantage. In a word, the ugly merchantman was metamorphosed into a bristling war ship, with a man at every point, and a broadside of cannon looking into the eyes of the pirates.

The latter, taken aback. recoiled a moment; but, before they had time for action, even for thought, the guns belched forth iron and fire, splintering the masts, cutting the rigging and sails as with knives, breaking the spars and the booms, and literally carving the schooner into pieces, and opening gulfs into which the waters rushed as through sluices, filling the hold, and admonishing the Rebels that their sole hopes of life lay in the ship's boat, or in wrestling with the sea.

The fire still continued, and the water was full of drift-wood. Many of the men jumped overboard, and the rest, launching the life-boat, jumped in, and held up a white handkerchief as a sign of surrender.

The St. Lawrence still continued the fire with small arms, but, directing their aim at the hulk, and not at the small boat, the crew, excepting four men, were not injured. In ten minutes from the firing of her first

gun, the vessel swayed heavily, and went under, carry·
ing down four men.

The officers of the St. Lawrence now discovered the
life-boat and the flag of humiliation. They dropped a
boat and made out to the Rebels, and finally passed
them on board ship, where they were ironed as fast as
received, and securely confined below.

In the engagement the St. Lawrence received two
shots, one in the foresail, the other in the quarter-deck.
She transferred her prisoners, thirty-seven in number,
to the Flag, on Sunday morning, and they were at once
taken to Philadelphia, where they were confined in the
Moyamensing prison to await the action of the proper
authorities.

These pirates were mostly Irishmen by birth, poorly
dressed, and appeared to have no regular uniform. As
far as appearances were concerned, they were admirably
fitted for their nefarious business.

The Petrel was formerly the United States revenue
cutter Wm. Aiken, and was surrendered in Charleston
harbor by her commander, on the 27th of December,
1860.

STORY XIX.

DEATH OF GENERAL LYON, AT THE BATTLE OF WILSON'S CREEK, AUGUST 10th, 1861.

GENERAL LYON had already received two wounds
and had his horse shot under him, but immediately
mounted another and continued giving orders.

The First Iowa. under Lieutenant-Colonel Merritt,

and part of the Kansas troops, were ordered to take the place of the First Missouri, who were almost exhausted, from over two hours severe fighting, and were in danger of being overpowered by a fourth body of fresh troops, now brought against them.

The Iowans and Kansans marched to the front with a firm tread, in excellent order, and, fighting like tigers, saved our army from overwhelming defeat. General Lyon saw and highly commended their indomitable bravery.

General Lyon now desired the men to prepare to make a bayonet charge immediately after their next fire; when the Iowans at once offered to go, and asked for a leader. There was no time to designate a leader; the enemy were advancing in force. "I will lead you! Come on, brave men!" exclaimed Lyon, placing himself in the van of the Iowans, and General Sweeney leading the Kansas troops.

The enemy advanced, discharged their pieces, and then retired before the destructive fire of our men. At this time, the brave General Lyon fell. He was immediately placed in an ambulance, to be carried to Springfield. General Sweeney being at the same time disabled by a shot in his right leg, the command devolved upon Major Sturgis.

The battle having commenced in front before six o'clock in the morning, and continued with but little intermission until eleven o'clock, and the enemy being finally driven from the field; Major Sturgis, upon learning that Captain Totten's cannon ammunition was nearly expended, ordered the ambulances, laden with wounded officers and soldiers, to move toward Spring-field; Lieutenant Dubois' battery having been sent back to the hill, at the north of the valley, to protect the retreat, in case the enemy should return.

The remnant of our brave army, though victorious in battle, then commenced returning to Springfield, in face of an enemy greatly superior in numbers, who were, however, so terribly whipped, as to be unable to make any attempt to follow.

This was one of the bloodiest battles on record. General Lyon's force was 5,200 men, while that of the enemy, as ascertained from their captured muster-rolls, was 23,000. Our loss was 223 killed, 721 wounded, and 291 missing. The Rebel loss was much greater.

The remains of General Lyon were placed in a metallic coffin, and in charge of his relatives and friends, accompanied by a military escort, were transported to Eastport, Conn., the place of his nativity, where they were interred with military honors and marked demonstrations of public regard.

Thus, in the prime of life, closed the career of one of the bravest and noblest men that ever devoted his life and energies to our country's service.

A wail on the wind.
From the far Western border :
Our nation is stricken
In grief and disorder !

A hero hath fallen !
The tidings how solemn !
Facing the foeman,
At the head of his column !

Brave Iowas called
For a hero to lead 'em.
To again front the battle
For the Union and freedom.

Its battle cry " onward !"
　　That phalanx all gory!
Brave Lyon now leads it,
　　To death, or to glory !

Never marched army-men
　　Braver or bolder,
Up to the canon's mouth,
　　Shoulder to shoulder.

" Charge, with the bayonet !
　　Cleave, with the sabre !
Thoughtless of danger,
　　And reckless of labor.

" No time is left us
　　With traitors to trifle !
Give them the contents
　　Of musket and rifle."
　　*　　　*　　　*　　　*　　　*
Lo ! the base Rebels,
　　Disorderly flying,
Mid the din of the battle,
　　And moans of the dying !

Thick o'er the battle-field,
　　Carnage is scattered !
Hundreds of heroes lie
　　Mangled and shattered !

Death sends his messenger,
　　Heavy and leaden,
Again Lyon's heart's blood
　　His armor doth redden !

He falleth. while flieth
　　Base traitors before him :
A victor he dieth,
　　And glory waves o'er him.

A wail on the wind
　　From the far Western border :
Our nation is stricken
　　In grief and disorder !

STORY XX.

ZAGONYI'S CHARGE.

It was a glorious fight. There is nothing more brilliant known to our history—perhaps, to any history. Wilson's Creek is doubly historic ground; upon it, on the 10th of August, 1861, occurred the terrible battle in which a thousand of our brave men poured out their blood like water; and the heroic Lyon laid down his life for the country which shall ever cherish his name in green and grateful remembrance; and eleven weeks after, on the head waters of the same stream, was made that charge of the Fremont Body-Guard, under the gallant Zagonyi, which will be ever coupled hereafter with that of the Light Brigade of Balaklava, when—

> "Into the jaws of death,
> Into the gates of hell,
> Rode the six hundred."

Time will not permit me to record any thing more than a few incidents of the battle, if battle it can be called; but it is clear beyond dispute, that 150 raw men, never before under fire, after a wearying ride of fifty miles, deliberately rode through a galling fire for more than a quarter of a mile, dismounted, tore down a fence, remounted and formed, all while the bullets were flying about them like hail, and then, with enthusiastic shouts for "Fremont and the Union," charged through and through a body of more than 1,000 cavalry and infantry, completely routing and dispersing them; that they then dashed into the city and chased the remainder of the flying Rebels through the streets for an hour and a half, until the last man of them was driven out of Springfield; in short, that 150 men defeated and drove 2,000 away, so effectually, that the little guard left behind was able to hold the town for two days, until the remainder of the army came up.

The loss of the Body-Guard, as far as could be ascertained at the time, amounted to 16 killed, 25 wounded, and 10 missing. Many who were slightly wounded were not included in these figures.

Major Zagonyi, who rode at the head of his men through the whole fight, did not receive a single scratch; though one bullet cut his clothing across the breast. One of his sergeants had three horses shot under him. Another of his men received one ball in a blacking-box, which he carried in his pocket; and a second bullet passed through his coat, vest, and shirt, but did not break the skin. Sergeant Hunter of Company C, had his horse shot in seven places; and more than two-thirds of all the horses were wounded.

On visiting the field on the west side of town, where the first change was made, I found the dead horses still lying upon the ground. The trees in the vicinity were cut and torn with balls, and thirty-six bullet holes were found in a single fence rail, and the ground was in many places still red with blood.

There were three companies of the body-guard in the engagement—A. B, and C. The latter was armed with Beal's revolvers, and sabres; the two former, in addition to those weapons, carried Colt's revolving carbines. After having once given all their fire, there was no time to reload, and the most effective work of the day

was done with the sabres. At the close of it, almost
every sabre of the command was stained with blood.

The funeral of fourteen of the body-guard, and two
of Major White's men, occurred on the 29th of October,
the third day after the fight, and was attended by the
major-general and his staff, a portion of the army, and
many of the people of Springfield. The bodies were
enclosed in plain, unpainted coffins, and all interred in
one grave, with military honors. The services were
conducted by the Rev. C. M. Blake, the staff chaplain.

The sixteen riderless horses, which followed the remains to the grave, told the cost at which the victory
was won; and while the dust was being committed to
dust, with the solemn and impressive Episcopal service,
there were few dry eyes among the stricken band who
had gathered together to do the last earthly honors to
their fallen comrades.

When Major Zagonyi was sent out to reconnoitre the
country, and if practicable, take possession of Springfield, it was not supposed that there were more than
three or four hundred Rebels there, as was actually the
case but a few days before. When he reached that
vicinity, and learned of their overwhelming numbers, it
would doubtless have been good generalship for him
to have fallen back, and wait for reinforcements. But
the idea had been so industriously given out, by those
who seemed to hate the commanding general of that
department, more than they loved the Union, that the
body-guard was a sort of kid-glove ornamental corps,
intended only to swell the retinue, and add to the display of General Fremont, and not fit for hard service;
that every man in it was eager to remove the unjust.
and ungenerous imputation. That they accomplished

it, none will deny, and if any think the cost great, let them remember where the blame lies.—COR. N. Y. TRIBUNE.

The following is Major Zagonyi's dispatch to General Fremont:

> Five miles south of Bolivar, Mo., ⎫
>   October 26th, 1 A. M.   ⎬

GENERAL:—I report, respectfully, that yesterday afternoon, at four o'clock, I met, in Springfield, from 2,000 to 2,200 of the Rebels, in their camp, formed in line of battle. They gave me a warm reception— warmer than I expected. But your guard, with one feeling, made a charge, and in less than three minutes, the 2,000 or 2,200 Rebels were routed by 150 men of the body guard.

We cleared out the city perfectly from every Rebel, and raised the Union flag on the court-house. It getting too dark, I concluded to leave the city, not being able to keep it with 150 men. Major White's men did not participate in the charge.

Allow me, General, to make you acquainted with the soldiers and officers. I have seen charges; but such brilliant unanimity and bravery, I had never seen, and did not expect it. Their war cry, "Fremont and the Union," broke forth like thunder.

Our loss is comparatively small; I expected to remain on the field with them all. I will write about particulars.

With the highest respect, your obedient servant,

CHAS. ZAGONYI,
Major Commanding Body-Guard.

ZAGONYI.

Bold captain of the body-guard,
    I'll troll a stave to thee!
My voice is somewhat harsh and hard,
    And rough my minstrelsy.
I've cheered until my throat is sore
For how our boys at Beaufort bore,
    Yet here's a cheer for thee!

I hear thy jingling spears and reins,
    Thy sabre at thy knee;
The blood runs lighter through my veins,
    As I before me see
Thy hundred men, with thrusts and blows,
Ride down a thousand stubborn foes,
    The foremost led by thee

With pistol snap, and rifle crack—
    Mere salvos fired to honor thee—
Ye plunge, and stamp, and shoot, and hack,
    The way your swords made free;
Then back again, the path is wide
This time. Ye gods! it was a ride,
    The ride they took with thee!

No guardsman of the whole command,
    Halts, quails, or turns to flee;
With bloody spur and steady hand,
    They gallop where they see
Thy leading plume stream out ahead,
O'er flying, wounded, dying, dead—
    They can but follow thee.

So, captain of the body-guard,
    I pledge a health to thee!
I hope to see thy shoulders starred,
    My Paladin; and we
Shall laugh at fortune in the fray,
Whene'er you lead your well-known way
    To death or victory.—G. H. BOKER.

STORY XXI.

CAPTURE OF FORT HATTERAS.

A NAVAL and military expedition was fitted out and sailed from Hampton Roads on Monday, the 26th of August, 1861, without notifying the New York reporters, and, consequently, the public were not advised of it, either North or South, in time to frustrate the purposes of the Government.

The destination of the armament was Forts Hatteras and Clark, which commanded Hatteras Inlet, the principal entrance to Albemarle and Pamlico Sounds, and key to the North Carolina interior coast, the principal rendezvous and headquarters of the pirates and smugglers.

The fleet consisted of the frigates Minnesota and Wabash, the sloop-of-war Pawnee, the Cumberland, the Susquehanna, the Monticello, the Harriet Lane, the steamers Adelaide and George Peabody, two propellers, a large number of schooners, barges, and other small craft. The fleet was under command of Flag-Officer Stringham. Its armament was upwards of 100 guns.

The land forces, commanded by General Butler, were shipped on board the Adelaide and George Peabody, and consisted of 500 of the Twentieth New York, Colonel Weber; 220 of the Ninth New York, Colonel Hawkins; 100 of the Union Coast Guard, Captain Nixon, and 60 of the United States Artillery, Lieutenant Larned commanding; constituting a total force of 880 men, designed to operate, in conjunction with the fleet, against the Rebel forts.

The fleet arrived off Hatteras Inlet late on Tuesday afternoon, and the next morning, at day-break, dispositions were made for an attack upon the forts by the fleet and for landing the troops, which was found to be a difficult matter, owing to the previous prevalence of southwest gales, which caused the breaking of a heavy surf upon the beach.

Though a laborious effort was made to land the troops, only 315 were landed, including 55 marines from the fleet and a number of regulars. Fortunately, a rifled 12-pounder cannon and a 12-pound howitzer were also landed, when, the boats all being broken up or swamped and the wind rising, further landing was rendered impracticable. The landing had been effected under cover of shells from the Monticello and Harriet Lane, and those who reached the shore were thoroughly wet.

The bombardment was commenced by the Minnesota, about two miles and a half distant, on Wednesday, at eleven o'clock, A. M., and she was soon after joined by the whole fleet.

The scene was magnificent. The bombardment from the fleet was incessant, and the shells pitched into the forts and exploded with terrible effect; the forts responding at long intervals. After about three hours, the nearest fort (Fort Clark) was silenced, and its flag struck, the garrison abandoning it and taking refuge in Fort Hatteras.

A small party of the Coast Guard, led by Mr. Wiegel, a volunteer aid, advanced and took possession of the abandoned fort, and raised the American flag.

The Monticello which, to protect the land force, had reached the inlet and unfortunately grounded, became

I	7

the object of a terrible fire from Fort Hatteras, to which she replied sharply with shell, and held her own for fifty minutes, in which time she threw fifty-five shells, partially silencing her assailants. She finally succeeded in getting off, and withdrew for repairs, having had seven 8-inch shells shot through her, one of them below water, and one or two men slightly bruised, but no others hurt.

As night was approaching, and the weather appeared threatening, prudence required the ships to make an offing. It was reluctantly done, leaving the troops on shore, a part of them in possession of Fort Clark, and the rest bivouacked on the beach near the place of landing, about two miles north of the forts.

At eight o'clock next morning, the fleet having approached as near as the depth of water would permit, the firing upon Fort Hatteras was renewed, first by the Susquehannah, and, in a few minutes, the fire of the entire fleet was concentrated upon that fort, which, for near half an hour, failed to reply, and after that its shots all fell short.

A large steamer came down the sound with reinforcements for the fort, but was prevented from landing by Captain Johnson, of the Coast Guard, who, with two guns that had been landed, and a 6-pounder found on shore, had constructed a sand battery, from which he opened fire upon the steamer, compelling her to retire.

The bombardment from the fleet continued without intermission till half-past eleven o'clock, when our shells began to range accurately upon the bomb-proof, where they were deposited with rapidity, and one of them actually passed down the ventilator into a room next to the magazine, where some three hundred terrified

Rebels had taken refuge from the bursting shells; but, fortunately for them, this unwelcome visitor failed to explode.

At this stage of imminent danger and great terror and excitement in the fort, a white flag was displayed in token of surrender; when our land forces under Colonel Weber, and those at Fort Clark, with loud shouts, started up the beach and were met by a flag of truce, and a signal was at the same time made for the flag-ship to cease firing.

General Butler, who was proceeding on board the propeller Fanny for the purpose of landing the rest of the troops, passed over the bar of the inlet into the channel just as the white flag appeared at the fort, and the Rebel steamer Winslow, with a large Secession force on board, which she had been prevented from landing, escaped up the sound, a shot from the Fanny failing to reach her.

General Butler then sent Lieutenant Crosby on shore to demand the meaning of the white flag. The boat soon returned bringing Mr. Wiegel, with the following note from the commandant of the fort:

"*Memorandum.* Flag-officer Samuel Barron, C. S. Navy, offers to surrender Fort Hatteras, with all the arms and munitions of war; the officers allowed to go out with side arms, the men, without arms, to retire.

"S. BARRON,
"Commanding naval defence, Va. and N. C.
"*Fort Hatteras, August* 29, 1861."

He also sent, at the same time, a verbal communication purporting "that he had in the fort 715 men, and 1,000 more within an hour's call, but that he was anxious to spare the effusion of blood." General Butler replied as follows:

"*Memorandum.* Benjamin F. Butler, Major-General United States Army, commanding, in reply to the communication of Samuel Barron, commanding the forces at Fort Hatteras, cannot admit the terms proposed. The terms offered are these—full capitulation; the officers and men to be treated as prisoners of war. No other terms admissible. Commanding officers to meet on board the flag-ship Minnesota, to arrange details,

"*August* 29, 1861."

Lieutenant Crosby returned in three-quarters of an hour, bringing with him Captain Barron, Major Andrews, and Colonel Martin, of the Rebel forces, who informed General Butler that they accepted the terms proposed by him, and had come to surrender themselves and their commands as prisoners of war. The General replied, that as the expedition was formed of the army and navy, the surrender must be made on board the flag-ship, to Flag-officer Sringham, as well as to himself. They then went on board the Minnesota, where articles of capitulation were signed.

The surrender was in conformity with General Butler's proposal, unconditional, saving the stipulation that the officers and men should receive the treatment due to prisoners of war.

The capture comprised Forts Hatteras and Clarke, 35 cannon, 1,000 stand of arms, five stands of colors, a quantity of ammunition, hospital stores, two schooners, one loaded with tobacco, and the other with provisions, one brig loaded with cotton, two light-boats, two surf-boats, 45 officers, several being of high rank, and 670 privates; the Rebels admitting a loss of 8 killed and 35 wounded. On our part there was no casualty whatever worthy of notice. This was owing mainly to our ships being for the most part out of range of their guns. The official report of the Rebel Major Andrews describes the firing from the fleet as being tremendous. He says: " The shower of shell in half an hour became literally tremendous, as we had falling into and immediately around the works, not less, on an average, than ten each minute; and the sea being smooth, the firing was remarkably accurate. One officer counted twentyeight shells as falling so as to damage us, in one minute, and several others counted twenty in a minute. * * * For three hours and twenty minutes Fort Hatteras resisted a storm of shells, perhaps more terrible than ever fell upon any other works. * * * One shell had fallen into the room adjoining the magazine, and the magazine was reported on fire."

Colonel Martin, who was in command at Fort Clark, says of the first day's operations, that Fort Clark was exposed to a "flood of shells," which poured upon it and the skirts of the adjacent woods for several hours, which "fire was promptly returned, until every charge of powder and every primer was exhausted, when a retreat to Fort Hatteras was ordered."

The troops having all been landed, General Butler took a formal surrender of the forts, with all the men and munitions of war; inspected the troops, to see that all the arms had been properly surrendered, marched them out, and embarked them on board the Adelaide; and march his own troops into the Fort, and raised the United States flag upon it, amid the cheers of the troops and a salute of thirteen guns, which had been shotted by the enemy.

In view of the great strength of Fort Hatteras, and its importance as the key to the Albemarle, General Butler held a consultation with Flag-Officer Stringham and Commander Stelwagen, when it was determined to hold possession of it.

General Butler thereupon left Colonel Hawkins, with the troops, in charge, and re-embarked the regulars and marines.

The prisoners were also embarked on the Minnesota, and all the necessary arrangements having been made Commodore Stringham, leaving the steamers Monticello and Pawnee inside the channel, in a position to command all approaches to the forts by the Sound, sailed from the inlet on the 30th of August, and arrived at New York Harbor on the 2d of September, where he was greeted with every demonstration of joy.

General Butler sailed on the Adelaide, Commander Stelwagen, with the wounded prisoners for Annapolis, and arrived at Washington city on the 1st of September, where at evening, he was serenaded at the National Hotel by a military band, and when he appeared was greeted with much enthusiam.

The ships of the fleet proceeded, some of them to their blockading stations, others returned to Fortress Monroe and other points, as directed. Thus ended successfully the Hatteras expedition, its results being of the highest importance.

MAJOR-GENERAL IRWIN MCDOWELL, of Ohio, was a graduate of West Point, of the class of 1838. He was twenty-third in a class of forty-five, of which Beauregard was second. He was promoted by brevet for gallantry at Buena Vista. He was in command of the Army of the Potomac at the first battle of Bull Run, of which disaster he made a very candid report.

STORY XXII.

THE FAITHFUL DOG OF SHILOH.

On Shiloh's hot-contested field.
The Rebels were constrained to yield :
Yet solemn truth requires to tell,
There many a Union hero fell.

There new-made mounds of earth disclosed
Where many a gallant one reposed ;
And one there was in quiet nook,
That might not, after, be mistook :

'Twas by his faithful comrades made,
And there Lieutenant Pfieff was laid.
For twelve long days since first he fell,
His faithful dog did guard it well.

*　　　*　　　*　　　*　　　*

From far off Illinoian plains,
His widowed wife sought his remains.
She came :—the faithful dog approached,
To learn what stranger-foot encroached—

Beheld her—and with eager mood,
Entreated her, as best he could,
To follow him without delay,
While he should lead the devious way.

He led, she followed o'er the ground,
Until at length they reached the mound
That he so long had guarded well,
Since that sad day his master fell.

Soon was the imprisoning clay removed,
And soon she clasped the form she loved.
As homeward she that form conveyed,
That faithful dog his best essayed,

At consolation and relief,
By sympathizing in her grief,
Evincing more than tongue could tell,
His sad lament for what befel.

STORY XXIII.

HOW A SCOUT LOST HIS BREECHES.

THE "Jessie Scouts" will no doubt occupy a page in the thrilling tales yet to be told. This company of youthful but hardy, circumspect, and fearless adventurers, was constantly employed for some dangerous duty; and their captain, an agile young fellow named Carpenter, was never better pleased than when engaged in some desperate affair, whether alone or accompanied by some of his men. One of the latter, S. J. Hale, lately returned from an expedition with a very lugubrious countenance, superinduced by the result of an adventure thus narrated:

Mounted on a swift horse, he was carrying dispatches, secreted on his person, to a certain post in this State, (Missouri,) and was somewhere in the vicinity of Waverly. He had ridden some ten miles, and was very disconsolate for want of an adventure, for the boys cannot sit patiently in their saddles if something stirring does not turn up occasionally. He made up his mind to stop the first suspicious looking individual he should meet, and had not long to wait.

An independent Secesh came along on a horse, carrying a shot gun and whistling "Dixie." Hale presented his revolver at the fellow and ordered him to dismount, which he did. The scout took possession of horse and gun, and saw the Rebel vanish in the woods. It was after this that the joke occurred which made poor Hale a wiser if not a happier man.

Lost in reverie he rode along, and unconsciously began to whistle Yankee Doodle, but had scarcely gone two bars of the tune, when out sprang from the woods a large and fierce-looking man, who, quick as thought, took a deadly aim at the young adventurer, within a few feet of his breast.

The scout was at his wit's end in a moment, and saw that he could not escape. To draw his revolver would have been madness, so he made no movement, but asked "Who are you?"

The Rebel's answer was, "I may be a ghost, but alive or dead, you can't fool this child; you're a Lincoln horde; come off that horse."

Off came Hale, and into the Rebel's hands soon went his pistols. The poor fellow thought he would now be allowed to go, but he was startled with the hoarse order of the Rebel—"Off with them boots!" and off came the boots.

"Off with them pants or die!" said the terrible Secesh, and off came the breeches. It didn't take the Rebel long to exchange his ragged habilaments for the sound ones which he had secured, and mounting his newly acquired horse he said, "Farewell, old codger; you're played out. Your company don't suit, and your suit is gone." A very quaint remark, but painfully true. Poor Hale's only remark was in the language of an old or new play, we don't remember which:

> " Done brown, by heaven!
> Let this pernicious hour
> Stand accursed in the calendar!
> Somebody catch me. I feel very faint.
> I'm very sick. Let me go home and die in comfort!"

The last thing Hale remembered of the Rebel was hearing him loudly sing:

> " In Dixie's land I'll take my stand,
> Wish you were in Dixie."

Over the subsequent travels of the breechesless young man we delicately throw a veil.

STORY XXIV.

CAPTURE OF PORT ROYAL, SOUTH CAROLINA.

On Tuesday, October 29th, 1861, the fleet, under command of Flag-Officer S. F. Dupont, sailed from Hampton Roads, numbering, with the army transports, fifty vessels. It was, in consequence of the delay in the arrival of some of the transports intended for conveying the troops of General T. W. Sherman's command, which constituted a principal feature of the expedition, that its departure was not effected sooner.

It was calculated that the passage to Port Royal would be effected in five days. at most; but, in consequence of adverse winds. and a perilous storm on the day and night of the 1st of November, in which the fleet was almost entirely dispersed, and two or three of the transports lost, (the men, however, all being saved, excepting seven.) the fleet did not arrive at Port Royal until the 4th of November, and then in straggling order.

Commodore Dupont says: "The fleet was utterly dispersed, and, on Saturday morning, one sail only was in sight from the deck of the Wabash. On the following day the weather moderated, and the steamers and ships began to re-appear. As the vessels re-joined, reports came in of disasters. I expected to hear of many; but, when the severity of the gale and the character of the vessels are considered, we have only cause for great thankfulness."

It was on Monday, at eight o'clock in the morning, that the Wabash (the flag-ship) anchored off the bar, with some twenty-five vessels in company and many more heaving in sight.

All the buoys and aids to navigation had been removed by the enemy, but the efficiency and skill of Commander Davis, the fleet captain, and Mr. Boutelle, assistant of the Coast Survey, with the steamer Vixen, soon found and buoyed out the channel, so that by three o'clock, P. M., the lighter transports and the gun-boats commenced passing the bar, and before dark, were securely anchored in the roadstead of Port Royal.

On Tuesday morning, a reconnoissance in force was made by the gunboats Octavia and Seneca and the steamship Flag, which drew the fire of the batteries on Hilton Head and Bay Point, sufficiently to show that the fortifications were works of strength and scientifically constructed.

Captain Davis and Mr. Boutelle having reported water enough for the Wabash to enter, she crossed the bar in safety, closely followed by the frigate Susquehanna, the Atlantic, Vanderbilt, and other transports of deep draft, running through that portion of the fleet already in.

The safe passage of the Wabash over the bar was hailed with gratifying cheers from the crowded vessels. She anchored, and immediately commenced preparing for action. But the delay occasioned by the planting of buoys, to designate shoals to be avoided, rendered it too late, in the judgment of Commodore Dupont, before it was possible to leave anchorage with the attacking squadron. The next day the wind blew a gale from the southward and westward, and the attack was unavoidably postponed.

At nine o'clock, A. M., November 7th, the flag-ship

made the signal to fall in and form in order of battle, the Wabash leading the main column, composed of the following vessels: Wabash, Susquehanna, Mohican, Seminole, Pawnee, Unadilla, Ottawa, Pembina and Vandalia. The starboard column was composed of the following vessels: Bienville, Seneca, Curlew, Penguin and Augusta.

At ten o'clock, A. M., the batteries on each side of the river opened fire on the head of the column, from long range heavy guns, which the flag-ship promptly replied to, and soon the action became general along the whole line, as the ships came within range.

At 10:30 the flag-ship winded the line, turning to the southward, when she engaged, for a few minutes, three Rebel steamers, within long range, up the river, which were soon put to flight, when she again proceeded in the order of battle down within close range of Fort Walker, on Hilton Head, when the firing became very spirited on both sides. After passing the batteries, the line was again winded in a circle, during which time our men kept up a steady fire.

"I kept under way," says the Commodore," and made three turns, though I passed five times between the forts. I had a flanking division of five ships to watch, and old Tatnall too, who had eight small, swift steamers ready to pounce in upon any of ours, should they be disabled. I could get none of my big frigates up."

The previous reconnoissance had satisfied all with the superiority of Fort Walker, and to that the Commodore directed his special efforts, engaging it at 800 yards, and afterward at 600. But the plan of attack brought the squadron near enough to Fort Beauregard to receive its fire, and the ships were frequently fighting the batteries on both sides at the same time.

. A well directed fire from the heavy guns of our gun boats and small steamers, soon drove the enemy from his defences, and so concluded a well contested fight, by a glorious victory. The defeat of the enemy ter minated in utter rout and confusion. Their quarters and encampments were abandoned, without an attempt to carry away either private or public property.

At half past two o'clock the American ensign was hoisted on the flag staff of Fort Walker, and on the next morning at sunrise, on that of Fort Beauregard. The ground over which the Rebels had fled was found strewn with the arms of private soldiers, and even the officers had retired in too much haste to be impeded with the incumbrance of their swords.

Landing the marines and a company of seamen, the commodore took possession of the abandoned ground, and held the forts on Hilton Head, till the arrival of General Sherman, to whom he transferred their com- mand.

With these forts were captured 43 pieces of cannon, most of them being of very heavy calibre, and the most improved design. Their sights were found graduated at 600 yards. Their rifled guns never missed. An 80-pounder rifle ball went through the mainmast of the Wabash, in the very centre, making an awful hole. They fought bravely, and their confidence was extreme that they could drive away their assailants.

When the Rebels once broke, the stampede was in- tense; and not a gun was spiked. In truth, says the Commodore, I never conceived of such a fire as that of this ship, on her second turn, and I am told that its

K

effect upon the spectators outside of her was intense. I learn that when they saw our flag on shore the troops were powerless to cheer, but wept. General Sherman was deeply affected, and the soldiers were loud and unstinting in their expressions of admiration and gratitude.

General Sherman says, I consider the performance a masterly one, and it ought to have been seen, to be fully appreciated.

After the works were reduced, I took possession of them with the land forces. The beautifully constructed work on Hilton Head was severely crippled, and many of the guns dismounted. Much slaughter had evidently been made there, many bodies having been buried in the fort, and some twenty or thirty were found a half mile distant.

The island, for many miles, was found strewed with the arms, and accoutrements, and baggage of the Rebels, which they threw away in their retreat. We also came into possession of about forty pieces of ordnance, and a large quantity of ammunition and camp equipage.

Our loss was reported by the Commodore, officially, at eight killed, and twenty-three wounded.

The moment General Drayton, the Rebel commander, took to his horse, in the panic of the 7th, his 200 servants went directly to the Wabash. This was worthy of notice as putting down the nonsense that the slaves were ready to fight for their masters.—DUPONT, et al.

SKETCH OF GENERAL T. W. SHERMAN.

GENERAL T. W. SHERMAN, commanding the land forces of the Port Royal expedition, entered the military service from the State of Rhode Island, and graduated at West Point, in 1836, the eighteenth in his class.

He was appointed a second lieutenant in the Third Artillery on July 1st, 1836; assistant commissary of subsistence, in March, 1837; first lieutenant of artillery, in March, 1838; captain, in May, 1846, and a brevet major in May, 1848, for "gallant and meritorious services, at the battle of Buena Vista," on the 23d of February, 1847.

Gardner's Military Dictionary says he was distinguished by his prudence and firmness in preventing a war with certain of the Sioux Indians, 1857.

He was for years in command of light artillery, well known as Sherman's Battery, and had always stood well, in the estimation of the army, for his skill and attainments as an artillerist.

On the breaking out of the Rebellion, when the new regiments were authorized to be added to the army, he was appointed a lieutenant-colonel of the Fifth Artillery.

He was among the first appointments of brigadier generals of volunteers; and soon after the battle of Bull Run he was assigned to the important duty of organizing the land forces of the Port Royal expedition, and established his Camp of Instruction at Hempsted, Long Island.

Prior to sailing on the Port Royal expedition, in consequence of an expected advance of the Rebels, his entire force was transferred to Washington.

STORY XXV.

CIRCUMSTANCES OF THE DEATH OF JOHN A. WASHINGTON—DESECRATOR OF A NOBLE NAME.

A CORRESPONDENT of the *Gazette*, writing from Cheat Mountain, Va., says: "I have the pleasure, and indeed it is a pleasure, to send you the news of the death of John A. Washington, who was killed yesterday afternoon, (September 15, 1861,) about seven miles south of Elk Water camp.

"The circumstances were as follows:—In company with three other officers he was approaching our fortifications with a view of making a reconnoissance. Secreted in the bushes by the road-side were a number of the 17th Indiana regiment, and, as Washington and his companions came up the road, the Indiana boys rose from their concealment and fired. Washington fell from his horse on the first round, having received three bullets, two of which passed entirely through his body, entering at the right breast; and one of the others was also hit, but the two remaining unhurt managed to get him away by supporting him on his horse.

"The body of Washington was conveyed to the quarters of Colonel Waggoner. He lived for the space of half an hour, and never spoke, save to utter once, 'O, my God!' The next day his body was sent to the Rebel camp under a flag of truce. In the pockets of Washington was found one hundred dollars in United States gold currency, and a splendid gold watch. His dress was new, and of the most elegant make, broadcloth coat and pants, and a white satin vest. His shoulder-straps denoted him to be a colonel—of one of the Virginia regiments, I suppose."

This was the same Washington who lived near Harper's Ferry, and figured somewhat as one of the unhurt victims of John Brown's raid. In the early stage of the war our authorities were so afraid of exasperating the Rebels that they strove to subdue them with bulrushes, as Homer's frogs fought the mice. Washington's money and watch were therefore taken from the captors and restored to his relatives, under cover of a flag of truce.

STORY XXVI.

PORT ROYAL CONTRABANDS.

THE negroes, as yet, show few symptoms of vindictiveness: but in two instances they have assisted in the capture of their former masters.

A Mr. Cuthbert, the owner of several large plantations on St. Helena Island and the main, was caught by Captain Falkner with the assistance of his own negroes. A small reconnoitering party, on the Coosaw river, met a boat containing half a dozen blacks and a white man, a German. This boat was seized, the blacks interrogated—they belonged to Cuthbert, and were going to meet him at a neighboring point.

Captain Falkner took the place of the captured white man, (whom he left in the care of his troops,) and ordered the negroes to row him back to their master. Another boat, containing a squad of Union men, fol-

lowed at a short distance. It was nearly dusk, and as
Falkner approached the place where Cuthbert stood
waiting his boat, the latter cried out, "Who comes
there?" The negroes answered and were recognized.

Captain Falkner at once jumped ashore with the
blacks and seized the Rebel. A scuffle ensued, for the
Southerner was armed, and a large and powerful man,
Falkner small. The negroes took no part, (they had
not yet gotten over their awe of a master,) and not till
the second boat arrived was Cuthbert secured. While
he was being rowed off, a prisoner in his own boat, and
by his own slaves, they burst out into singing, to the
tune of one of their own rude hymns, making the ver-
sicles as they went along :

> "O massa a Rebel we row him to prison, hallelujah.
> Massa no whip me any more, hallelujah.
> We hab no massa now, we free, hallelujah.
> We hab de yankees dey no run away, hallelujah.
> O! all our ole massas run away, hallelujah.
> O! massa gwine to de prison now, hallelujah."

Cuthbert, who had come to the island for the purpose
of preventing the escape of his slaves, was a lieutenant
of the boat—a patrol established for protecting the
coast at once against the Nationalists and the negroes.
He had, in conversation with Captain Falkner, scrupu-
lously maintained that the negroes loved their masters,
and wanted no freedom; but when the exulting chants
were sung in his hearing, he acknowledged that so long
as the Union forces remained, the South Carolinians
were in danger from their slaves. He was sent North
a prisoner.

STORY XXVII.

STORY OF THE WRECKS.

THE following account of the fate of the wrecked transports, during the terrible gale of the 1st of November, 1861, condensed from the correspondence of the *Tribune*, is deemed a proper appendage to the preceding account of the capture of Port Royal:

As our fleet slowly straggled into the harbor of rendezvous, after that most fearful tempest, and as we noted the continued absence of one after another of our noble vessels, we reluctantly made up our unwilling minds to the sad belief that at least six of our smaller steamers had gone down: the ferry-boats Ethan Allen and Commodore Perry, the transports Union, Peerless, Governor and Belvidere.

There was also much anxiety about the Ocean Express, though as she was a large and staunch sailing ship, it was hoped that she had merely been blown out of her course, and would weather the gale and yet make her appearance.

This latter vessel was, to a great extent, the right arm of the expedition, for she carried all the heavy cannon with which it was proposed to make our Palmetto foothold good. Upon the same ship also, by a strange oversight of the chief of ordnance (Captain McNutt), had been placed the entire stock of gunpowder with which it had been intended to fill the magazines, for the use of the siege-trains that might be organized from Port Royal for the benefit of Charleston or Savannah.

Should the Ocean Express be lost, the army would be so crippled as to be almost powerless for offensive operations, until new supplies could be sent. If such a great loss should come to the knowledge of the enemy, it was easy to see what advantage might be taken of it. The act of loading all the stores of such an indispensable nature on a single ship, was one so strange as hardly to be credible of an old and experienced officer, and the condemnation of the mistake was as universal as was the feverish anxiety regarding the fate of the ship. This strange proceeding was, however, subsequently accounted for when, on a medical examination, held by request of his friends, the officer was pronounced insane.

The anxiety was less concerning the other vessels than perhaps it otherwise would have been, from the fact that, with one exception, they carried no men beside their own crews. On board the Governor, however, were Major John G. Reynold's battalion of marines, 340 men, all told.

The Peerless was an English steamer, of small size, and had on board 87 live beef-cattle, for the use of the army.

The Ethan Allen and Commodore Perry were two ferry-boats, formerly employed on the Williamsburg ferries, and were of the same pattern and size as those that ply on the East river. It is a matter for surprise that they were ever deemed adequate to weather Hatteras in a November gale. However, they were to attempt the passage, and were intended to be employed in landing troops, after the fleet had reached its destination.

The Belvidere had on board horses and commissary

stores; and the Union had also a few head of cattle, and quartermasters' stores.

The fleet began to arrive in Port Royal harbor on Sunday night, but no one of the above missing vessels was seen until Thursday morning, when the Ocean Express came in, to the great relief of all.

Meanwhile, the most doleful accounts had reached us of the others. It was asserted that the Governor had gone down with 200 marines; this number, by degrees, came down to 20, at which point it remained till some of the rescued men arrived, to set the matter right. The other missing vessels were all believed to have gone down.

It was afterward ascertained, however, that the Union went ashore on the coast of North Carolina, and all her crew were saved, though 73 soldiers were made prisoners, there being a few in her. The Belvidere, after such a struggle with the storm as few ships ever live to tell of, came safely out. The two ferry-boats, the Ethan Allen and Commodore Perry, finding they could not weather the gale, put back for Fortress Monroe, which place they finally reached. The Pearless and Governor both went down, under the following circumstances:

The steamer Governor started from Fortress Monroe with the rest of the fleet, on Tuesday, October 29th, and proceeded pleasantly enough until she encountered the gale, which began on Thursday night, and which soon increased to a tempest.

On Friday she was struck by a number of heavy seas, which made crashing work with every thing on deck. Beyond carrying away the deck-load, and smashing up some of the lighter wood-work, no serious damage was done, until three, P. M., Friday; when seven or eight terrible seas, in quick succession, struck her, and broke her hog-braces.

In a few minutes another sea carried her smoke-stack overboard, thus, for the moment, adding the terrible danger of *fire* to the perils of the winds and waves. At eight, P. M., the steam-pipe burst; and at two, A. M., on Saturday, the packing of the cylinder blew out, thus completely disabling the engines.

At four, A. M., the rudder-chains broke, leaving her, for a time, totally unmanageable. The tiller was presently rigged, but in a few minutes the rudder-head broke short off, depriving the vessel of all her steering apparatus, and leaving her a helpless wreck on the water, in one of the hardest gales that ever blew on this coast.

After a few hours of agonizing suspense, during which, all on board made up their minds that death awaited them, speedy and certain, they spoke the gunboat Isaac Smith, which had been attracted by the Governor's signals of distress, and the bark Young Rover. Both promised to stay by her; but in the tremendous sea then running, neither could render the slightest assistance. The Rover, however, cheered their sinking hearts, by telling them that a large frigate was bearing down to their relief.

The men went into ecstacies of extravagant joy when the frigate hove in sight. She proved to be the Sabine, and Captain Ringgold promised to do every thing in his power for their aid—a promise he most nobly redeemed.

By order of Captain Ringgold, the two ships were fastened together by two powerful hawsers. The Sabine then veered out chain enough to bring her stern within thirty feet of that of the Governor. Two heavy spars were then rigged from the stern of the Sabine, in the direction of the sinking ship, and were there made securely fast.

The spars were projected nearly over the bows of the Governor, but they rose and fell with each tremendous swell, so that it would have been hopeless for any person to cross from one ship to the other by crawling along the spars; this, however, had not been intended, but a safer plan was adopted.

From the ends of the spars were lowered strong ropes, rigged to run easily through pulley-blocks; at the end of the rope which dropped on board the Governor a running loop was made, and the crew of the Sabine manned the other end. All things being ready, the loop was made fast under the arms of a man, the crew of the Sabine gave a quick run aft, and in less time than it takes to tell it, the man was raised in the air and swung on board the frigate.

Thirty men were thus saved when both hawsers broke and the ships separated. The Governor was then brought close under the quarter of the Sabine, and about forty more leapt to her deck, and the others, all, excepting a corporal and six men, were finally assisted on board. Of those lost, four were washed over, in trying to cross on the hawsers from ship to ship; one was crushed between the ships, and the other three slipped overboard and were drowned. They saved all their muskets but twenty; 10,000 cartridges and some clothing were lost.

The Peerless was a small steamer, chartered to be used in the shallow waters of the Southern rivers and creek. She had on board 87 beef-cattle, was caught in

in the gale, and made signal of distress, when the Star of
the South ran down to her aid, and going too close, ran
into the Peerless, doing her much damage. The captain then lightened the ship by throwing the cattle overboard; but the ship continuing to sink, he was obliged
to leave her. The crew were all taken off by the
Mohican. The captain was the last to leave her—she
went down within an hour.

STORY XXVIII.

ROMANCE OF THE WAR—A GALLANT DEED AND CHIVAL ROUS RETURN.

IN a movement of Stoneman's cavalry, in May, 1863,
the advance was led by Lieutenant Paine, of the 1st
Maine cavalry. Being separated by a considerable distance from the main body, he unexpectedly encountered
a superior force of Rebel cavalry, and his whole party
were taken prisoners. They were hurried off as rapidly as possible to get them out of the way of our
advancing force, and, in crossing a rapid deep stream,
Lieutenant Henry, commanding the Rebel force, was
swept off his horse.

As none of his men seemed to think or care anything
about saving him, his prisoner, Lieutenant Paine, leaped
off his horse, seized the drowning man by the collar,
swam ashore with him, and saved his life, thus literally
capturing his captor. He was sent to Richmond with
the rest of the prisoners, and the facts being made
known to General Fitzhugh Lee, he wrote a statement
of them to General Winder, the Provost Marshal of

Richmond, who ordered the instant release of Lieutenant Paine, without even parole, promise or condition, and, we presume, with the compliments of the Confederacy, and he arrived soon after in Washington.

This act of generosity, as well as justice, must command our highest admiration. There is some hope for men who can behave in such a manner. But the strangest part of the story is yet to come. Lieutenant Paine, on arriving in Washington, learned that the officer, whose life he had thus gallantly saved, had since been taken prisoner by our forces, had just and been confined in the Old Capitol prison. The last we heard of him he was on his way to General Martindale's headquarters to obtain a pass to visit his beneficiary and benefactor.

Such are the vicissitudes of war. We could not help thinking, when we heard this story, of the profound observation of Mrs. Gump: "Sich is life, vich likewise is the hend of hall things hearthly." We leave it to casuists to determine whether, when these two gallant soldiers meet on the battle-field, they should fight like enemies, or embrace like Christians? For our part, we do not believe that their swords will be any the less sharp, nor their zeal any the less determined, for this haphazard exchange of soldierly courtesy.

STORY XXIX.

THE "CONTRABAND'S" MISTAKE.

WHILE General McClellan commanded our army in Western Virginia, a stout male "contraband" suddenly
L

disappeared from his master in an inexplicable manner. He was afterward discovered harmlessly pursuing the avocation of cook in the camp of the 19th Ohio.

Sambo was suddenly confronted with his master, in the General's presence.

Quoth our legal military friend, Lieutenant-Colonel Key, " What's your name, boy? "

" Pompey Johnson, sah." replied Sambo.

" Where are you from?" continued the Colonel.

" Johnsontown, Cumb'land County, State ob Ohio," said the negro, with sublime audacity,

" Do you know that man?" asked the Colonel, designating Sambo's master.

The darkey eyed his master, coolly, from head to foot, as if he was preparing to swear to his inches, and, without winking, responded—

" No, sah—dun' 'no him; neber seed him afore—stranga to me, sah."

" Why, you rascal," interposed his master, " I raised you—bought you when you were nine years old; everybody in town knows you're my nigger."

" Dun' 'no you, sah! Stranga to me, sah! I'se free cullud pussun, sah! Cum from 'hio, sah, wid the sogers."

The neighbors identified Pompey as the claimant's chattel, and he was remanded to servitude, when he suddenly regained his consciousness, and retired obediently. He had been captured from his master, a Secessionist, by some of the lads of the 19th Ohio, who desired him for a cook, and had instructed him to play the part he assumed. The darkey, however, mistook the name of the county he was to hail from, substituting Cumberland for Trumbull.

STORY XXX.

BATTLE OF CHESNABURG.

THE affair commonly known as the "Battle of Ches
naburg," which occurred in the Kanawha campaign of
1861, is deserving of a place in our war history.
General Cox's division had been moving from place
to place, and finally encamped in the vicinity of Spiral
Knob. No enemy in force had for some time appeared
and the army was eager for a fight.

One evening a celebrated scout from a neighboring
State went out, and had proceeded about seven miles,
when he came upon the pickets of the enemy. Crawling up to the encampment, he alarmed the sentinels,
who gave chase, but finally eluding them, he returned
to camp with the joyful tidings that several thousand
Secessionists were encamped in a cornfield, about seven
miles off.

Upon receipt of the news, the countenances of the
officers and men beamed with delight at the prospect
of a fight. It was at once decided that the Secesh
should be attacked the same night, and the colonel of
the regiment to which the scout belonged claimed the
honor of leading the attack, as one of his men had
discovered the enemy.

That evening, at dress parade, the order was read to
the attacking force to march at a certain hour. The
gallant colonel, not wishing that any should be forced
to fight who were disinclined, and that he should not
be embarrassed by any cowardly spirits, addressed his
men, telling them that all such as were afraid could

remain behind. The men were worked up to a good fighting pitch, and when the hour for marching came, all were found in their places,

The regiment moved off, each man determined to win or die, and was followed by a supporting force, at a proper distance. Silently, they marched for several miles, with the determined tread of men who were resolved on victory or an honorable death. The road was rugged and crooked, winding around mountains and through ravines, as only mountain roads can.

When near the camp of the vile Secesh, General M., who had command of the whole force, rode to the front and engaged in conversation with the colonel commanding the advance. Having attained the summit of a mountain ridge, which gave a view of the opposite hills, they soon espied the pickets of the enemy. The lines were formed and everything put in readiness for a charge, when General M., raising himself in his stirrups, exclaimed: "Why, Colonel, *those are my pickets! and, by golly, that is my camp!*"

The effect of this announcement may be better imagined than described. Just think of two or three thousand men being roused from their slumbers at midnight, marched seven miles over one of the worst roads in creation, and then being brought up before their own camp!

The matter was finally explained. The road they had followed ran in an easterly or southeasterly direction from the camp, then winding round among the mountains, ran directly west, and came out into the road at the south end of the encampment. The scout had also followed the same road, and came very near being caught by his own friends, in his own camp.

This ludicrous affair has been appropriately christ-
ened, and will hereafter be known, in the Cheat Mountain region, as the Battle of Chesnaburg.

STORY XXXI.

RUNNING THE GAUNTLET OF FORTS JACKSON AND ST. PHILIP.

THE expedition for the capture of New Orleans, under
Major-General Benjamin F. Butler of the land forces,
and Flag Officer Farragut of the naval forces, and Captain D. D. Porter of the mortar flotilla, being in the
lower Mississippi, on the morning of the 17th of April,
1862, passed up and anchored on the west shore. The
advance vessels were about a mile below a chain barrier,
which the enemy had stretched across the river on hulks,
but which proved not very difficult of removal.

The purpose of the Commodore was to bombard the
forts, Jackson and St. Philips, from about half a mile
above our position, the forts being distinctly visible
from our mast heads.

The hulls of the mortar boats were screened by
woods, and the masts were disguised with evergreens,
a precaution adopted by the sailors, so that from
the forts they were scarcely distinguishable from the
trees.

Fire rafts were sent down by the rebels, designed to
destroy our fleet, but were prevented by the precaution-
ary measures of Captain Porter.

Failing to reduce the forts after six days of incessant

fire, having commenced on the 18th, Flag Officer Farragut determined to attempt their passage with his whole fleet, except that portion of it under the immediate command of Captain Porter, known as the mortar fleet, being the Harriet Lane, Westfield, Owasco, Clifton and Marine, also the Jackson, towing the Portsmouth. This flotilla was to remain below, so that when the Commodore should have effected his passage above the forts, the enemy would be placed between two fires, with his supplies from New Orleans cut off, thus rendering his surrender merely a question of time.

About eleven o'clock P. M. of the 23d, the Itasca signaled that the chain was clear, and that the fleet could proceed when ready. The night was moderately dark, and the mortar vessels kept up an incessant roar.

The first division of the fleet was lying along the right bank of the river, the second division was formed on the left bank, while the third division was in the centre of the lines. The whole were to sail in the following order:

1st Division, FLAG OFFICER FARRAGUT *commanding.*

Hartford. COM. WAINRIGHT.   *Brooklyn,* CAPT. T. T. CRAVEN.
Richmond, COM. ALDEN.

2d Division, CAPT. BAILEY *commanding.*

Cayuga, LIEUT. HARRISON.   *Verona,* COM. C. L. BOGGS.
Pensacola, CAPT. MORRIS.   *Katahdin,* LIEUT. PREBLE.
Mississippi, COM. SMITH,   *Kneodout,* COM. RANSOM.
Oneida, COM. J. P. LEE.   *Wissahickon,* LIEUT. A. A. SMITH.

3d Division, CAPT. BELL *commanding.*

Sciota, CAPT. H. H. BELL.   *Itasca*
Iroquois.   *Winona,* LIEUT. EDW. NICHOLS.
Pinola.   *Kennebec.*

At one o'clock A. M. on the 24th, all hands were

called, hammocks stowed, and everything put in order
to weigh anchor at two o'clock.

At two o'clock two red lights at the Hartford's mizen
peak announced the time to get under way. The second
division from some cause did not start at the signal, and
the whole were delayed half an hour.

At three o'clock the moon arose, and a silvery path
was bright before us upon the placid waters; and in
thirty minutes we were gliding over it swiftly to the
conflict; while the signal fires of the enemy, enhancing
the lunar light, rendered our approach distinctly visible
to them.

The advance column, led by the gunboat Cayuga,
Captain Bailey, approaching Fort St. Philip at a quarter
to 4 o'clock, both forts opened their fire. At ten minutes to four o'clock, having brought her guns to bear,
the Cayuga opened fire with grape and shrapnel on Fort
St. Philip. At four o'clock she passed the line of the
fort, and encountered eleven gunboats above.

Meanwhile the rest of the fleet were not idle; the
Oneida and Verona coming up, pitched gallantly into
the fight. The flag ship Hartford joined in the fight at
five minutes to four, replying to Fort Jackson with a
nine inch shell, soon followed by rapid broadside firing,
the other vessels of the division following suit; while
to add to the deafening noise the mortar boats inces-
santly belched forth their destructive missiles with continuous roar.

Shot, shell, grape and canister filled the air. Steadily
we steamed on, giving them shell; the forts firing rifled
shot and shell, ten inch, columbiads forty-two, thirty-two,
and twenty-four pounder balls; and at the same time
thirteen steamers and the floating battery Louisiana,

were pouring into and around us a hailstorm of iron, perfectly indescribable.

Their steamers were crowded with troops who fired volleys of rifle balls at us with but little effect. One of them neared us, containing some 200 men, when our howitzer opened on her, and Captain Proome, of the Marine Corps, also opened upon her with two nine-inch guns, when was heard an explosion, terrific yells, a careen, and that fellow was done for.

The Verona sunk six of them in succession, and was herself sunk by a ram. The Cayuga, as before stated, encountered a fleet of them, which she succeeded in discomfitting, either sinking, capturing, firing, or driving them ashore. At half past five o'clock, having been under a terrific fire for an hour and twenty minutes, the Hartford passed the forts badly cut up, and saw several Rebel steamers which had encountered the Cayuga, and other boats of the advance, in flames along each side of the river. The Hartford passed up to the quarantine, which had previously surrendered to Captain Bailey, of the Cayuga.

In the afternoon, Commander Farragut dispatched Captain Boggs, of the Verona, to Captain Porter, with the following letter:

"DEAR PORTER: We had a rough time of it, as Boggs will tell you; but, thank God, the number of killed and wounded was very small, considering. This ship had two killed, and eight wounded. We destroyed the ram in a single combat between him and the old Mississippi; but the ram backed out when he saw the the Mississippi coming at him so rampantly, and he dodged her and ran on shore, whereupon Smith put two or three broadsides through him and knocked him all to pieces. The ram pushed a fire-raft on to me, and in trying to avoid it I ran the ship on shore. He again pushed the fire-raft on me, and got the ship on fire all along one side. I thought it was all up with us, but we put it out, and got on again, proceeding up the river, fighting our way.

"We have destroyed all but two of the gunboats, and these will have to surrender with the forts. I intend to follow up my success, and push for New Orleans, and then come down and attend to the forts, so you hold them in *statue quo* until I come back. I think if you send a flag of truce and demand their surrender, they will yield, for their intercourse with the city is cut off. We have cut the wires above the quarantine, and are now going ahead. I took three or four hundred prisoners at Quarantine. They surrended, and I paroled them not to take up arms again. I could not stop to take care of them.

"If the General will come up to the bayou and land a few men, or as many as he pleases, he will find two of our gunboats there to protect him from the gunboats that are at the forts. I wish to get to the English Turn where they have not placed a battery yet, but have two above New Orleans. They will not be idle, and neither will I. You supported us nobly.

"Very truly, yours,

"D. C. FARRAGUT.

"To Captain D. D. PORTER.
    "Commanding Mortar Flotilla."

Captain Boggs, the bearer of this letter, late commander of the Verona, stated that before the Verona sunk, she destroyed, alone, six of the Rebel steamers, of which he learned the names of four, viz.: the Wm. H.

Webb, Palmetto, Phenix, and Jackson. As he passed
the forts, the Verona, as well as all the other vessels,
received their fire. The Richmond, and one or two
more of the large steam-sloops, slackened speed, and
poured three or four broadsides each into the enemy.

The Verona, after discharging two broadsides, passed
on a mile or two above, and came in contact with
several Rebel gunboats, by which she was attacked,
two or three assailing her at once, butting her with their
iron-cased prows, and making several large holes in her.

Captain Boggs fought them bravely with his guns as
long as his vessel floated, and drove the Rebel steamers
ashore, where they were fired by their own crews. One
of his shot disabled still another steamer, by making a
hole in her boiler, when she surrendered to the Oneida,
which took her officers and crew prisoners.

The Verona's last guns were fired when her decks
were under water, and no clothing or property of any
kind on board was saved. She lost three of her crew
killed, and seven wounded. Eleven Rebel steamers,
including the ram, were destroyed, and the captain of
the ram captured.

After the fight, the whole squadron that passed the
forts, numbering twelve vessels, repaired to the Quarantine anchorage, seven miles above the fort. There the
dead were buried, and the wounded cared for. Our
killed and wounded was estimated, by Captain Boggs,
at about one hundred and twenty-five; the enemy's loss
was thought to be enormous.

Captain Porter, acting on the suggestion of Commodore Farragut, sent Captain Guest, with a flag of truce,
up to the forts, with a demand for an unconditional
surrender. As the captain approached Fort St. Philip,

his flag was fired on several times, when he immediately returned. Half an hour after, a gig came down from the Rebel fort, bearing a white flag and a Rebel lieutenant with a motley crew. After learning the nature of our demand, he went back to the fort, and soon returned again with an answer from Colonel Higginson that our terms were inadmissible, and that the forts would never surrender.

Soon after the Rebel answer had been received by Captain Porter, the bombardment of the forts was renewed by him, and continued until the mortar fleet was ordered down the river on the approach of the burning ships and the ram Manassas, with a view to obtaining greater sea room for advantageous manœuvring.

The larger part of the squadron having passed the forts, cheers of exultation, vehemently reiterated, made the welkin ring.

Of the gallantry, courage and conduct of this heroic action, unprecedented in naval warfare, considering the character of the work and the river, too much cannot be said.

At eleven o'clock on the morning of the 25th, the fleet weighed anchor and steamed up the river for New Orleans, leaving the Kineo and Wissahickon to guard the quarantine and keep possession of the canals leading out to the sea.

The sequel of this story, involving the surrender of the forts, I shall render very briefly. It had been arranged between the flag-officer and General Butler, that in case the forts were not reduced, and a portion of the fleet succeeded in passing them, that the General should make a landing from the Gulf side, in rear of the forts at the quarantine, and from thence attempt Fort St. Philip by assault, while the bombardment was continued by the fleet.

The General went with his troops to Sable Island, twelve miles in rear of Fort St. Philip. The 26th Massachusetts Volunteers, Colonel Jones, were then shipped on board the light draught steamer Miami, and taken within six miles of the fort, and from thence, with the aid of some thirty row-boat, conveyed four and a half miles further, the men, a part of the way, dragging the boats singly, themselves waist-deep in water. The enemy not considering this mode of attack possible, took no measures to oppose it. We occupied at once both sides of the river, effectually cutting them off from all supplies, while we made our dispositions for the assault. Captain Porter had sent two schooners into the bayou to cut off all escape, and General Phelps had two regiments in the river below. Thus surrounded, and the men in mutiny, the forts surrendered to Captain Porter on the 28th of April, and were at once occupied by General Butler.

STORY XXXII.

CAPTURE OF NEW ORLEANS.

LEAVING the Kneodout and Wissahickon to guard the quarantine and keep possession of the canals which lead out seaward, the fleet started up the river for New Orleans, at eleven o'clock, A. M., of the 24th of April, 1862.

For miles from their anchorage they found, on both sides of the river, the houses were decorated with white flags, and in many instances, tattered and torn American ensigns waved over fishing luggers and houses, while the people expressed their joy by hearty greetings, and waving of handkerchiefs. The precaution had been taken of cutting the telegraph wires every few miles, but the people of Orleans had been early warned of the fall of the forts, and made preparation to give the invaders a characteristic reception.

As the fleet proceeded, the negroes of the plantations left their labors and flocked to the levee, in apparent ecstacies of joy at its approach, ludicrously bowing, courtesying, and tossing hats and caps in the air.

During the afternoon dense columns of smoke were visible in the direction of New Orleans, indicating that something was on fire. The flames continued all the evening. At eight o'clock the fleet anchored eighteen miles below the city.

Getting under way again at half past five, A. M., on the 25th, we soon passed five large ships, laden with cotton, nearly consumed, evidently the source of the smoke and flames seen the evening before. At a quarter to eleven the Chelmette batteries were discovered on each side of the river, the one mounting ten guns, the other eight. They both opened fire on our advance, but were silenced in a few minutes, with the loss of one man overboard.

"This last affair," says Farragut, "is what I call one of the elegancies of the profession—a dash and a victory."

The river was filled with ships on fire, and along the levee were burning vessels, no less than eighteen being on fire at one time, and others were being fired as fast as

M

the torch could be applied. A terrible rain storm came on and the fleet came to anchor at one o'clock, P. M.

The view from the decks was such as will probably never be witnessed again. A large city lay at the mercy of our fleet. Its levee was crowded by an excited mob. The smoke of the ruins of millions of dollars worth of cotton and shipping at times concealed the people.

While men were hastening up the levee, firing ships and river craft as fast as possible, others were rushing to and fro. Some, who cheered for the Union, were fired upon by the crowd; men, women and children being armed with pistols, knives, and various weapons.

Some cheered for Jeff. Davis and Beauregard, using the most insolent and defiant language toward the old flag: order being a thing past and forgotten.

At two o'clock, Captain Bailey went on shore, bearing a flag of truce, for the purpose of communicating with the authorities. As the boats drew near the levee, the mob cursed the old flag and everything pertaining to it. It was with the greatest difficulty that the naval officers reached the City Hall, where the City Council, the Mayor and Major-General Lovell were awaiting their arrival.

Flag-Officer Farragut sent word to the authorities that he demanded the surrender of the City of New Orleans, and assured them of the protection of the "old flag." The city being under martial-law, of course the civil authorities could do nothing; but General Lovell, with much pomposity and bluster, replied that he would never surrender. But, on being informed that the city was in our power, he agreed to evacuate the city with his troops, numbering some ten or fifteen thousand, and leave matters to the civil authorities.

Captain Bailey and his aid, Lieutenant Perkins, then returned to the boats, suffering many insults and indignities by the way, as also did the officer in charge of the boats in their absence.

The next morning Mayor Monroe sent his secretary and chief of police to Commodore Farragut, to say that he would convene the Council at ten o'clock, and give him an answer: that the general had retired, and that he had resumed the duties of his office as mayor, and would endeavor to preserve order in the city and prevent the destruction of property.

Flag-Officer Farragut sent the mayor a letter by his secretary, demanding a surrender of the city, in conformity with the demand made by him the day previous, through Captain Bailey. This second letter was as follows:

United States Flag-ship Hartford, }
off New Orleans, April 26, 1862. }

To his Excellency the Mayor of the City of New Orleans.

SIR:—Upon my arrival before your city, I had the honor to send to your honor, Captain Bailey, U. S. N. second in command of the expedition, to demand of you the surrender of New Orleans to me, as the representative of the Government of the United States. Captain Bailey reported the result of an interview with yourself and the military authorities. It must occur to your honor, that it is not within the province of a naval officer to assume the duties of a military commandant. I came here to reduce New Orleans to obedience to the laws of, and to vindicate the offended majesty of the Government of the United States. The rights of persons and property shall be secured.

I, therefore, as its representative, demand the unqualified surrender of the city, and that the emblem of the sovereignty of the United States be hoisted over the city hall, mint and custom-house, by meridian this day, and all flags and emblems of sovereignty, other than this of the United States, be removed from all the public buildings by that hour.

I particularly request that you shall exercise your authority to quell disturbances, restore order, and call upon all the good people of New Orleans to return at once to their vocations; and I particularly demand that no person shall be molested in person, property or sentiments of loyalty to their Government.

I shall speedily and severely punish any person or persons who shall commit such outrages as were witnessed yesterday, by armed men firing upon helpless women and children, for giving expression to their pleasure at witnessing the "old flag."

I am, very respectfully,

D. G. FARRAGUT,
Flag-Officer Western Gulf Squadron.

To this demand, the mayor replied at length, in what may be termed a subdued tone of insolence and arrogance in distress. Professing to give expression to the universal sentiment of his constituents, he says:

"The city is yours by brutal force, not by my choice or the consent of its inhabitants. It is for you to determine what will be the fate that awaits her. As to hoisting any flag not of our own adoption and allegiance, let me tell you that the man lives not in our midst whose hand and heart would not be paralyzed at the mere thought of such an act. Nor could I find, in my whole constituency, so desperate and wretched a renegade as would dare to profane with his hand the sacred emblem of our aspirations. * * * *

" You have a gallant people to administrate during your occupancy of this city, a people sensitive to all that can in the least affect their dignity and self-respect. Pray, so, do not fail to regard their susceptibilities. * * * Your occupying the city does not transfer allegiance from the Government of their choice, to one which they have deliberately repudiated, and that they yield the obedience which the conqueror is entitled to extort from the conquered."

Flag-Officer Farragut then sent the following:

U. S. FLAG-SHIP HARTFORD. at anchor, off City of New Orleans, April 26.

To his Honor, the Mayor of New Orleans :

Your Honor will please give directions that no flag but that of the United States will be permitted to fly in presence of this fleet, so long as it has the power to prevent it; and as all displays of that kind may cause bloodshed, I have to request that you will give this communication as general circulation as possible.

D. G. FARRAGUT,
Flag Officer

At ten o'clock the Commodore sent on shore Lieutenant Kortz, of the navy, and Lieutenant Brown, of the marines, with a marine guard to hoist the flag on the Custom-house, but the excitement was so great that the Mayor and councilmen thought it would produce a conflict, and great loss of life.

At eleven o'clock, pursuant to General Orders, all the officers and crews of the fleet assembled "to return thanks to Almighty God, for his great goodness and mercy in permitting them to pass through the events of the last two days with so little loss of life and blood."

Early on the same morning a boat's crew were sent to hoist the flag on the Mint, which having been done it was speedily torn down by one W. B. Mumford, assisted by the Rebels, Lieutenant Holmes, Sergeant Burns, and James Reed. They took the flag in triumph up St. Charles street, where it was torn in shreds and distributed.

General Butler, after taking possession of the forts on the 28th, and finding them defensible, and well provisioned, and a good store of ammunition, left the 26th regiment Massachusetts volunteers in garrison, and proceeded up the river with his main forces, to occupy New Orleans, being informed of its capture.

On arriving at New Orleans, General Butler reported officially, "I find the city under the dominion of the mob. They have insulted our flag, torn it down with indignity. This outrage will be punished in such manner as in my judgment will caution both the perpetrators and abettors of the act, so that they shall fear the stripes, if they do not reverence the stars of our banner."*

General Butler, on assuming the authority of the city, issued his proclamation and caused it to be offered for publication to the several newspaper offices, but they all refusing, the guard took possession of the True Delta office, sent for northern printers, set it up, put it in the form, and worked it off in the edition.

The main noticeable points of the proclamation, were the following:

* Mumford, the principal in the outrage, was afterwards hung for it.

All persons in arms against the United States were required to surrender.

All ensigns, flags, and devices, tending to uphold any authority whatever, save the flag of the United States, and of foreign consulates, must be suppressed.

All persons still holding allegiance to the Confederate States to be held as rebels and enemies.

All rights of property to be held inviolate, subject to the laws of the United States.

All inhabitants enjoined to pursue their usual avocations.

The circulation of Confederate bonds to be suppressed.

All assemblages of persons in the streets by night or day to be suppressed.

All requirements of martial law to be enforced as long as United States authorities deem necessary.

STORY XXXIII.

GENERAL BUTLER IN NEW ORLEANS.

THE following incident, illustrating General Butler's mode of dealing with refractory cases at New Orleans, during his administration there, is vouched for by the very best authority.

A merchant of that city, who was a Secessionist of that stamp that took great pleasure in spouting about "Picayune Butler," found himself with arms in his hands on the Rebel side of the lines, after the taking of New Orleans.

But he was under the necessity of writing frequently to the agent who had his property in charge. In his letters he frequently indulged in execrations of General Butler, and in one of them expressed a warm sympathy for men suffering under his tyrannous rule there, saying, that he believed a personal chastisement could be inflicted on Butler, and offering his friend and agent five thousand dollars to do the job.

It happened that this letter was seen by Butler, "and contents noted." Soon afterward the order was issued requiring all persons who wished to hold their estates in that city, real and personal, to register their names and take the oath of allegiance.

The merchant in question had too much to lose, and slipping within our lines again, endeavored to make himself at home around the city, as though he had never been away; but while busy at the preparatory work, General Butler's orderly waited on him with a polite invitation to call at headquarters. He did so, suspecting nothing.

General Butler received him very kindly, and begged to show him something of interest; taking the letter in question from his desk, he asked him if that was his handwriting and signature; and the convicted hater of Picayune Butler could do no less than own up.

General Butler then said to him, that as he was evidently a man of substance, with money to spare for good purposes, he might give his $5,000 to the fund for the support of the poor loyalists, as he had not been able to secure the threshing that he first proposed to pay it out for, and that he might have twenty-four hours in which to place the money in that fund, or go to the fort below, and wear a ball and chain.

The man made haste to liquidate, and registered himself on the side of General Butler's authority thereafter.

STORY XXXIV.

RUNNING THE VICKSBURG BLOCKADE.

ON the 1st of February, 1863, it was determined that the rams Monarch and Queen of the West should run past Vickburg on the following morning, at daybreak. For some cause the Monarch did not raise steam at the proper time, nor join the attempt, and the Queen did not get off as soon as was expected.

At six o'clock she started, under a full head of steam. She was under command of Colonel Ellet, who aided in capturing Memphis, in June previous. The Vicksburgers were evidently not taken by surprise, as they opened fire promptly on the ram. The Queen was four miles distant from Vicksburg when she started.

When she had proceeded half a mile, a signal-light was hoisted on the cupola of the Vicksburg Courthouse, and in five minutes three batteries opened. The Queen kept steadily on her way, the guns bearing on her increasing in number, momentarily, until finally, every battery seemed playing. Her progress was so rapid, that the batteries could not get range, with any degree of accuracy. Out of two hundred shots fired, only three took effect. Her capstan was shot away. One 7-inch shell lodged in the state-room, but did not explode. Had it done so, Colonel Ellet thought the ram would have been destroyed. No one on board was hurt.

The Queen attempted no reply to the batteries, but ran into the gun-boat Vicksburg, at the wharf, striking her forward of the cook-house, damaging her to some extent.   In less than one hour from starting, the Queen of the West was safely anchored below the city, at the mouth of the new cut-off.   She carried two long Parrot guns, and the intention of running her below, was to cut off steamboat communication between Vicksburg and Port Hudson.

STORY XXXIV.

ASSASSINATION OF GENERAL ROBERT L. McCOOK.

ON the 5th day of August, 1862, as General McCook was on his way with his brigade from Hazel Green to Winchester, Tennessee, when about six miles from Salem, Alabama, contiguous to the State line, it being about ten o'clock in the morning, he fell a victim to guerrillas.

He was riding in an ambulance, or small wagon, being ill, having been sick about six weeks, and was accompanied by Captain Hunter Brooke, who was nursing him.   He was not in advance of his command, as has been erroneously stated, but between regiments, the 18th regulars and part of the 1st Ohio cavalry, having preceded him.   His usual escort of twelve of the 1st Ohio cavalry were in attendance.

While on the road, they were attacked by a party of men in citizen's clothes, and were fired upon by them, some fifteen or twenty times; the men rushing out of the brush, by the road side, where they had lain secreted, and undiscovered by the advance regiments.

Unfortunately, the General had sent three of his

escort with orders to different parts of the brigade, and three others off the road to select a suitable camping-ground, thus reducing his escort to six.

As the guerrillas made for the ambulance, during the firing, the remainder of the escort fled, without firing a shot; seeing which, the driver of the ambulance attempted to escape them by running it half or three-quarters of a mile, but finding escape impossible, he stopped by running it against a bank; when General McCook and Captain Brooke both rose up and raised up their hands in token of having surrendered.

The assassin, John A. Gurley, rode up, (being fifteen or twenty yards in advance of the rest of the party,) and fired three shots from a revolver. The first shot took no effect, the second shot passed through Captain Brooke's coat, and the third shot struck General McCook in the left side, just at the lower rib, while he was in an upright position, with his hands raised.

After the performance of this dastardly deed, Gurley rode on, and rejoined his command about twelve o'clock at New Market, where Captain Brooke, who had been taken along as a prisoner, charged him with it, and he admitted that he did it.

Another Rebel rode up after Gurley ceased firing, and aimed his gun, when the General told him re-proachfully, "You needn't shoot; I am already fatally wounded." The ball had passed entirely through his body, fatally tearing the intestines.

The main body of the guerrillas pursued the fleeing escort, but three or four remaining with their victim.

Captain Brooke and Gurley drove the General to the house where he died. He lived about twenty-four hours after being wounded, and retained his consciousness to the last, though frequently unable to speak, from the dreadful pain he suffered. He stated that when the party came up to the house, *the occupants, men, women and children, clapped their hands in approbation of the Rebel achievement.*

The whole brigade arrived at the house, about an hour after he was wounded. The men came up in double-quick, panting and shouting for vengeance. The effect of the sad sight, of their mortally wounded General, upon them, was most distressing. All day and night the faithful soldiery were grouped about the house, waiting their turns to bid a last farewell to their commander. Neither among the officers or men was there a dry eye, or a lip not quivering with anguish. A more moving scene has rarely been witnessed. The brigade did not resume its march until the General had breathed his last.

Retribution—terrible retribution was dealt by the 9th Ohio. The hands of the men that cheered Rebel murderers will clap no more. With fire and sword and bayonet, the scene of the foul assassination was reduced to a state of desolation, from which it will not recover until time will have swept away the remembrance of the death of Robert L. McCook.

The corpse of General McCook was taken to Nashville on the 7th day of August, and from thence removed to Ohio, his State. Captain Brooke was taken from the Rebel house soon after his arrival there, and was paroled the next day, and came within our lines, but not in time to accompany the corpse.

ELEGY

There's a wail o'er the land, for the brave McCook,
  And tears to his mem'ry are flowing,
To mingle and swell the sacred brook—
  A tribute the nation is owing!

He hath fallen, alas! by a traitorous foe—
  The hell-born Confederation:
And freedom bewaileth the dastardly blow,
  Which in gloom hath enshrouded a nation!

Brave heroes he leadeth to battle no more,
  The foremost and head of the column;
Yet still he *precedeth*, as ever before—
  To the tomb! oh! how truthful and solemn!

Then tears to the mem'ry of the brave McCook,
  Whose fair fame surviveth in story;
Whose name is enrolled in freedom's fair book,
  And whose spirit hath gone up to glory!

STORY XXXVI.

A CUTE YANKEE TRICK.

A GOOD "Yankee trick" was played off in February, 1862, on some twenty-five or thirty Baltimore Secession aspirants. They were anxious to spirit their way to "Dixie," and agreed with a Yankee captain, owner of a schooner, to land them in Virginia for two hundred and fifty dollars. This he agreed to, stipulating that they should fork over the sum in advance. They agreed. A given night approached, when the sly craft was in waiting at a designated point, over the river, some miles from Baltimore.

N   10

The aspiring Dixeyites arrived, paid their money, and went aboard all in jovial spirits. Sails were spread, and off went the schooner, to plow her way through the briny deep, while those who had taken passage exclaimed—

> "Nor care what land thou bringest us to
> So not again to ours."

The night was long, dark, and dreary, but while stars yet were peeping, the Yankee captain made a point on the Maryland shore, told his passengers it was Virginia, landed them safely, and advised them to make the best of their way toward Richmond, when he pushed off and was soon out of sight.

Morning broke, but only to reveal the sad consciousness that these recruits for Jeff. Davis and Beauregard were still on Maryland soil, minus their money, and in a worse condition than when they started.

Every day or two, for a while, brought back to his Baltimore home, one or more of these cheerless wanderers, in an awful dilapidated condition. Whether or not our *Yankee Salt* succeeded in getting another such cargo, is considered extra-problematical.

MAJOR-GENERAL WILLIAM S. ROSECRANS, of Ohio, was fifth in the class of 1842, numbering fifty-six. Being a professor at West Point, during the entire period of the Mexican war, he was kept away from battle until that of Rich Mountain, where, by his skill and bravery, was most unquestionably achieved the brilliant victory accredited to General McClellan. His subsequent achievements, as commander of the Army of the Cumberland, at Murfreesboro' and Chickamauga are matters of well-known history.

STORY XXXVII.

THE FEDERAL MAJOR AND TEXAN WIDOW.

A ROMANTIC STORY.

THE following amusing episode, as the sequel will show, lately occurred on a trip to New Orleans, as related by a gallant captain of the 27th Army Corps.

He says:—"We had a very pleasant trip down to the Crescent City, with some political prisoners from the Department of the Missouri, and persons who were allowed to pass into the Confederate lines to see their relations, look after their property, &c.

"Among the exiles was Ashton P. Johnston of St. Louis, Marmaduke, late of the Convention, Rev. Father Donnelly, of St. Joseph, and other of less import.

"Among the 'voluntaries' were young maids and old maids, wives and widows. Among the young maids was one who *confidentially* told me that she was going to Mobile to be married. It looked to me very much like *sending supplies to the enemy;* but I couldn't '*help*' it, so let it go. They nearly all came to this place in charge of Captain Dwight, Assistant-Inspector General of the Department of the Missouri.

"In the party was a young widow. 'Pretty!' In my judgment she was interesting—when was a young and pretty widow not? Being young, pretty, and a widow, is it strange that a young officer, to whose care she was intrusted, should extend to her all the courtesies and attention proper and consistent with his official position? It was not strange; nor was it strange that in return for his kindness, and at his solicitation, she should confide to him the tale of her woes.

"She was from Mexico; her husband had been conscripted in Texas, into the Rebel army; had died, leaving her the sole proprietress of numerous droves of mustangs, and the mother of two small children, (mostly boys and girls.)

"Her spirits and her person, draped in the habiliments of mourning, for the length of time deemed proper, she resolved to quit the place where each familiar object reminded her of the time spent in conjugal felicity with the dear departed one; that one 'gone to a ranch from which there was no return;' so all the personal property, with the exception of some unruly mustangs, who refused to be 'cotched,' and some colored individual, who, having heard of the Proclamation, refused to be considered personal property, and wouldn't be 'catched neither,' was converted into Confederate tr— cash, and the ranch vacated.

"At Metamoras the Confederate money was exchanged for gold, passage secured on a Spanish vessel to Havana, which was soon bounding across the Gulf. Tears were shed, as on leaving one's native land they always will be; but it was all for the best; a residence upon the beautiful island of Cuba, a place in the affections and family of the dear relations who anticipated her coming; quiet walks beneath fragrant orange groves; the air of that delightful and salubrious climate, would go far in dispelling the gloom which shrouded her young and ardent soul.

"But, alas! for the orange groves, and ambrosial atmosphere, a storm arose, the ship was driven into an inlet off the coast of Florida, was taken by our blockading squadron off Key West, for a blackade runner, and sent to New York, where, after an examination, she was released, and sent on her way.

"The fair widow, having escaped the dangers of the sea, resolved not to venture again, till her nerves had regained their wonted firmness. Having friends at St. Louis, she resolved to visit that city. Arriving there —there she remained until the fall of Vicksburg and Port Hudson, and the consequent opening of the Mississippi river, when she resolved to attempt Havana, this time via New Orleans. Major B. was on the boat. The major, you must know is a very gallant man. The ladies, dear creatures, will fall in love with him. In fact, the citadel of their affections invariably capitulates when he lays siege.

"The major was introduced to the fair widow by the captain in charge, and he had a soul to sympathize with her in her affliction, so to his special care she was consigned. It was soon a mutual discovery that their tastes and sympaties were similar. Did he admire any particular scenery along the shores?—ditto, she. Together they would pass hours in some retired place upon the guards of the boat, in sweet interchange of thought and sentiment.

"He had never met one before for whom he had formed an attachment so sincere, and she, from the moment when first introduced, felt that she saw in him the realization of her hopes. In him she saw the only one who should ever catch the untamed mustangs, and again bring joy to the ranch.

"Thus did this enamored pair pass the long hours of the journey. Arrived in New Orleans. Would the major be so kind as to secure her rooms at the hotel,

and to make some inquiry after her uncle, who resided
somewhere in the city? Of course he would. Mine
host of the St. Charles provided the proper apartments.
and the widow duly domiciled therein, the Major sallied
forth to make inquiries after "our uncle," in which he
was entirely unsuccessful; not being able to find any
gentleman of that name. The widow felt sad, was dis-
appointed.

"Her uncle was formerly a man of wealth and influence, and she had not calculated upon having any
difficulty in finding him; but this cruel war had changed
everything; and then the beautiful eyes of the fair and
and fascinating widow filled with tears.

"It grew rather embarrassing to the Major. He was
expecting to meet his wife, who was waiting in the city
for him, having come around via the Gulf. But the
fair creature whose head was reclining upon his shoulder,
and whose heaving bosom was beating against his own,
knew nothing of that; she only knew as she said, that
in that great city, among strangers, without the Major
her heart would break.

"How benevolent the Major's intentions may have
been, we can only conjecture, for unlooked for events
will sometimes play the deuce with one's arrangements.
At least it was so in this case. The fact was, the wife
of the Major learning of his arrival made inquiries, and
ascertaining that he had taken No. ——, resolved upon
a pleasant surprise for him, so with two of the little
majors in tow she proceeded to No. ——. Passing an
adjoining room she overheard the voice of the one
sought for, and thinking there must be some mistake
in the number of the room, and that where that familiar
voice was heard must be the right one, she pushed
open the door and entered.

"Whether the scene which met her eye, was calculated to increase her faith in the constancy of her spouse, or otherwise, we leave those who are able to judge to decide. We do know, though, that the Major's baggage was removed to another part of the house before many hours had expired, and that he was the recipient of a note from the clerk of the house to the following effect:

"'DEAR MAJOR:—Having unexpectedly found my uncle, I will relieve you and yours from any further care upon my part, if you will be so kind as to settle the bill which the clerk will present to you. Adios. L.

P. S. Not having sold my gold yet, it is inconvenient for me to refund you the —— dollars which you so kindly loaned to me.   L.'

"The major is a wiser man: he looks meek, but will fire up upon any allusion being made to mustangs or Spanish widows."

COLONEL LORIN ANDREWS.

FEW braver and more patriotic men than Lorin Andrews ever lived. At the breaking out of the Slaveholders' Rebellion, he was the first man in Ohio to tender his services to Governor Tod. Knowing what would be necessary, he did not wait for the requisition to be made on the State for troops, but hastened to offer his services in whatever position the Governor might designate. He was appointed Colonel of the 4th Infantry, Ohio volunteers, under the President's requisition, served with the regiment in Western Virginia, with ardor, ability, and fidelity, until he was taken sick in August, 1862, when he returned to his family in Gambier, and died in September following, lamented by all who knew him. The following is submitted as a tribute to his memory:

A good man hath fallen !
   A brave man lies low !
And sad is our sorrow,
   And deep is our woe !

Though Kenyon bewail him,
   In sadness and gloom,
'Twill nothing avail him,
   Low in the dark tomb !

No more will he heighten
   The fame of her glades ;
Nor with science enlighten
   Her classical shades.

Ye vot'ries of learning !
   Well may ye deplore
So sad a bereavement
   To freedom and lore !

At the call of our country
   He flew to her aid :
He mounted his charger,
   And wielded his blade

How faithful in friendship !
   How stern in his wrath !
And woe to the Rebel
   That countered his path !

His courage undaunted,
   And "onward" his word,
His faith in dry powder,
   And trust in the Lord.

But life's toilsome battle,
 With him is now o'er ;
Since death has disarmed him,
 He armeth no more.

He hath ceased from his labor,
 He heareth no call,
His pistols and sabre
 Now hang in the hall.

The good man hath fallen—
 The brave man lies low !
And sad is our sorrow,
 And deep is our woe !

STORY XXXVIII.

HOW THE POWDER WAS SAVED FROM EXPLODING.

DURING the engagement the Gunboat Valley City was fighting two Rebel boats at once, working her guns on both sides, when a shell entered her port-bow, passed into her magazine, knocked the head off a half-barrel of powder, and exploded in a locker, which was filled with blue-lights, rockets, and Coston signal lights.

The fire-works were ignited at the instant, and, in the close box, burnt with fury, filling the magazine with sulphurous fumes. The quarter gunner, instead of leaving his post, as most men would have done, at such a terrible juncture, immediately sat upon the open barrel, to keep the sparks from falling into the powder.

Captain J. G. Chaplin, commander of the vessel, called all hands to fire-quarters, but seeing that this would take too many from the guns, said he would go into the magazine himself, and extinguish the fire. Without a moment's hesitation, he jumped into the perilous place, and giving orders to keep up the fight, he passed up powder with one hand, and buckets of water down with the other, until the fire was quenched.

On entering the magazine and seeing the gunner sitting so quietly on the powder-barrel, he thought he was either shirking his duty, or bewildered by fear, and asked him sternly what he was doing there. "Ah, Sir," said the splendid fellow, "this 'ere shell have stove off the head of the barrel, and if I get up, a little spark might fall in, and blow us all to smithereens in a minute." Courage like this of Captain Chaplin and his quarter gunner has seldom been shown in any navy, and their conduct should be noted among the brightest incidents of the war.

> Search the wide world over, and still you will find
> In our army and our navy, are the bravest of mankind.

STORY XXXIX.

GENERAL BUTLER'S ACCOUNT OF HIS RECRUITING OPERA-TIONS IN LOUISIANA.

EXTRACTED FROM HIS TESTIMONY BEFORE THE COMMITTEE ON THE CONDUCT OF THE WAR.

"I ISSUED an order that any Confederate soldier, who chose to desert and leave the Rebel army, might come into New Orleans and register his name.

"There had come into New Orleans, up to this time, something over 6,000 men, who had been soldiers in the Rebel army, and registered themselves as paroled prisoners; so that I had in New Orleans nearly twice as many men who had been soldiers in the Confederate army as I had of Union soldiers.

"I had asked for leave, which had been granted, to recruit my regiments. I recruited in Louisiana all my old regiments up to the full standard; raised two new white regiments, and four companies of cavalry—all of men living in Louisiana. They fought bravely at Baton Rouge. Out of 460 men of the 14th Maine, who were in line, 200 of them were recruits from Louisiana. They, of course, were healthy men, not having suffered the troubles either of Camp Parapet or Vicksburg.

"I ordered $8 a month to be paid out of the provost fund to the widows and mothers of quite a number of Louisiana soldiers that were killed under our flag, because I knew it would take a long time to get it from Washington, and I wanted to encourage others to enlist. The provost fund was made up of fines and forfeitures, sales of confiscated property, and two dollars charged for each pass, &c.

"I asked for liberty to raise 5,000 native Louisianians, and raised nearly that number, including recruits in the old regiments. White recruiting began then to fall off, because of the high wages beginning to be paid for white labor on the plantations, in order to save the sugar crop where the negroes had left.

"I had written to Washington for reinforcements, but they replied that they could not give me any, though they wrote that I must hold New Orleans at all hazards. I determined to do that, if for no other reason, because the Rebels had offered a reward for my head, and it would have been rather inconvenient to me to have lost it.

"Upon examining the records, I found that Governor Moore, of Louisiana, had raised a regiment of free colored people, and organized and officered it; and I found one of his commissions. I sent for a colored man, as an officer of that regiment, and got some fifteen or sixteen of the officers together—black, and mulatto, light and dark colored—and asked them what they meant by being organized under the Rebels.

"They said they had been ordered out, and could not refuse; but that the Rebels had never trusted them with arms. They had been drilled in company drill. I asked them if that organization could be resuscitated, provided they were supplied with arms. They said that it could. Very well, I said, then I will resuscitate that regiment of Louisiana militia.

"I, therefore, issued an order, stating the precedent furnished by Governor Moore, and in a week from that time, I had in that regiment a thousand men, reasonably drilled, and well-disciplined; better disciplined than any other regiment I had there, because the blacks had always been taught to do as they were told. It was composed altogether of freemen; made free under some law.

"There was a very large French and English population in Louisiana. I ascertained that neither French nor English law permitted French or English subjects to hold slaves in a foreign country. According to the French law, any French citizen holding slaves in a foreign country, forfeits his citizenship. According to the British law, any Englishman holding slaves in a foreign country, forfeits one hundred pounds.

"I, thereupon issued an order, that every person should register himself; the loyal as loyal; French subjects, as French subjects; English subjects, as English subjects, &c., under their own hands, so that there could be no mistake in the books of the Provost Marshal. That was accordingly done.

"I then said to those who claimed to be French and English subjects: 'According to the law of the country to which you claim, by this register, to owe allegiance, all the negroes claimed by you as slaves are free, and being free, I may enlist as many of them as I please.' And I accordingly enlisted one regiment and part of another, from men in that condition.

"We had a great many difficulties about it. But the English Consul came fairly up to the mark, and decided that the negroes claimed as slaves by those who had registered themselves as British subjects, were free; so that I never enlisted a slave. Indeed, it was a general order, that no slave should be enlisted.

*   *   *   *   *   *   *

"I sent an expedition under General Weitzel to Donaldsonville, and swept down through that country to Berwick Bay; drove out the enemy, who were there in considerable force, and brought the whole of that region, from one end to the other, within the Union lines.

*   *   *   *   *   *   *

"In taking possession of that district, which had heretofore been in possession of the enemy, we obtained possession of a region of country containing more sugar plantations, and more slaves, than any other portion of Louisiana. Some 15,000, perhaps 20,000 slaves came, by that one expedition, under our control; and, as Congress had passed a law declaring that all slaves held by Rebels, in regions that after-

o

ward should come into our possession, should be free, all those slaves became free.

"I enlisted a third regiment, and two batteries of heavy artillery, from among those negroes thus made free. Two of these colored regiments were employed in guarding the Opelousas Railroad, running from Algiers to Berwick Bay, and when I left there they were still thus employed.

＊   ＊   ＊   ＊   ＊   ＊   ＊

"I turned over to my successor, of soldiers, 17,800, including the black regiments, though I had but 13,700 to start on."

STORY XL.

SCENE IN THE CAPITOL GROUNDS, WASHINGTON.

AN amusing scene is represented by a newspaper correspondent, as having occurred in August, 1862, in the capitol grounds at Washington. He says:

While on the steamer Adelaide, the Fortress Monroe boat from Baltimore, I became acquainted with a Mr. Graves, an English gentleman from Manchester, who was on his way to the fortress for the purpose of making a visit to the army of the Potomac. When the army evacuated Harrison Landing he started for Washington, and it was within half an hour after he left there, that an amusing scene occurred, of which the following is his own version.

He entered the capitol grounds and asked an officer whom he met, what that magnificent structure was used for? (meaning the capitol.)

"That," answered the officer, "is the bakery for the United States army. (The basement was in fact appropriated for that purpose at that time.) This singular answer somewhat took Mr. Graves aback, who, remonstrating at what he considered an unwarrantable joke, under the circumstances, received for reply, "That is the only answer you will get, sir, and if you don't like it you must take your own remedy." When the gentleman asked his name, "John Smith," answered the officer. Highly incensed at this second indignity, Mr. Graves demanded his card, producing his own.

The officer now appeared to wish to get rid of the matter, turning on his heel in the direction of the capitol exclaiming "Pshaw!" The Englishman followed him up the steps of the capitol. On reaching the top, the officer turned round and said, "Well, sir, what are you following me for? What do you want?" "I want your name," answered Mr. Graves, "and I will follow you till I learn what it is." The officer ordered him to leave the place, but to no purpose. Both parties appeared to be getting excited, when fortunately, at this instant a door opened, and Captain Darling made his appearance. "Captain Darling," commanded the officer, "take this man away." Captain Darling at once advanced and took charge of Mr. Graves. "I demand that you tell me the name of that officer," said Mr. Graves, "before I leave." "That," said Captain Darling." is General Halleck, commander-in-chief of the American army." The Englishman wilted.

STORY XLI.

NARROW ESCAPES.

At the battle of Fort Henry, a soldier had the plate of his belt struck by a bullet, and the U in the U. S. entirely obliterated : and yet he was unhurt.

Another had the pictures of his wife and mother in separate cases in his side pocket, and a ball passed through both, and lodged in the inside one; the cases thus saving his life. He sent them to his wife by express.

A member of the 8th Missouri had a half dollar in his pocket, which was struck with so much force as to bend the edges together and enclose the ball.

A colonel of one of the regiments found four of his men hid behind a stump, and riding up with great gravity, asked them if that stump needed so large a guard. At that instant a cannon ball sent it a kiting, without hurting one of them.

A private soldier received ten wounds, and yet sat on a log and loaded and fired as long as he could see the enemy.

Among the wounded who arrived in Louisville after the battle of Murfreesboro, was Joseph Rock, a private in Company B, 23d Kentucky, aged eighteen years, who was in the thickest of the fight. He was shot in the right breast, a Minnie ball striking the buckle of his suspender, driving it through a portion of the lungs, and lodging under the skin in his back. The surgeon cut through the skin and took out the ball and buckle, which were fastened together. Beside this, he had three balls to pass through the leg of his pants; and the stock of his gun was shivered by a ball while he was taking aim. He was lodged in hospital No. 4, and when last heard from was rapidly recovering from his injuries.

At the battle of Fort Donelson, Peter Morton, of the 13th Illinois, had the case of his watch, which he wore in his upper vest pocket, immediately over his heart, torn away by a canister shot, and the watch still continued to keep time.

STORY XLII.

ENLISTING NEGROES.

THE following matter of fact occurred at Nashville, as stated by the *Nashville Union:*

A slaveholder from the country approached an old acquaintance, also a slaveholder, residing in the city, and said: "I have several negro men lurking about here, somewhere. I wish you would look out for them, and when you find them do with them as if they were your own."

"Certainly I will," replied his friend.

A few days after the parties met again, and the planter asked, "Have you found my slaves?"

"I have."

"And where are they?"

"Well, you told me to with them as if they were my own, and as I made my men enlist in the Union army, I did the same with yours."

The astounded planter absquatulated.

STORY XLIII.

A HEROIC UNION GIRL.

Paducah, *February* 11, 1862.

In these times of terror and peril in this district, some of the most heroic acts have been performed, but perhaps the noblest of all was enacted a few days since, by a young lady of Graves County, well known to the writer, Miss Anna Bassford. Her father and family are devotedly for the Union; the old man having information that the notorious H. C. King, (expelled from our Legislature for treason,) and his robber band, intended to visit the house for the purpose of taking horses, guns, &c., hid his gun, and brought his horses to this place.

While here, three of King's robber band visited the house, demanded the gun, and alarmed Mrs. Bassford, who ordered a son, some fifteen years old, to find the gun, and deliver it to them. The boy, after considerable search, found the gun; the robbers then demanded a pistol, which they were informed belonged in the family; whereupon the daughter, some seventeen years old, told them she knew where the pistol was, but they could not get it.

The robbers insisted, with loud, vulgar oaths, but the girl was determined; and seeing they were foiled in this, they ordered the feeble, sickly boy to mount up behind one of their clan, as they intended to take him to Camp Beauregard, in place of his "d—d Lincolnite father."

The boy and mother in tears, protested, but to no

effect, and the boy was in the act of mounting, when the heroic sister stepped between her brother and the robbers, and, drawing, cocking, and presenting the pistol, ordered her brother to the house, and with eagle-piercing eye fastened on the robbers, and death-dealing determination in her countenance, dared them to hinder or touch her brother, and she would lay the one that did so dead at her feet. Suffice it to say, the three brigands scampered off, and left the family without further molestation.

STORY XLIV.

A GALLANT STAND BY AN ILLINOIS COMPANY.

DURING the Rebel raid in West Virginia, in the spring of 1863, an event occurred worthy of record. Captain Wallace, Company G, 23d Illinois, in command of a part of his company and a detachment of Company A, 14th Virginia, under Captain Smith, in all eighty men, occupied a church at the mouth of Greenland Gap, so advantageously placed as to command the gap, and compel the enemy to capture it before they could advance. From morning until dark this brave little force withstood a Rebel force of fifteen hundred men.

Three times the enemy charged up to the church, and were repulsed. Five out of eight of the officers of their first battalion were killed or wounded in the first charge. The number of the enemy slain was more than the whole force opposed to them. "Bravely they fought—long and well," but sorrowful to relate, as night drew on, the enemy took advantage of the shade to fire the building. Even then the undaunted braves refused to surrender, and it was not till the blazing roof fell in, that they yielded. Glory to the fallen heroes. General Kelley pronounces it one of the most gallant affairs of the war.

STORY XLV.

BALLOONING EXTRAORDINARY.

RELATED BY AN EYE-WITNESS.

On the 11th of April, 1862, at five o'clock P. M., an event, both thrilling and amusing, occurred at our camp in front of Yorktown. The commander-in-chief had appointed Fitz-John Porter to conduct the siege. He was a soldierly New Hampshire gentleman, of the regular army, had fought gallantly in Mexico, was forty years of age,—handsome, enthusiastic, ambitious, and popular. He had made several ascensions with Professor Lowe, and learned to go aloft alone.

One day he ascended thrice, and seemed as cosily at home in the firmament, as upon the solid earth. It is needless to say that he grew careless, and on this particular morning, leaped into the car, and demanded the cables to be let out with all speed. I saw, with some surprise, that the flurried assistants were sending up the great straining canvass with a single rope attached.

The balloon was but partially inflated, and the loose folds opened and shut with a crack like that of a musket. Noiselessly, fitfully, the yellow mass rose into the sky, the basket rocking like a feather in the zephyr;

and just as I turned to speak to a comrade, a sound from overhead, like the explosion of a shell, and something striking me across the face, laid me flat upon the ground.

Half-blind and stunned, I staggered to my feet, but the air seemed full of cries and curses. Opening my eyes ruefully, I saw all faces turned upward, and when I looked above—the balloon was adrift. The treacherous cable, rotted with vitriol, had snapped in twain: one fragment had been the cause of my downfall, and the other trailed, like a great entrail, from the receding car, where Fitz-John Porter was bounding upward, upon a Pegasus that he could neither check nor direct.

The whole army was agitated by the unwonted occurrence. From battery No. 1, on the brink of the York, to the mouth of Warwick river, every soldier and officer was absorbed. Far within the Confederate lines the excitement extended. We heard the enemy's alarm-guns, and directly the signal flags were waving up and down our front.

The General appeared directly over the edge of the car. He was tossing his hands frightenedly, and shouting something that we could not comprehend.

"Open the valve!" called Lowe, in his shrill tones: "climb—to—the—netting—and reach—the valve—rope."

"The valve!—the valve!" repeated a multitude of tongues, and all gazed with thrilling interest at the retreating hulk, that still kept straight upward, swerving neither to the east nor the west.

It was a weird spectacle—that frail, fading, oval, gliding against the sky, floating in the serene azure. the little vessel swinging silently beneath, and a hun-

dred thousand martial men, watching the loss of their
brother-in-arms, but powerless to relieve, or recover
him. Had Fitz-John Porter been drifting down the
rapids of Niagara, he could not have been so far from
human assistance. But we saw him directly, no bigger
than a child's toy, clambering up the netting, and
reaching for the cord.

"He can't do it," muttered a man beside me; "the
wind blows the valve-rope to and fro, and only a spry,
cool-headed fellow can catch it."

We saw the General descend, and appearing again
over the edge of the basket, he seemed to be motioning
to the breathless hordes below, the story of his failure.
Then he dropped out of sight, and when we next saw
him, he was reconnoitring the Confederate works,
through a long, black spy-glass.

A great laugh went up and down the lines, as this
cool procedure was observed, and then a cheer of ap-
plause ran from group to group. For a moment it was
doubtful that the balloon would float in either direction; it seemed to faulter like an irresolute being, and
moved reluctantly southeasterly, toward Fortress Monroe. A huzza, half uttered, quivered on every lip.
All eyes glistened, and some were dim with tears of
joy. But the wayward canvass now turned due westward, and was blown rapidly toward the Confederate
works. Its course was finally direct, and the wind
seemed to veer often, as if contrary currents, conscious
of the opportunity, were struggling for the possession
of the daring navigator.

The south wind held mastery for a while, and the
balloon passed the Federal front, amid a howl of despair
from the soldiery. It kept right on, over sharp-shooters,

rifle-pits, and outworks, and finally passed, as if to deliver up its freight, directly over the heights of Yorktown.

The cool courage, either of heroism or despair, had seized upon Fitz-John Porter. He turned his black glass upon the ramparts and masked cannon below, upon the remote camps, upon the beleagured town, upon the guns of Gloucester Point, and upon distant Norfolk.

Had he been reconnoitering from a secure perch at the tip of the moon, he could not have been more vigilant: and the Confederates probably thought this some Yankee device to peer into their sanctuary, in despite of ball or shell.

None of their great guns could be brought to bear upon the balloon; but there were some discharges of musketry that appeared to have no effect, and finally, even these demonstrations ceased. Both armies in solemn silence were gazing aloft, while the impurturable mariner continued to spy out the land.

The sun was now rising behind us, and roseate rays struggled up to the zenith, like the arcs made by showery bombs. They threw a hazy atmosphere upon the balloon, and the light shone through the net-work, like the sun through the ribs of the skeleton ship, in the "Ancient Mariner." Then, as all looked agape, the air craft "plunged and racked and veered," and drifted rapidly toward the Federal lines again.

The hallelujah that now went up shook the spheres, and when he had regained our camp-limits, the General was seen clambering up again, to clutch the valve-rope. This time he was successful, and the balloon fell suddenly, so that all hearts once more leaped up, and the cheers were hushed.

Cavalry rode pell-mell from several directions, to reach the place of descent; and the General's personal staff galloped past me like the wind, to be the first at his debarkation. I followed the throng of soldiers with due haste, and came up to the horsemen in a few minutes.

The balloon had struck a canvass tent with great violence, felling it as by a bolt, and the General, unharmed, had disentangled himself from innumerable folds of oiled canvass, and was now the cynosure of an immense number of people.

While the officers shook his hands, the rabble bawled their satisfaction in hurrahs, and a band of music marching up directly, the throng of foot and horse gave him a vociferous escort to his quarters.

STORY XLVI.

INCIDENTS OF THE BATTLE OF CHANCELLORVILLE.

FROM Captain William D. Wilkins, (of the staff of General A. S. Williams, commander of a division of the Twelfth Army Corps,) who was wounded and taken prisoner at the battle of Chancellorville, and subsequently paroled and returned to Detroit, the *Free Press* learned some interesting particulars.

The captain was placed in charge of a squad and taken to a plank road in the rear, where he met General Jackson and staff. Jackson had at this time formed a column of attack on the plank road, with the design of flanking our army, and obtaining possession of the

United States Ford, which would undoubtedly have resulted in the total discomfiture of our army. The column consisted of 15,000 men and three batteries of artillery.

Jackson was sitting on his horse at the head of the column, surrounded by his staff. He had a peculiarly sad and gloomy expression of countenance, as though he already had a premonition of his fate. It was but fifteen minutes later that he was mortally wounded.

As they came into his presence, the guard announced "a Yankee officer." Captain Wilkins asked if it was Major-General Thomas J. Jackson? On being answered in the affirmative, he raised his hat. General Jackson said, "A regular army officer, I suppose; your officers do not often salute ours." Captain Wilkins replied, "No, I am not: I salute you out of respect to you as a gallant officer." He then asked his name and rank. On being informed, he further inquired what corps and commanders were opposed in front. Captain Wilkins replied that as an officer he could not return a truthful answer to such questions. Jackson then turned to the guard and ordered them to search him.

He then had in the breast pocket of his coat Hooker's confidential orders to corps commanders, giving a plan, in part, of the campaign, the countersigns of the field for a week in advance, and the field returns of the Twelfth Corps on the preceding day. These were all exceedingly important papers.

Fortunately, before the guard could carry the orders into execution, a terrific raking fire was opened on Jackson's column by twenty pieces of artillery, commanded by Captain Best, from an eminence on the plank road. The first eight or ten shots flew over the

P

heads of the column. The men and gunners dismounted, leaving their horses and guns. Our artillery soon got the range with more precision, and the shell and round shot ricocheted and plowed through this dense mass of the enemy with terrific effect. Shells were continually bursting, and the screams and groans of the wounded and dying could be heard on every side.

As an instance of the terrible effect of this fire, one of the guard was struck by a solid shot just below the hips, sweeping off both his legs. A battery came dashing up, but when they got into the vortex of the fire, the gunners fled, deserting their guns, and could not be made to man them. An officer, splendidly mounted and equipped, attempted in a most gallant manner to rally them. A ball struck him on the neck, completely severing his head from his body, and leaving his spinal column standing. His body rolled to the ground and and his horse galloped to the rear.

One of the shells struck a caisson full of artillery ammunition, which exploding, ascended in a crater of various colored flame, and showered down on the heads of the men below a mass of fragments of shot and shell. The loss inflicted by this fire must have been terrible; placing considerably over one thousand men *hors de combat*, and effectually breaking up the contemplated attack of the column.

An officer of Jackson's staff subsequently stated that it was about fifteen minutes after this that General Jackson with staff advanced to the front, to reconnoiter our position; having accomplished which, he returned by a different path toward his own men, who mistaking his approach for that of a party of our cavalry, fired upon him, killing and wounding four of his staff, and wounding Jackson, once in the right arm, and twice in the left arm and hand.

While Captain Wilkins was being taken to the rear, he devoted his attention to disposing of the important papers which he had on his person. He dared not take them from his pocket to attempt to tear them up, but constantly kept his hand in his pocket, and worked the papers into a ball, and as they were passing along, got them into his bosom, and finally into the pit under his arm, where he carried them all that night.

The next morning the guard halted to get their break-fast, and a soldier was trying to kindle a fire to cook some coffee which they had taken from our men. The wood was damp and the fire refused to burn. The soldier swore at it until his patience gave out, when Captain Wilkins asked him if he would not like some kindlings, and handed him the important papers. The soldier took them, and not dreaming of their import-ance, used them to kindle his fire.

STORY XLVII.

STORY OF GENERAL McCLELLAN.

THE Washington Correspondent of the *Philadelphia Inquirer*, is responsible for the following story of General McClellan, while in command of the army of the Po-tomac: "General McClellan was in the habit of riding around occasionally, in citizen's dress, accompanied by a few of his staff. One day he was walking through one of the encampments, and passing the rear of the tents, he saw a bucket of coffee standing near a fire. He asked what it was, and one of the soldiers said 'coffee.' 'It looks more like slops,' he replied. 'Oh,' said the soldier, 'it is not fit to drink, but we have to put up with it, and our other food is not a bit better.' 'Well, whose fault is it?' he asked. 'Oh, our Quartermaster is drunk most of the time, and when he is not, he is studying how to cheat.'

"McClellan passed on, and seeing more evidence of the dirty and slovenly manner in which the Quartermaster conducted his operations in his tent, he accosted him with the remark that the men were complaining of bad treatment from him. The Quartermaster flew into a passion, and swore it was none of his business; and he had better not come sneaking around trying to make mischief. McClellan answered him, telling him he had better be cautious how he talked. Quartermaster replied, 'Who are you, that you assume so much apparent authority?' 'I am George B. McClellan, and you can pack up your traps and leave.' The Quartermaster was struck dumb, and McClellan turned and left him.

"That evening the Quartermaster left to the tune of the 'Rogue's March,' played by some of the boys who had got wind of it. He was superseded by a Quartermaster who did not 'get drunk and cheat.' The story was soon circulated around some of the camps, and the officers kept on the lookout for the General, and of course did not have much lying around loose: and the men were ready to risk their lives at the cannon's mouth for the man who *did care* how they were provided for."

MAJOR-GENERAL McCLELLAN.

George B. McClellan, the son of a physician of Philadelphia, was born in that city, December 3d, 1826. He entered West Point Academy at the age of sixteen, and graduated at twenty, as brevet Second Lieutenant of Engineers. He served in the Mexican war, with a company of sappers and miners, as Second Lieutenant, was breveted First Lieutenant at Contreras, and Captain after the capture of the City of Mexico.

After the war he remained on duty with the sappers and miners, at West Point, until June, 1851. He next served as Engineer at the construction of Fort Delaware.

In the spring of 1852 he was assigned to duty under Major R. B. Marcy, in the Expedition for the Exploration of Red River. Thence he was ordered direct to Texas, as Senior Engineer on the staff of General Persifer F. Smith, and was engaged on the coast of Texas, on surveys of Rivers and Harbors.

In 1853 he was ordered to the Pacific coast, in command of the Western Division of the Survey of the North Pacific Railroad route. He returned to the East in 1854, on duty connected with the Pacific survey.

The following year he received a commission in the 1st Regiment of Cavalry, and was sent to Europe as a member of the Military Commission, to the seat of war, in the Crimea, and in Northern Russia.

He resigned in January, 1857, to take the position of Vice-President and Chief Engineer of the Illinois Central Railroad, which he held about three years, and relinquished for the presidency of the Ohio and Mississippi Railroad Company, of which he also acted as General Superintendent; and was acting in that capacity when the rebellion broke out.

In the month of April, 1861, he was appointed Major-General of the Ohio State forces, mustered into the United States service April 23d of that year, and on the 14th of May, ensuing, was commissioned as Major-General in the United States army, and assigned to the Department of Ohio, including Western Virginia. Since then his course is of public notoriety.

STORY XLVIII.

LITTLE EDDIE THE DRUMMER BOY OF EAST TENNESSEE.

I have a sad tale worth relating,
    And stating to you;
And more so, by my estimating,
    Because it is true.
'Tis about little Eddie, the drummer,
    And young refugee;
Whose mother, with him was a comer
    From East Tennessee.

'Twas a few days before we had orders,
    Brave Lyon to join.
And march to where Wilson's creek borders
    Missouri's fair line,
That our drummer was sick and unable
    More duty to do,
When a " contraband," stalwart and sable,
    Our lines ventured through.

Then straightway the " boy" was arrested,
    And marched to the tent;
Where our captain politely requested—
    " For what was you sent ?"
He replied that he knew of a drummer,
    Would like to enlist,—
A boy who was lately a comer
    From Tennessee —East.

The captain commanded, "inform him,
>> I'll give extra pay,
If he'll be on the ground in the morning,
>> For marching away."
A good-looking middle aged woman,
>> Next morning was seen,
With a lad, sharp and sprightly uncommon,
>> Not more than thirteen.

Her story was briefly narrated—
>> A poor refugee,
By murderous Rebels unmated,
>> In East Tennessee—
She sought in St. Louis a sister,
>> Her burden to share;
But she had unluckily missed her—
>> Not finding her there.

She craved but the boon of a station.
>> For her drummer boy;
Then she, in some honest vocation,
>> Her time would employ.
Thus having rehearsed her brief story,
>> The captain looked grum:
" Fear not," cried the lad, "it's my glory,
>> And sure I can drum."

Said the captain, " Well, well, (to the sergeant,)
>> " The fifer must come,
Go tell him our business is urgent,
>> And bring you the drum."
By side of the long legged fifer.
>> From far Illinois,
He seemed a diminutive cypher,
>> That refugee boy.

Stooping down from his tall elevation,
>> To see who had come.
The fifer made interrogation,
>> " My man can you drum?"

"Yes, sir; O I wish that last summer,
     You'd been there to see,
How for brave Captain Hill I was drummer,
     In East Tennessee."

The fifer struck up, (for his trying.)
     A beautiful tune;
Which at once set his drum sticks a flying,
     Like hail stones in June.
Was it fifing, or piping. or tooting,
     Of difficult chime,
The drummer boy skillfully put in,
     The rub-a-dub time.

Says the captain, "good madam, I'll take him,
     Pray what is his name?"
" Edward Lee," she said. "do not forsake him,
     Return him the same."
Said he. " In six weeks we'll restore,
     It cannot be more;
Should he 'scape all the dangers before him,
     And may-be in four."

Said she. " I trust him in your keeping."
     And fast fell her tears—
She kissed Eddie, and went away weeping,
     With motherly fears.
We marched, and were soon in that battle,
     Too dreadful to tell,—
Boomed the cannons, and muskets did rattle,
     And brave Lyon fell!

The night after that terrible hissing
     Of balls in the air,
Little Eddie was counted as missing,
     But no one knew where.
*   *   *   *   *   *
On guard as the morning was breaking,
     Soon to my ears come,
The sound, there could be no mistaking,
     The sound of his drum.

That sound, when permitted to follow,
        Little Eddie, I found,
With his back to a log in the hollow,
        His seat was the ground.
His drum, which was hanging quite near him,
        On a bush that grew there,
He beat that his comrades might hear him,
        And come to his care.

He saw me, and then stopped his drumming,
        As quick as you'd think—
"O corporal. I'm glad of your coming,
        O, give me some drink !"
I turned to the brook for some water,
        My canteen was dry—
"O, corporal," he cried do not loiter,
        And leave me to die !"

Returning I quickly discovered
        That both of his feet,
As he sat with his limbs all uncovered,
        Were shot off complete !
He drank, then said, "do but assure me
        You don't think I'll die !
This man said the surgeon could cure me,
        This man that's near by."

I perceived that a Rebel lay near him,
        Whose spirit had fled :
Pitying Eddie, he had tried to cheer him,
        Himself was now dead.
He was shot in his bowels, (so said he,)
        And crawled along there,
And trying to save little Eddie,
        He died without care.

He had taken his buckskin suspender,
        And corded each limb
Of Eddie so careful and tender—
        The Lord pity him !

While hearing this pitiful story.
  And viewing the scene,
The foe rushed upon us, all gory,
  Adown the ravine.

The leader took up little Eddie,
  And quickly we sped,
And soon reached their camp, when already
  The poor boy was dead!
His mother, now wailing and mourning,
  A poor refugee;
God grant her a happy returning
  To East Tennessee.

STORY XLIX.

VENTURESOME AND SUCCESSFUL SCOUTING EXPEDITION.

CAPTAIN S. BARD, with a scouting party of twenty-eight horsemen, left Covington about four o'clock on Sunday evening, taking the Independence pike, and when about eight miles out, branching off to the right.

The night being fine, they rode the greater part of the time, and after having gone a distance of about twenty-seven miles, they returned, passing near a little settlement called Ficksville. Captain Bard was at this time a hundred yards in advance of his party, and came upon an armed horseman. As he approached him, he opened with—"Good morning."

"Good morning," replied the horseman.

"Is there any danger about here?" said Captain Bard.

"From whom?"

"Why, from the Federals."

"Oh, no," was the reply; "there's no danger of them

about here; there is none of them in this neighborhood."

"Think not?" said Captain Bard; "suppose you deliver up your fire-arms;" and at this moment he pulled
out a pistol and pointed it directly at the Rebel Captain,
for such he appeared to be.

"Why, you are joking, ain't you?" said Reb.

"No; I'm in earnest; I want them right away." The
latter part of the sentence was delivered in an emphatic
manner; and Captain Butternut, (for he would not give
his name,) unbuckled his belt, in which were the pistols,
a Colt's navy revolver, and a five-nick cartridge pistol,
and delivered it to Captain Bard, at the same time remarking:

"Caught at last, after eighteen months' service. I'll
go along."

A Rebel private near by yielded himself a prisoner
at once. By this time a number of Bard's men had
come up.

STORY L.

A FEMALE SOLDIER AND HER EXPERIENCE.

In the month of May, 1863, a young woman arrived
at Chicago from Louisville, Ky., whose history is thus
related in the Chicago Post:

"She gave her name as Annie Lillybridge, of Detroit,
and stated that her parents reside in Hamilton, C. W.
Last spring, (1862,) she was employed in a drygoods
store in Detroit, where she became acquainted with a
Lieutenant W———, of one of the Michigan regiments,

and an intimacy immediately sprang up between them. They corresponded for some time, and became much attached to each other. Some time during the ensuing summer Lieutenant W———, was appointed to a position in the 21st Michigan Infantry, then rendezvousing in Ionia county.

"The thought of parting from the gay lieutenant nearly drove her mad, and she resolved to share his dangers and be near him. No sooner had she resolved upon this course than she proceeded to act. Purchasing male attire she visited Ionia, enlisted in Captain Kavanah's Company, 21st Regiment. While in camp she managed to keep her secret from all—not even the object of her attachment, who met her every day, was aware of her presence so near him.

"Annie left with her regiment for Kentucky, passed through all the dangers and temptations of a camp-life, endured long marches, and sleeping on the cold ground without a murmur. At last, before the battle of Pea Ridge, in which her regiment took part, her sex was discovered by a member of her company, and she enjoined secresy upon him, after relating her previous history.

"On the following day she was under fire, and from a letter in her possession, it appears she behaved with marked gallantry, and by her own hand shot a Rebel captain who was in the act of firing upon Lieutenant W———. But the fear of revealing her sex continually haunted her.

"After the battle, she was sent out with others to collect the wounded, and one of the first corpses found by her was the soldier who had discovered her sex. Days and weeks passed on and she became a universal

favorite with the regiment; so much so, that her Colonel
(Stephens) frequently detailed her as regimental clerk
—a position that brought her in close contact with her
lover, who at this time, was Major, or Adjutant of the
regiment.

"A few weeks subsequently, she was out on picket
duty, when she received a shot in the arm that disabled
her, and notwithstanding the efforts of the surgeon, her
wound continually grew worse. She was sent to the
hospital at Louisville, where she remained several
months, when she was discharged by the post surgeon,
as her arm was stiffened and rendered useless.

"She implored to be permitted to return to her regiment, but the surgeon was unyielding, and discharged
her. Annie immediately hurried toward home. At
Cincinnati she told her secret to a benevolent lady, and
and was supplied with female attire.

"She declares that she will enlist in her old regiment
again, if there is a recruiting officer for the 21st in
Michigan. She still clings to the Lieutenant, and says
she must be near him if he falls, or is taken down sick;
that where he goes, she will go; and when he dies, she
will end her life by her own hands."

An anecdote is reported characteristic of the brave
McCook. When advancing in Tennessee, the Rebel
General Buckner sent to him by a flag of truce a message, the purport of which was, that unless he withdrew
his troops from the State, within fifteen days, he, (Buckner,) would annihilate them. Our gallant general's
only reply was a *cannon-ball*, which he gave to the
emissary, telling him to deliver it to Buckner.

Q

LIEUTENANT-GENERAL U. S. GRANT.

LIEUTENANT-GENERAL ULYSSES S. GRANT was born at Point Pleasant, Ohio, April 27, 1822, and graduated at West Point in 1843, (twenty-first of a class numbering thirty-nine members,) as brevet second lieutenant in the Fourth Infantry.

In the Mexican war he participated in Taylor's battles at Palo Alto, Reseca de la Palma, and Monterey, Afterward his regiment joined Scott at Vera Cruz, and Lieutenant Grant took part in every engagement up to the city of Mexico, receiving brevet first lieutenant and captain for meritorious conduct at the battle of Molino del Rey and Chepultepec.

At the close of the war his regiment went to Oregon, where he was promoted to a captaincy, but resigned in 1853, and settled in St. Louis. In 1859 he removed to Galena, Ill., where he was engaged in commercial business when the rebellion broke out. He was among the first to offer his services to Governor Yates, and was made colonel of 21st Illinois Volunteers, with which he went into service in Missouri.

In the summer of 1861, he was made brigadier-general, and assigned to the district of Cairo. He immediately occupied Paducah, Kentucky; stopped the flow of supplies for the Rebels up the Tennessee and Cumberland; moved soon after on Belmont, Mo., opposite the Rebel stronghold at Columbus, Ky., from which place he was driven only after a desperate fight, by a largely superior force of Rebels.

In February, 1862, he led the land forces sent against Fort Henry, but did not participate in the victory; the

gunboats having done the work before he got there.
Thereupon he marched forthwith upon Fort Donelson,
which place he besieged and assaulted, and on the 16th
of February, the Rebels raised the white flag. (Pillow
and Floyd having stolen off during the night, with 5,000
men, leaving Buckner to surrender,) and sent to Grant
for terms.

He replied that the surrender must be unconditional,
or he would instantly move on the works. This short
and soldierly answer gave him the *sobriquet* of Unconditional Surrender Grant, the initials being the same as
of his real name. This fortunate and fairly won victory was rewarded by a major-general's commission.

In April he reached Pittsburg Landing, Buell being
in his rear with reinforcements, for which, however, the
Rebels did not wait, but made a furious onslaught
upon Grant, who was forced back to the shelter of the
gunboats, where he resisted Johnson with success.

The next day Buell came up, and the Rebels got a
severe flogging at what they call the battle of Shiloh,
their commander, General Albert S. Johnson, being
killed. His subsequent operations, culminating in the
capture of Vicksburg, and the opening of the Mississippi river, are fresh in the public mind.

General Grant is a plain man, about five feet nine
inches in height, has sandy hair and whiskers, blue
eyes, a firm, determined mouth, well shaped nose, and a
complexion that shows the effects of exposure. He has
a good form, and stands squarely on his feet. He never
uses profane language, is almost a model of temperance,
with the exception of continual smoking.

He is of a taciturn habit, attending closely to business,
methodical and cautious, though full of daring and dash,

if need be, and prides himself on his horsemanship.
Fortunately General Grant is a soldier, and nothing but
a soldier, having no aspirations for political preferment.

Congress having by law revived the rank of lieutenant-general, President Lincoln appointed General Grant
to that high office, and on the 9th day of March, 1864,
commissioned him, in presence of the entire cabinet,
General Halleck, and several others: addressing him as
follows: "General Grant—in consequence of the nation's
appreciation of what you have done, and its reliance
upon you for what remains to do in the existing great
struggle, you are now presented with this commission,
constituting you lieutenant-general in the army of the
United States. With this high honor devolves upon you,
also, a corresponding responsibility. As the country
herein trusts you, so under God it will sustain you. I
scarcely need to add that with what I here speak for
the nation, goes my own hearty, personal concurrence."
General Grant replied in appropriate terms.

STORY LI.

DEATH OF COLONEL J. L. KIRBY SMITH, OF THE 43D I. O. V.

Soon in the battle of the 4th inst. (battle of Corinth,
October, 1862), Colonel J. L. Kirby Smith, of the 43d
Ohio fell, with a mortal wound. I have not words to
describe the qualities of this model soldier, or to express
the loss we have sustained in his death. The best testimony I can give to his memory, is the spectacle witnessed by myself in the very moment of battle, of stern,
brave men, weeping like children, as the word passed,
"Kirby Smith is killed."—[GENERAL STANLEY'S RE-
PORT—BATTLE OF CORINTH.]

Let tears cease to flow—in vain we deplore him,
The night-cloud of death has forever closed o'er him:
Dim is the eye late so radiant with fire,
As perish'd the son, so perish'd the sire !*

He was young. he was pious. and dauntlessly brave:
A spirit more beautiful God never gave;
While genius and science beamed forth from his mind,
Truth, honor, and love, in his heart were enshrin'd.

His present, how brilliant ! his future how grand !
Hope saw him the peer of the first in the land:
Death smote him in battle; light turn'd into gloom,
And hope, and the hero now sleep in the tomb !

The pride of the army; fond lover and son,
Too soon for his country. his proud race was run !
But ah! who can paint the sad anguish in store,
For the mother and maiden who'll see him no more !

The patriot's affection will hallow his name,
The love of his comrades will cherish his fame:
For the cause of his country his life-blood was given;
His, the homage of earth, and the glory of heaven.   [S.]

The 43d Ohio Regiment was on the left of Fort Robinett, and on the left of the 63d, under the ridge; but when the desperate attempt to storm that redoubt was made by the Rebels, under Texas Rogers, we were brought into action by changing front forward on the first company, which rested on the fort; and this enabled us to pour in a cross fire, which sent the Rebel column staggering to the rear.

The loss of our regiment (the 43d) in the few moments required to execute that movement, attests the hazard of the move, and the steadiness, and daunt-

---

* Colonel Smith's father was slain in storming a battery at Molino del Ray, in Mexico.

less courage of the men who made it. Here, within the space of ten minutes, ninety of our boys were smitten to the earth by a hurricane of lead. Here fell dead several of our best and bravest officers, among the first of whom, was our brave and accomplished Colonel, J. L. Kirby Smith, than whom, no more perfect soldier or heroic man has yielded his life during this bloody war.

Colonel J. L. Kirby Smith was a native of New York, and was in the twenty-fifth year of his age when he fell, mortally wounded, by a bullet passing through his jaw, and coming out under his ear. He lingered in great suffering, in a state of consciousness, but unable to speak, until Sunday evening, when he died.

His remains were taken to Ohio for interment, by Lieutenant Colonel Swayne, of the 43d.

He graduated at West Point in 1857, and held a Lieutenant's commission in the regular army upon the breaking out of the rebellion; when he was appointed Colonel of the 43d Ohio Infantry, which he organized at Mount Vernon, and took the field in February, 1862, and served with distinction in General Pope's command, throughout the *Island-Number-Ten* campaign. As a military man, he had few if any superiors among all the Ohio colonels. His loss to the regiment is irreparable.

Colonel Smith's father, Captain E. Kirby Smith, was killed at the head of his company in Worth's terrible charge at the battle of Molino del Rey, Mexico, shot through the head. Father and son have shared a soldier's fate, both fallen in the fray, battling for the right. The same volley which wounded Colonel Smith, also killed Captain J. M. Spangler, of Company A, and also mortally wounded Adjutant Charles C. Heyl, of Columbus, an intimate friend of the Colonel.

STORY LII.

THE HERO OF CORINTH.

PRIVATE ORRIN B. GOULD, of Co. G, 27th Ohio, was
the hero of the Battle of Corinth. The following letter
to Governor Tod, from Colonel John W. Fuller, commander of Brigade, gives the history of young Gould's
heroic conduct. It has been announced that the Governor had promoted him to a captaincy, and though
severely wounded, his recovery was not despaired of.
Colonel Fuller's letter is as follows:

"Headquarters. 1st Brigade, 2d Division,
" Army of the Mississippi.
"Near Ripley, Miss., October 9th, 1862.

"To the Governor of Ohio:

"SIR,—I have the honor of forwarding to your Excellency, the "Battle-Flag" of the 9th Texas Regiment,
which was captured by a private of the 27th Ohio Infantry, at the battle of Corinth, October 4th, 1862.

"The Rebels, in four close columns, were pressing with
gallantry, amounting to recklessness, upon the Ohio
Brigade, with the evident intention of breaking our
lines, when the terrible and incessant fire of our men
drove them back in the utmost confusion.

"The 6th Texas bore down upon the left centre of the
27th Ohio, with this flag at the head of their column,
and advanced to within six or eight yards of our lines,
when Orrin B. Gould, a private of Company G, shot
down the color-bearer, and rushed forward for the
Rebel flag.

"A Rebel officer shouted to his men to 'save the
color,' and at the same moment put a bullet into the

breast of Gould, but the young hero was not to be intimidated. With the flag-staff in his hand, and the bullet in his breast, he returned to his regiment, waving the former defiantly in the faces of the enemy.

"After the battle, when visiting the hospitals, I found young Gould stretched upon a cot, evidently in great pain. Upon seeing me his pale face was instantly radiant with smiles, and pointing to his wound, he said, 'Colonel, I don't care for this, since I got their flag.'

"I have the honor to be your Excellency's obedient servant,

"JOHN W. FULLER,
"Colonel commanding 1st Brigade, 2d Division.
"HON. DAVID TOD,
"Governor of Ohio."

STORY LIII.

IRON CLAD BREASTWORKS.

WHILE search was being made of the passengers on the central train, one evening in June, 1863, a soldier noticed that a lady's dress appeared more full breasted than it naturally should be; and his quick eye also detected the fact that the artificial contents of the lady's bosom were pressed out against the folds of the dress, so as to make it almost certain that pistols were there.

He was a very polite soldier, and in the most gentlemanly manner approached the lady and said: "Madam, I want those revolvers." She replied indignantly: "Sir, I am a respectable woman, and have no revolvers." The soldier again said, very coolly: "Madam, I wish you to give me those revolvers, and pointed to her bosom. She again denied that she had any.

Without further parleying, the soldier, in discharge of his duty, thrust his hand into the place of concealment and drew out a revolver, and kept on repeating the operation until seven were captured. Then gathering up the pistols, he politely remarked to the lady: "Madam, your breastworks seem to have been iron clad."

STORY LIV.

FUN IN CAMP.—A DOG STORY.

A RICH story is told of the boys in the 2d Vermont regiment. It seems that the men of a certain New Jersey regiment had repeatedly stolen the fresh meat from the Vermont boys in the night, and appropriated it to their own use. Some of the Vermont boys thereupon killed a dog, dressed it neatly, and hung it up in the quartermaster's department.

The Jerseys, mistaking it for mutton, stole it, as usual, and bore it off in triumph. The Vermonters were on the watch, and ascertained that it was served up the next day upon the table of the Jersey officers.

The joke soon became public, and the Jerseys were greeted, when they visited the camp of the Vermonters, with a "bow-wow," by way of friendly salutation.

The point of this practical joke, as we were told it at the camp of the Vermonters, where the affair occurred, is omitted in the above narrative. The dog which the mischievous wags converted into mutton, for the benefit of their foraging New Jersey neighbors, was a fine Newfoundlander, belonging to the New Jersey colonel. The story in camp goes that a leg of the sacrificed animal was served up at his master's own table.

STORY LV.

THE OTHER SIDE OF THE DOG STORY.*

HAVING given an amusing account (page 189) of the joke practiced by the 2d Vermont regiment on the 26th New Jersey, it is but just to give the Jersey boys the benefit of their version of the matter, by which it appears that the Vermonters were, after all, the victims of their own enterprize. It is as follows:

A long-legged, long-bodied, long-tailed feminine canine, for several weeks had roamed throughout the ranks of the brigade, like the ghost of "Snarleyow," keeping the soldiers awake by her midnight howlings. The butchers of the 2d Vermont caught, killed and dressed the canine, hanging the carcass on a tree in a grove fronting the camp of the 26th, as a bait for the Jersey boys, who they fondly hoped would take it for mutton. This probably would have been the case, had not a Jersey teamster, William Fagan, while loading the slaughtered beeves of that morning, observed their proceedings, and placed the 26th upon their guard. Some of their boys, thereupon, under cover of twilight, took the carcass into camp, and transmogrified it into very nice looking *head-cheese*, which was retailed the next day through the Vermont camps at ten cents a roll.

The Vermonters missed the carcass, and presumed, of course that the "Jerseys" had swallowed the bait. But it is not difficult to picture their dismay, when the jubilant question, "How are you dog?" was answered

---

* The reader is notified that the compiler does not vouch for the truth of this or Story LIV.

with the significant reply, "How are you head-cheese?"
The latent influence of the head-cheese reposing uneasily
upon their Green Mountain stomachs, displayed itself
in "bow-wow," whenever a Jerseyman hove in sight.
The "Jerseys" solaced themselves in whistling for the
lost canine, but she never reappeared.   And thus were
the biters bitten.

STORY LVI.

JENKINS' MODE OF PAROLING PRISONERS.

ON the arrival of the Rebels at Hagerstown, in their
great raid of 1863, a lieutenant and five men, wearing
the Federal uniform, crept out of the house where they
had been hiding, and gave themselves up to be paroled.
They told Jenkins that they did not wish to fight any
longer against their Southern brethren.   The reply of
the general must have greatly astonished the cowardly
traitors.   He indignantly rejected their claim of brother-
hood; told them that if he had a twenty-fifth cousin
as white-livered as they were, he would kill him and set
him up in his barn-yard to make sheep own their lambs;
and concluded by detailing six "good lusty fellows
with thick boots" to "parole" the recreant Federals by
vigorously kicking them out of the camp, to the west
border of the town.

It is said that the Rebel soldiers were highly tickled
with the scene, and highly approved of Jenkins's mode
of paroling cowards.   The six miserable poltroons must
have felt very differently.   What an encouraging prospect it must have been for Federal deserters.

STORY LVII.

REV. GRANVILLE MOODY, COLONEL OF THE 74TH OHIO.

COLONEL MOODY was one of the most popular Colonels in Middle Tennessee. The Secesh call him "the Go-Devil-Preacher-Colonel." His popularity is attributable to a peculiar manner he has of taking hold of things.

Shortly after the Colonel was ordered to "occupy, hold, and possess," Franklin, Tennessee, one of the larger sized Seceshers came into his office on business, and during a conversation which ensued, informed the Colonel that he was "a liar." The Colonel threw out his right, took him in the "tater trap," and brought his man.

The Colonel was out taking a walk one evening. He observed his black charger in the distance, coming at full speed, and, as he approached, was surprised to see that he was mounted by an individual dressed in butternut clothes. The Colonel sprang into the middle of the street, and as the horse was passing, seized the rein with one hand, and ye breast of ye butternut with the other, bringing said butternut to the ground, head foremost, as he checked the steed. Had the Colonel missed his hold he would never have seen his charger again, for the rider was a Rebel horse thief.

A Rebel, while under arrest, complained that armed men stood about him all the time, stating that if he just had a chance, he could whip as many Yankees as would come at him fair. The Colonel ordered, "Sergeant, put down that gun, put away that pistol and belt. Now, sir," addressing the fighting Secesh, "try that fellow; you shall have fair play. I give you my word and honor, if you can whip him, you sha ll not be interfered with." Butternut backed out, and acknowledged that he had just been acting the fool.

The Colonel was never known, but in a single instance, to give up property of any kind he had once taken, and that instance was when a Secesh woman declared that the last words of her dying husband were, "wife, take care of them three bags of salt." One of the bags of salt was returned.

The Colonel took possession of all surplus provender that could be found in his reach; if it belonged to a Union man, he gave a Government receipt for it; but if it belonged to a Rebel, that was the end of it.

STORY LVIII.

COLONEL LAWSON'S PAROLE.

A St. Louis paper of December 20th, 1862, gives the following good story of Colonel Lawson. It seems that he was captured some two weeks previous to that date, by an irregular body of the Rebels, alias guerillas, numbering nearly one hundred. At first they threatened to shoot him, but finally decided to release him on parole. Upon investigation, it proved that of the Rebels who then had him in charge—about a dozen—not one could write a parole, or any thing else. Through their whole youth they had never been subjected to the pernicious influence of free schools.

R   13

At last they requested Colonel Lawson himself to make out the parole and sign it. He immediately wrote an agreement, solemnly pledging himself never to take up arms against *the United States of America*, or in any way give aid and comfort to their enemies,—signed it, and was set at liberty. He made the best of his way to our lines, and was not overtaken.

It is surmised that when that parole fell into the hands of some Rebel officer who *could read*, it evoked a good many maledictions upon the head of the "Yankee trickster."

STORY LIX.

A PRACTICAL JOKE ON GEN. NELSON'S MULE TEAMSTER.

OUR boys are furious for practical jokes, and are constantly on the watch for subjects. One was recently found in the person of a new teamster, who had the charge of six large, shaggy mules. John was the proprietor of two bottles of old Bourbon—a contraband in camp—which a wag discovered, and resolved to possess. Being aware that the driver's presence was an impediment to the theft, he hit upon the following plan to get rid of him:

Approaching the driver, who was busy currying his mules, he accosted him with—"I say, old fellow, what are you doing there?"

"Can't you see?" replied John, gruffly.

"Certainly," responded wag, "but that is not your business. It is after tattoo, and there is a fellow hired here, by the General, who curries all the mules and horses brought in after tattoo."

The mule driver bit at once, and desired to know where the hair-dresser kept himself. Whereupon he was directed to General Nelson's tent, with the assurance that there was where the fellow "*hung out.*"

"You can't mistake the man," said wag; "he is a large fellow, and puts on a thundering sight of airs for a man in his business. He will probably refuse to do it, and tell you to go to the devil; but don't mind that, he has been drinking to-day. Make him come out *sure.*"

Jehu posted off, and entering the tent where our Napoleon of the 4th Division sat in deep reverie, probably considering the most expeditious method of expelling the Rebel Buckner, from his native State, slapped him on the back with force sufficient to annihilate a man of of ordinary size. Springing to his feet, the General accosted his uninvited guest with—"Well, sir, who are you, and what the devil do you want?"

"Old hoss, I've got a job for you now; six mules to be curried, and right off, too," said the Captain of mules, nothing daunted at the flashing eye of the General.

"Do you know whom you are addressing, sir?" asked the indignant commander.

"Yes," said John, elevating his voice to a pitch which rendered the words audible a square of; "you are the fellow hired by Uncle Sam to clean mules, and I won't have any foolishness. Clean them mules and I'll give you a drink of busthead."

"You infernal villain!" exclaimed the General, now perfectly furious, "I am General Nelson, commander of this Division!"

John placed the thumb of his right hand against his nose, and extending his fingers, waved them slowly, in a manner supposed by some to be indicative of great wisdom. The General's sword leaped from its scabbard, and John from the tent just in time to save his head.

Our boys drank the "big mule driver's health" in the Bourbon, the story soon got out, and became the popular joke of the season.

STORY LX.

A COSTLY MISTAKE. 1862.

Among the civilian prisoners captured at Rogerville, East Tennessee, was a gentleman from Connersville, Indiana, who had been visiting Richmond on army business. He seemed to be impressed with the belief that the Rebels regarded it as an offence worthy of death, to hail from a Northern city, and that when he fell into their hands, the hour of his dissolution drew nigh.

During Saturday night, while we were all quietly bunking in a corn-field, guarded by Confederate cavalry, the unsophisticated hoosier determined to rid himself of all the "evidence of his guilt," which he had in his possession. The night was very dark and cloudy. Indiana drew out his pocket-book, and after fumbling over it for some time, took therefrom what he thought was a pass from Governor Morton, authorizing him to leave his native State.

He had now, as he thought, got hold of the instrument destined to betray him even unto death.   He resolved to annihilate it, and placing it in his mouth, set his vengeful teeth to work to reduce it to a state of undecipherable pulp.   This done, with one masterly exhalation, he sent the "quid" over a neighboring fence, and with an easy conscience slept till morning.

During Sunday he had occasion to look over his private papers, and soon found, to his dismay, that Governor Morton's pass was still in his possession, but that a bank draft for three hundred dollars was missing!   He had masticated the wrong document, much to his own pecuniary loss.

STORY LXI.

A TALK WITH A REBEL AT FORT DONELDSON.

WHEN I got back to my command, I found one of our lieutenants had Colonel Hanson, of the Kentucky 2d, in custody.   He was a rough-looking customer, dressed in citizen's dress, short, muscular, and blear-eyed—he looked to me as a fit person to command a band of pirates.   He said he wanted somebody to tell him where to march his men, that he was tired of waiting.

He acted and talked like one having a "heap" of authority, and not much like a prisoner.   Finding no one to give him, immediately, the information he desired, he became sociable.

"Well," said he, "you were too hefty for us."

"Yes, but you were protected by these splendid defences."

"Your troops fought like tigers."

"Do you think now one Southern man can whip five Northern men?"

"Not Western men," he replied, doggedly. "Your troops are better than Yankee troops—fight harder—endure more. The devil and all hell can't stand before such fellows. But we drove you back."

"Why didn't you keep us back?"

"You had too many reinforcements."

"But we had no more troops engaged in the fight than you had."

"Well, you whipt us, but you haven't conquered us. You can never conquer the South."

"We don't wish to conquer the South; but will restore the stars and stripes to Tennessee, if we have to hang ten thousand such dare-devils as you are."

"Never mind, sir, you will never get up to Nashville."

"Then Nashville will surrender before we start."

"Well, well, the old United States flag is played out —we intend to have a right Government down here."

"What am I to understand by a right Government?"

"A Government based on property, and not a damned mechanic in it."

"Do these poor fellows, who have been fighting for you, understand that they have no voice *in the 'right Government' that you seek to establish?*"

"They don't care. They have no property to protect."

> Fling the striped bunting out !
> Never, never let it drag !
> Rally, rally freemen stout,
> Underneath the starry flag !

STORY LXII.

COLONEL STRAIGHT'S CAVALRY RAID INTO GEORGIA, IN
APRIL, 1863.

COLONEL A. D. STRAIGHT, of the 51st Indiana Volunteers, in command of a brigade of about 1,700 men, for
special service, left Murfreesboro', on the 7th or 8th of
April, 1863, to receive an outfit at Nashville.

At Nashville, instead of horses, they received, in part,
about nine hundred worn-out Government mules and a
few young, unbroken ones. Thus imperfectly outfitted,
they embarked on the 10th of April, on transport steamers, and proceeded down the Cumberland to Palmyra,
from whence they marched over land to Fort Donelson.

This march tested the bottom of the animals, proving
them deficient in all respects. The expectation had
been, that the men would be able to secure a better
mounting by capturing horses on their route; but the
guerillas, having preceded them, left but small opportunity for that operation.

From Fort Donelson they marched to Fort Henry,
where the troops re-embarked for Eastport, on the Tennessee River, about 190 miles above Fort Henry, where
they left the boats and started to join General Dodge's
forces, at Bear Creek, Alabama. The day after reaching Dodge's command, they advanced to Tuscumbia, the
Rebels leaving after slight skirmishing, Colonel Straight's
brigade bringing up Dodge's rear. After a stay of a
day and a half with the General, for some more broken-
down mules, Colonel Straight's brigade left Tuscumbia,
at midnight, for Russellville, which was reached in six

hours; the main body proceeding on to Mount Hope, to capture some horses, ascertained to be near there.

But the owners of the horses, apprised of their approach, conveyed the animals to the mountains, where they were securely secreted from our scouts. The next day the whole brigade left Mount Hope for Moulton, and, during their march, heard heavy cannonading in the direction of Town Creek, which was afterward ascertained was from Dodge's forces advancing on that place, it being his purpose to engage the enemy, and divert their attention from Colonel Straight, and prevent their pursuing him, till he could advance into the heart of their country, beyond their reach; but heavy rains and the swollen state of Town Creek prevented the General from crossing it.

Colonel Straight's command reached Moulton at dusk, and left at midnight for the Cumberland Mountains; his whole force not yet being mounted, one hundred men having to march on foot, greatly impeded his progress.

While crossing the mountains, *contraband* information enabled them to capture a sufficient number of horses and mules to mount those of the men who were yet on foot.

Having been about two days in the mountains, just as the troops had taken up their line of march, early in the morning, they were attacked by General Forrest, who had overtaken them, with 2,200 men and two pieces of artillery.

They, however, went on about three miles, to Day's Gap, where they dismounted, formed in line of battle, and, after a sharp conflict of about two hours, repulsed the rebels, capturing their artillery and a few prisoners.

Colonel Straight pursued them but a short distance, as being so much better mounted, they soon distanced him.

Having buried the dead and cared for the wounded, Colonel Straight resumed his line of march south, and having advanced about twelve miles, was again overtaken by Forrest, who had been strongly reinforced by a brigade of well-mounted infantry, with a battery of six pieces, under the command of Colonel Roddy.

The attack was immediately renewed, in hopes of overwhelming Colonel Straight's command with their superior numbers; but, to their mortification, they were repulsed two or three times, in a contest of three hours' duration, with heavy loss.

In this engagement Colonel Straight made use of the guns he had captured in the morning, as long as possible, but subsequently spiked them and left them on the field, having no suitable ammunition for them, and no spare horses for their removal.

This fight lasted till after dusk, when Forrest not renewing the attack, Colonel Straight resumed his line of march, being within eighty miles of the Georgia line.

While on the field, after the fight, the narrator of the particulars thus far stated (H. R. King. Ass't Surgeon, 51st Penn'a Vols.) was taken prisoner, while looking after the wounded, in company with Brig.-Surg. Wm. L. Peck, who barely escaped a similar fate.

Mr. King was taken before Forrest, who inquired of him, "what General commands your forces?"—to which Mr. King replied, "he is not a General, but a Colonel— Colonel Straight." Forrest seemed surprised at this, and remarked that the Colonel was "as brave a man as he ever had to contend against!"—that "he understood his business well, showing excellent generalship in the posi-

tions he selected; and that he was surprised at Colonel
Straight's holding out so long as he did, against superior odds."

At Huntsville, Mr. King heard General Forrest
remark to some citizens, that he never could have
taken Colonel Straight's command, had his men been
well mounted. Mr. King also learned that the force
pursuing Colonel Straight was 4,000 men, with a
battery.

After Mr. King was captured, he informs us that he
knew nothing more of the proceedings of Colonel
Straight's brigade, until he met him and his officers in
Libby Prison, in Richmond, Va. The following is given
by Mr. King, as a brief statement given him by Colonel
Straight's officers :—

"After the last battle, above alluded to, Colonel
Straight again started, marching toward Rome, Ga., and
Forrest, as I was told, having telegraphed General
Bragg to send a brigade on to Rome, followed him,
and overtook him at Bluntsville, where another fight
ensued, Forrest being again repulsed.

"Skirmishes now occurred every day, until out troops
were within a few miles of Rome, when another fight
took place, at Cedar Bluff, where Colonel Straight
fought Forrest until all his available ammunition was
exhausted—some of it having been wet in the hold of
the boat, while on the river—and the mules were completely worn out, so that they would not move, either
by coaxing or beating.

"Colonel Straight was therefore compelled to surrender, which he did, on condition that the officers
should retain their side-arms, and be paroled, and exchanged immediately. Nevertheless, as soon as he and

his officers had been removed from General Forrest's command, their side-arms were taken from them.

"Previous to his surrender, Colonel Straight sent three hundred of his men (the only ones in his command who were mounted on horses) to destroy some bridges and a large rolling-mill, all valued at about two millions of dollars, which they accomplished.

"The officers in Colonel Straight's command," continues Mr. King, "justify him in all that he did, express themselves well pleased with his management of the troops, say that he acted as bravely and as nobly as a man could act, and are extremely desirous to continue under his command."

Had it not been for the rise in Town Creek, which prevented General Dodge from crossing, and engaging the enemy, as originally planned, Colonel Straight would have been able to have succeeded in his expedition ; and would, notwithstanding, had his men been well mounted, as was admitted by Forrest, himself. Our entire loss in all the engagements, was seven killed and fifty-eight wounded. The rebel loss was one hundred killed and four hundred wounded, which Mr. King says he ascertained while within their lines.

STORY LXIII.

A HEROIC INCIDENT.

A young man in our employ, says the Mansfield (Ohio) Herald, in April, 1863, received a letter recently, announcing the death of a former school fellow, named

Austin Macy, of Montgomery County, Ohio, by the Rebels in Kentucky. The letter gives the following details of the courageous manner in which he met his fate, and we doubt if the annals of the war, so prolific of heroism, can parallel young Macy's audacious gallantry.

Macy belonged to an Ohio regiment, stationed at Camp Dick Robinson, Kentucky, and was sent out with a detachment on a scouting expedition. After a time he became separated from his party, and soon discovered a party of Secesh, who did not notice him. Concealing himself, he fired on and succeeded in killing seven of them, before they saw where he was hidden.

There being no further chance, Macy attempted to escape, but unfortunately, his horse threw him, severely injuring and disabling him. He was thereupon easily captured by the Rebels, who deliberately shot him seven times, wounding and mangling him in a most dreadful manner, but not killing him. He was still able to raise up and shoot his eighth man! An end was then put to this gallant hero by bayonetting him, and his mangled remains were then thrown into a mudhole. He was in his twenty-second year.

The above particulars were obtained from a Union woman, who witnessed a part of the affair, which occurred on her farm. She plead unsuccessfully with the leader of the Rebel party, for the privilege of burying Mr. Macy's corpse. He had not the humanity to grant her request.

When once a man descends to be a wicked heartless Rebel,
His remnant of humanity is scarcely worth a pebble :
From lesser to outrageous crimes—the length and breadth of evil,
And heighth and depth of infamy, his progress shames the devil.

STORY LXIV.

A SAD AND REMARKABLE INCIDENT.

IN the second year of the war, a private in the 19th Indiana regiment was tried by a court-martial for deserting his post, and found guilty, the punishment for which is death. His execution was deferred for some time, and he was kept in a painful state of suspense. At last the day was fixed for his execution, and five regiments were drawn up in line to witness it, while a file of twelve men were in advance to execute the sentence of death by shooting him.

The prisoner was led forward blindfolded, and the usual words of preparation and command were given, in a low, measured tone, by the officer in command. During the interval between the commands—"Take aim," and "Fire," and before the last was given, a horseman rode rapidly up the road, waving in the air a paper, which was understood by all to be a reprieve. Covered with dust and perspiration, the horseman rode hurriedly up to the officer in command, and delivered to him what really proved to be a reprieve.

The shout "reprieve" fell upon the poor soldier's ear, which was already strained to the utmost, in anticipation of hearing the last, and final word that was to usher his soul into the presence of his Creator—it was too much for him, and he fell back upon his coffin, apparently dead. The bandage was removed from his eyes, but reason had taken its flight, and he became a hopeless maniac. He was discharged from the army, and sent home to his friends.

His death had really never been intended, but it was necessary for the good order and discipline of the army, to make an impression upon not only himself, but the whole brigade; for which purpose the forms of the execution were regularly gone through with in its presence, and the reprieve arrived in good time, as intended.

It was sought by this means to solemnly impress upon the minds of the soldiers, the necessity of a strict observance of duty and obedience, under the penalty of an ignominious death. It was a fearful ordeal for the deserter, and it is questionable whether to him the completion of the tragedy would not have been better than the actual result.

STORY LXV.

DARING EXPLOIT,

ONE of the most daring and successful exploits of the war, was performed by four men, on Saturday night, May 1st, 1863, on Rock creek, in Wayne county, Kentucky. Benjamin Burk, a citizen; Hudson Burk, a discharged soldier; James Burk, of Wolford's cavalry, and a citizen named James Davis, having received intimation of a band of twenty-eight men, under command of Captain Evans, of the famous band of Rebel robbers, that infested Wayne and Clinton counties, known as Champ Ferguson's men, having stopped at the house of Jonathan Burk to spend the night, determined to attempt their capture.

Four men against twenty-eight fiends, who had reveled in the blood of innocent neighbors, for a year— think of it! It seemed like madness, yet the attempt was made. Coming to a sentinel, who stood guard over their thirty-one horses, Davis ordered him to surrender his gun, which the coward did, and received in return a blow from it that knocked his brains out. The way was now clear to the house, where the remainder of the party were asleep. Surrounding the dwelling, they at once raised a hideous yell, crying, "Wolford! Wolford!" at the top of their voices.

The Rebels awakened by the noise, supposed that Wolford's cavalry, whom they dreaded as they did death, was upon them, sprang from their beds, leaving their clothes and guns behind, and rushed for the doors.

Out they rushed with nothing on but their shirts and drawers, some without the latter even, to take leg-bail. Hudson Burk met Captain Evans at the door; both fired at the same time. Burk was slightly wounded in the head, but the infamous Evans was instantly killed. Four others were slain, and the remainder of the party escaped.

They abandoned every thing; all their horses, personal property, guns, and several thousand dollars in greenbacks, in addition to a considerable amount of Confederate money. Nothing remained for the victorious few to do, but to gather up the fruits of their victory, which they divided with William Milligan, a prisoner, whom they had released from the clutches of the marauders.

STORY LXVI.

ROMANCE OF THE WAR.—A HEROINE,

THE following narrative appeared in the *Louisville Journal* early in May, 1863:

A few weeks since, a captain, accompanied by a young soldier apparently about seventeen years of age, arrived in this city in charge of some Rebel prisoners.

During their stay in the city, the young soldier alluded to had occasion to visit headquarters, and at once attracted the attention of Colonel Mundy as being exceedingly sprightly, and possessed of more than ordinary intelligence. Being in need of such a young man at Barracks No. 1, the colonel detailed him for service in that institution.

A few days subsequently, however, the startling secret was disclosed, that the supposed young man was a young lady, and the fact was established beyond doubt by a soldier who was raised in the same town with her, and knew her "parents." She "acknowledged the corn," and begged to be retained in the position to which she had been assigned; having been in the service ten months, she desired to serve during the war. Her wish was accordingly granted, and she is still at her post.

On learning the facts above stated, we took occasion to visit the barracks, and was introduced to "Frank Martin," (her assumed name) and gleaned the following incidents connected with her extraordinary career during the past ten months.

Frank was born near Bristol, Pa., and her parents reside in Alleghany city, where she was raised. They

are highly respectable people, and in good circumstances.
She was sent to the convent in Wheeling, Va., at twelve
years of age, where she remained until the breaking out
of the war, having acquired a superior education, and
all the accomplishments of modern usage.

She visited home after leaving the convent, and after
taking leave of her parents, proceeded to this city in
July last, (1862, with the design of enlisting in the 2d
East Tennessee Cavalry, which she accomplished, and
accompanied the army of the Cumberland to Nashville.
She was in the thickest of the fight at Murfreesboro,
and was severely wounded in the shoulder, but fought
gallantly, and waded Stone river into Murfreesboro, on
the memorable Sunday on which our forces were driven
back. She had her wound dressed, and here her sex
was disclosed, and General Rosecrans made acquainted
with the fact.

She was accordingly mustered out of the service,
notwithstanding her earnest entreaty to be allowed to
serve the cause she loved so well. The general was
very favorably impressed with her daring bravery, and
superintended the arrangements for her safe transmis-
sion to her parents. She left the army of the Cumberland resolved to enlist again in the first regiment she met.
When she arrived at Bowling Green she found the 8th
Michigan there and enlisted; since which time she has
been and is now connected with it.

She is represented as an excellent horseman, and has
been honored with the position of regimental bugler to
the regiment. She has seen and endured all the pri-
vations and hardships incident to the life of the soldier,
and gained an enviable reputation as a scout, having
14

made several wonderful expeditions, which were attended with signal success.

Frank is only eighteen years of age, quite small, and a beautiful figure. She has auburn hair, which she wears quite short, and large blue eyes, beaming with intelligence. Her complexion is naturally very fair, though slightly bronzed at present from exposure. She is exceedingly pretty and very amiable. Her conversation denotes more than ordinary accomplishment, and what is stranger than all, she appears very refined in her manners, giving no evidence whatever of the rudeness which might naturally be expected from her late associations.

Frank informs us that she has discovered a great many females in the army, and is now intimately acquainted with a young lady who is a lieutenant in the army. She has assisted in burying three female soldiers at different times, whose sex was unknown to any but herself.

STORY LXVII.

SIEGE OF VICKSBURG—ADVENTURES OF A REBEL DISPATCH BEARER.

THE *Mobile Register* published the following interesting letter, from the "father of Lamar Fontain," (a pious old Rebel.)

Lamar is almost continually in the saddle, and employed in very hazardous enterprises. His last feat of arms was the most daring he has yet performed.

He left my house May 24th, 1863. under orders from

General Johnston to bear a verbal dispatch to General Pemberton, in Vicksburg, and to carry a supply of percussion caps to our troops in that besieged city. I parted with him, hardly hoping ever to see him again; for I knew that Vicksburg was closely invested on all sides. The enemy's lines of circumvallation extend from Snyder's Bluff, on the Yazoo, to Warrenton, on the Mississippi, and the rivers, and their opposite shores, are filled and lined with their forces.

He was well mounted, and was burdened with forty pounds of percussion caps, beside his blanket and crutches. He has no use of his broken leg, and cannot walk a step without a crutch; and in mounting his horse, he has to lift it over the saddle with his right hand. But he accomplishes this object with much dexterity, and without assistance. I loaned him a very fine saber, with a wooden scabbard, to prevent rattling, and a very reliable revolver, which has never missed fire, when loaded by me.

The family were called together for prayers, and we prayed fervently, that the God of our fathers would shield him from all danger, and enable him to fulfil his mission to Vicksburg successfully, and give him a safe return. I then exhorted him to remember, that if it was the will of God for him to live, and serve his country, all the Yankees owned by Lincoln could not kill him; but if it was the Divine will that he should die, he would be in as much danger at home as in Vicksburg, and death would certainly find him, no matter where he might be.

I charged him to use his best endeavors to kill every one of the jackalls who should attempt to stop his course, or to come within reach of his sword or pistol.

He crossed Big Black River that night, and the next day got between their lines and the division of their army, which was at Mechanicsburg. He hid his horse in a ravine, and ensconced himself in a fallen tree, over-looking the road, during the day. From his hiding place, he witnessed the retreat of the Yankees, who passed him in considerable haste and confusion.

After their columns had gone by, and the night had made it safe for him to move, he continued his route in the direction of Snyder's Bluff. As he entered the telegraphic road from Yazoo City to Vicksburg, he was hailed by a picket, but dashed by him. A volley was fired at him by the Yankees. He escaped unhurt, but a Minnie ball wounded his horse mortally.

The spirited animal, however, carried him safely to the bank of the Yazoo River, where he died, and left his rider afoot. He lost one of his crutches in making his escape, it being jerked from him by the limb of a tree, and he had no time to pick it up.

With the assistance of one crutch, he carried his baggage, and groped along the Yazoo, until he pro-videntially discovered a small log canoe, tied by a rope, within his reach. He pressed this into his service, and paddled down the river until he met three Yankee gun-boats coming up to Yazoo City.

He avoided them by running under some willows overhanging the water, and lying concealed until they passed. Soon afterward he floated past Snyder's Bluff, which was illuminated, and alive with Yankees and negroes, participating in the amusement of a grand ball of mixed races.

He lay flat in his canoe, and could hardly be dis-tinguished from a piece of drift-wood—and he glided safely through the gunboats and barges of the amalgamationists. He reached the backwater of the Mississippi before day, and in the darkness missed the outlet of the Yazoo, and got into what is called "Old River."

After searching in vain for a pass into the Mississippi, day dawned, and he discovered his mistake. He was forced to conceal his boat and himself, and lie by for another day. He had been two days and nights without food, and began to suffer the pangs of hunger.

At night he paddled back into the Yazoo, and descended it to the Mississippi, passing forty or fifty of the Yankee transports. Only one man hailed him, from the stern of a steamboat, and asked him where he was going. He replied that he was going to his fishing lines.

In the bend, above Vicksburg, he floated by the mortar fleet, lying flat in his canoe. The mortars were in full blast, bombarding the city. The next morning he tied a white handkerchief to his paddle, raised himself up, in the midst of our picket-boats at Vicksburg, and gave a loud huzza for Jeff. Davis, and the Southern Confederacy, amid the *vivas* of our sailors, who gave him a joyful reception, and assisted him to General Pemberton's headquarters.

After resting a day and a night in the city, he started out with a dispatch from General Pemberton to General Johnston. He embarked in his same canoe, and soon reached the enemy's fleet below the city. He avoided their picket-boats on both shores, and floated near their gunboats. He passed so near one of these, that through an open port-hole he could see men playing cards and hear them converse.

At Diamond Place he landed, and bade adieu to his

faithful "dugout." After hobbling through the bottom
to the hills, he reached the residence of a man who had
been robbed by the savages of all his mules and horses,
except an old, worthless gelding, and a half-broken colt.
He gave him the choice of them, and he mounted the
colt, but found that he traveled badly.

Providentially he came upon a very fine horse in the
bottom, tied by a blind-bridle, without a saddle. As a
basket and old bag were lying near him, he inferred
that a negro had left him there, and that a Yankee
camp was not far distant. He exchanged bridles, and
saddled the horse, and mounted him, after turning loose
the colt.

After riding so as to avoid the supposed position of
the Yankees, he encountered one of them, who was returning from a successful plundering expedition. He
was loaded with chickens, and a bucket of honey. He
commenced catechising Lamar, in true Yankee style,
who concluded it best to satisfy his curiosity, by sending him where he could know all that the devil could
teach him.

With a pistol bullet through his forehead, Lamar left
him, with his honey and poultry lying in the path, to
excite the conjectures of his fellow-thieves.

He approached with caution the next settlement,
where he hired a guide, for fifty dollars, to pilot him to
Hankerson's Ferry, on Big Black River, which he
wished to reach near that point, without following any
road. The fellow he hired proved to be a traitor.

When he got near the ferry, Lamar sent him ahead
to ascertain whether any Yankees were in the vicinity.
The conversation and manners of the man had excited
his suspicions, and as soon as he left him he concealed

himself, but remained where he could watch his return. The man was gone much longer than Lamar expected; but returned, and reported that the way was open, and that no Yankees were near the ferry.

After paying him, Lamar took the precaution to avoid the ferry, and to approach the river above it, instead of following the guide's directions. By this he flanked a force of the Yankees posted to intercept him; but as he entered the road near the river bank, one of them, who seemed to be on the right flank of a long line of sentinels, suddenly rose up within ten feet of him, and ordered him to halt.

He replied with a pistol shot, which killed the sentinel dead, and, wheeling his horse, galloped through the bottom up the river; but the Yankees sent a shower of balls after him, two of which wounded his right hand, injuring four of his fingers. One grazed his right leg, cutting two holes through his pantaloons, and another cut through one side of my sword scabbard, spoiling its beauty, but leaving a mark, which makes me prize it more highly.

Seven bullets struck the horse, which reeled under him, but had strength and speed enough to bear him a mile from his pursuers, before he fell and died. Lamar then divided his clothes and arms into two packages, and swam Big Black River safely.

He did not walk far before a patriotic lady supplied him with the only horse she had—a stray one, which came to her house after the Yankees had carried off all the animals belonging to the place. On this he reached Raymond, at two o'clock in the morning, changed his horse for a fresh one, carried his dispatch to Jackson that morning, and rejoiced us all by an unexpected visit the same day.

STORY LXVIII.

THE BATTLE OF GETTYSBURG.

On the 13th of June, 1863, General Lee attacked and captured Winchester, its armament, and part of the garrison. He then crossed the Potomac, near Williamsport, and directed his march upon Harrisburg General Hooker followed on his right flank, covering Washington and Baltimore.

On reaching Frederick, Maryland, on the 28th of June, General Hooker was, at his own request, relieved from the command, and Major-General Meade appointed in his place. The army of the Potomac was at this time mainly concentrated at Frederick.

On the 29th General Meade put his army in motion, and at night was in position, its left at Emmittsburg and right at New Windsor. The advance of Buford's cavalry was at Gettysburg, and Kilpatrick's Division at Hanover, where it encountered Stuart's cavalry, which had passed around the rear and right of our army, without meeting serious opposition.

On the 30th, the 1st, 3d, and 11th Corps were concentrated at Emmittsburg, under General Reynolds, while the right wing moved up to Manchester. Buford reported the enemy in force on the Cashtown road, near Gettysburg, and Reynolds moved up to that place on the 1st of July. He found our cavalry warmly engaged with the enemy, and holding him in check on the Cashtown road. Reynolds immediately deployed the advanced Division of the 1st Corps, and ordered the 11th Corps to advance promptly to its support.

Wadsworth's Division had driven the enemy back some distance and captured a large number of prisoners. when General Reynolds fell mortally wounded.

The arrival of Ewell's Corps, about this time, by the York and Harrisburg road, compelled General Howard, upon whom the command devolved, to withdraw his force, the 1st and 11th Corps to the Cemetery Ridge, on the south side of Gettysburg.

About seven, P. M., Generals Sickles and Slocum came on the field with the 3d and 12th Corps, which took position, one on the left and the other on the right of the new line. The battle, for the day, however, was over.

General Meade arrived on the field during the night with the reserves, and posted his troops in line of battle, the 1st Corps on the right, the 11th Corps next, then the 12th Corps, which crossed the Baltimore pike, the 2d and 3d Corps on the Cemetery Ridge, on the left of the 11th Corps.

The 5th Corps, pending the arrival of the 6th, formed the reserve. On the arrival of the latter at two o'clock, P. M., it took the place of the 5th, which was ordered to take position on the extreme left.

The enemy massed his troops on an exterior ridge, about a mile and a half in front of that occupied by us.

General Sickles, misinterpreting his orders, instead of placing the 3d Corps on the prolongation of the 2d, had moved it nearly three-fourths of a mile in advance; an error which nearly proved fatal in the battle. The enemy attacked this Corps and the 2d with great fury, and it was likely to be utterly annihilated, when the 5th Corps moved up on the left, and enabled it to reform, behind the line it was originally ordered to hold,

T

The 6th Corps and part of the 1st, were also opportunely thrown into this gap, and succeeded in checking the enemy's advance. About sunset the Rebels retired in confusion and disorder. About eight, P. M., an assault was made from the left of the town, which was gallantly repelled by the 1st, 2d and 11th Corps.

On the morning of the 3d we regained, after a spirited contest, a part of our line, the right of which had been yielded to sustain other points on the 2d. About one, P. M., the enemy opened an artillery fire of 125 guns on our centre and left. This was followed by an assault of a heavy infantry column on our left and left centre. This was successfully repulsed with terrible loss to the enemy.

This terminated the battle, and the Rebels retired, defeated, from the field. The opposing forces in this sanguinary conflict were nearly equal in numbers, and both fought with the most desperate courage. The commanders were also brave, skillful, and experienced, and both handled their troops on the field with distinguished ability; but to General Meade belongs the honor of a well-earned victory in one of the greatest and best fought battles of the war.

The victory, however, like others gained by the army of the Potomac, under other commanders, was not followed up with the promptness requisite for the realization of the greatest results, and on the morning of the 14th of July, it was found that Lee, with his army, had crossed to the south side of the Potomac. His rear guard, however, was attacked by our cavalry, and suffered considerable loss.

Our loss in this short campaign was very severe, viz.: 2,834 killed, 13,709 wounded, and 6,643 missing, in all

23,186. We captured 3 guns, 41 standards, 13,621 prisoners, 28,178 small arms.

The entire loss of the enemy is unknown; but judging from the numbers of his dead and wounded left on the field, it must have been much greater than ours.

MAJOR-GENERAL GEO. G. MEADE.

THE Commander-in-Chief of the Army of the Potomac, Major-General George G. Meade, was born in Spain, in 1816, during the temporary sojourn of his parents in that country. His father was a Pennsylvanian. He entered the Military Academy at West Point, from the District of Columbia, in September, 1831, graduated July 1st, 1835, and was appointed Second Lieutenant in the 3d Artillery; but resigned on the 26th of October, 1836. May 19th, 1842, he was appointed Second Lieutenant of the Topographical Engineers.

In the Mexican war he distinguished himself at the battle of Palo Alto: was brevetted a First Lieutenant for gallant conduct at Monterey, and in August, 1851, attained the full rank of First Lieutenant; and was appointed Captain, May 19th, 1856; and on the 31st of August, 1862, Brigadier-General of Volunteers.

Being assigned to the command of a brigade in General McCall's division, he accompanied it to the Peninsula, where he distinguished himself in the battles of Beaver Dam, Gaines' Mills, and Nelson's Farm. In the latter, he was wounded by a fragment of a shell, which passed through his right side.

He was thought to be mortally wounded, and on the day of the battle of Malvern Hill he was placed on a steamer to be sent north to his family. His wound proved less serious than had been supposed, and he recovered in time to command a division in the battles of South Mountain and Antietam, where he again distinguished himself.

He was also in the battle of Fredericksburg, and at Chancellorville he commanded the 5th Corps.

When General Hooker was wounded at Antietam, General McClellan placed General Meade in command of the Corps which had just been deprived of its heroic leader. During the action, General Meade received a slight contusion from a spent grape-shot, and had two horses killed under him. He distinguished himself greatly, during the battle, by deeds of daring and valor.

On the 28th of June. 1863, Major-General Hooker, at his own request, was relieved of the command of the Army of the Potomac; and General Meade being appointed to succeed him, assumed the command of that army, which was then principally concentrated at Frederick, Md. This was just previous to the sanguinary battle of Gettysburg, the particulars of which are given in Story LXVIII., to which the reader is referred.

In army circles, General Meade has the reputation of being an able, cool-headed, energetic officer; and what is equally to the purpose, his whole heart is in the cause of the Union.

He is a fine-looking man, of nearly six feet stature, with vigorous constitution, and correct habits. His soldiers always admired him, and relied confidently upon his nerve and skill, in action.

At the critical period of his assuming the command of the Army of the Potomac, he was so perfectly acquainted with it, as to be able to put it in motion, with the least possible delay, and achieved a most glorious result.

STORY LXIX.

BARBARA FRIETCHIE.

Up from the meadow rich with corn,
Clear in the cool September morn,
The clustered spires of Frederick stand,
Green-walled by the hills of Maryland.

Round about them orchards sweep,
Apple and peach trees fruited deep;
Fair as a garden of the Lord,
To the eyes of the famished rebel horde.

On that pleasant morn of the early Fall,
When Lee marched over the mountain-wall—
Over the mountains winding down,
Horse and foot into Frederick town,

Forty flags with their silver stars,
Forty flags with their crimson bars,
Flapped in the morning wind: the sun
Of noon looked down and saw not one.

Up rose old Barbara Frietchie then,
Bowed with her fourscore years and ten;
Bravest of all in Frederick town,
She took up the flag the men hauled down:

In her attic-window the staff she set,
To show that one heart was loyal yet;
Up the street came the Rebel tread,
Stonewall Jackson riding ahead.

Under his slouched hat left and right,
He glanced: the old flag met his sight.
"Halt!" the dust-brown ranks stood fast.
"Fire!" out blazed the rifle blast,

It shivered the window, pane and sash,
It rent the banner with seam and gash;
Quick as it fell from the broken staff,
Dame Barbara snatched the silken scarf.

She leaned far out on the window sill,
And shook it forth with a royal will :
" Shoot, if you must, the old gray head,
But spare your country's flag," she said.

A shade of sadness, a blush of shame,
Over the face of the leader came ;
The nobler nature within him stirred
To life at that woman's deed and word :

" Who touches a hair of yon gray head
Dies like a dog ! march on !" he said.
All day long, through Frederick street
Sounded the tread of marching feet :

All day long that free flag tossed
Over the heads of the Rebel host ;
Ever its torn folds rose and fell
On the loyal minds that loved it well.

And through the hill-gaps sunset light
Shone over it with a warm good-night :
Barbara Frietchie's work is o'er,
And the Rebel rides on his raids no more.

Honor to her ! and let a tear
Fall for her sake on Stonewall's bier ;
Over Barbara Frietchie's grave,
Flag of freedom and union wave !

Peace and order and beauty draw
Round thy symbol of light and law ;
And ever the stars above look down
On thy stars below in Frederick town !

                              JOHN G. WHITTIER.

-------- ◆◆◆◆ --------

" Then fling out our flag most high to-day,
    Triumphant 'mid the clang of war ;
  And death to him who shall betray
      One single stripe or star."

STORY LXX.

CAPTURE, TRIAL AND EXECUTION OF COLONEL LAWRENCE WILLIAMS AND LIEUTENANT WALTER G. PETERS, OF THE REBEL ARMY.

FRANKLIN, TENN., *June 9th*, 1863.

WHEN the history of this most bloody war is fully written, few, if any incidents will be of more thrilling interest than the capture, trial, and execution of Colonel Williams and Lieutenant Peters. We had been besieged for four or five days by General Forrest, our communications with Nashville cut off, and most of the time fighting, and were almost hourly looking for a general assault upon our feeble garrison. Colonel Baird, of the 85th Indiana, had made the best possible disposition of our forces, and all were resolved to sell Franklin as dearly as possible.

But on the night of the 8th of June, the dull monotony of dodging shells was relieved, and excitement was carried to the highest pitch, as two fine-looking officers, dressed in what appeared the Federal uniform, and mounted on splendid horses, rode up to Colonel J. P. Baird's headquarters and introduced themselves as Colonel Anton and Major Dunlap, of the United States regular army.

They stated that they had, a few days before, been ordered by the War Department to report to General Rosecrans for duty as special inspectors of the army of the Cumberland: that they had entered upon their new field of duty the day before, fully equipped and accompanied by two orderlies.

They showed proper papers from Adjutant General Thomas, and General Garfield, chief of Rosecrans' staff, and stated that after leaving Murfreesboro they took the direction of Eaglesville; and when near that place they stopped for dinner, and while at dinner they were surprised by a party of about twenty Rebel scouts, who captured their orderlies, and were so near capturing them as to make it necessary to leave their coats and other baggage; that they were unfortunately out of funds, and wished the loan of fifty dollars of Colonel Baird, that they might go to Nashville to refit themselves before going further on duty.

Colonel Baird, although very suspicious that all was not right, felt compelled to recognize them, with such perfect papers from so high a source. He gave them the fifty dollars and a pass to Nashville, upon receiving which, the two started off at full speed in the direction of Nashville.

But they had scarcely disappeared in the dark, when Colonel Watkins, of the 6th Kentucky Cavalry, and Colonel Baird both felt such intense anxiety lest they might be imposed upon, that it was instantly resolved to pursue and arrest the two gents, and hold them until they could learn from General Rosecrans the truth of their statements.

As no time was to be lost, the gallant Colonel Watkins, accompanied by a single orderly, started in pursuit, and dashing forward toward our pickets, luckily came in sight of the gentlemen. The colonel hailed them and ordered them back to Colonel Baird's headquarters. Undoubtedly the first impulse of these daring spies was to resist, which they could have done desperately, as they were both well armed; but the cool courage of Colonel Watkins induced them to return. Colonel Williams afterwards stated, that he put his hand on his pistol to shoot Colonel Watkins, but the hope of not being detected as a spy, caused him to desist.

After their arrival at headquarters, Colonels Baird and Watkins questioned them very closely, but could get no clue to anything that would raise a reasonable suspicion, until General Rosencrans telegraph that he had no such officers in his department.

The prisoners were then informed that they were suspected, and were under arrest until they could properly explain themselves. They showed correct maps of our lines, and seemed well acquainted with all the officers of the regular army.

Their persons were then searched, and the first thing upon examining the sword of the Colonel Anton, revealed the fatal marks, C. S. A; the die was cast and the blood rushed to the cheeks of the almost petrified prisoners. They acknowledged that they were trapped, and at once confessed their real names, rank and position.

The colonel acknowledged himself to be Colonel Lawrence Williams of the 2d Regular Cavalry, at the breaking out of the War, and was recognized by Colonel Watkins as a fellow soldier of that regiment: he had entered the confederate service, and was now chief of artillery on General Bragg's staff. That he entered upon this most hazardous enterprise, fully aware of his fate if detected; but refused to disclose the nature of his business.

The younger man said he was Lieutenant Walter G. Peters, of General Wheeler's staff, and showed some

15

excitement; but Colonel Williams was perfectly cool after the first moment of detection.

Colonel Baird now telegraphed the facts to General Rosecrans, and received the laconic reply, to try the prisoners by court-martial, and if found guilty, hang them at once, to prevent all possibility of Forrest's profiting by their information. Now came the severe struggle; the prisoners had confessed their guilt, but to hang two such men, of their rank, was a terrible task, but Colonel Baird was equal to the emergency, and knowing the exigencies of the service, proceeded promptly to obey General Rosecrans order.

A court-martial was called by Colonel Baird to sit at once: the charges and specifications were duly presented, and the court thus sitting, at the dead hour of night, after carefully and patiently hearing the confessions and other evidence, performed the sad and painful duty of finding the prisoners guilty of being spies, and Colonel Baird, under General Rosecrans' order, approved the finding, and sentenced Colonel Williams and Lieutenant Peters to be hung by the neck until dead!

At four o'clock on the morning of the 9th of June, Colonel Baird informed the prisoners of their awful fate, and could not refrain from shedding tears as he announced it to them. Colonel Williams received his sentence with the most perfect coolness; but begged that as his father had fallen in our country's service at Monterey, in the Mexican war, that he might be shot, and asked mercy for Lieutenant Peters; but under Rosecrans' imperative order no clemency could be shown.

After the sentence of the prisoners was announced, they began to prepare to meet their fate. They made their wills, and wrote letters to their friends full of the deepest affection and tenderness. A chaplain was called, and the prisoners partook of the sacrament, and joined in prayer with great fervency. They did not attempt to sleep, but spent the whole time in either writing or conversing.

At the request of Colonel Williams, Colonel Watkins took charge of his effects, which consisted of eleven hundred and seventy-five dollars in Confederate money, a fine watch, and some private papers. Lieutenant Peters had very few effects about his person, the only one of importance being a gold locket, containing a likeness of his wife, with a fine gold chain attached. He requested it to be buried with him, which was faithfully done.

At nine o'clock in the morning, Captain Alexander, who had taken charge of the execution, reported the scaffold and gallows ready. The infantry and cavalry were formed in hollow square about the place of execution: at half-past nine the prisoners were brought forward by the guard. They marched with firm tread, and mounting the scaffold, took an affectionate leave of each other, when the halters were placed about their necks, and they were launched into eternity.

Thus two officers, who were born and bred gentlemen, one a regular army officer of the United States service, who had been educated and given position by our Government, expiated their crimes of treason against the Government they were taught to love and respect, and were bound in honor and duty to defend.

Protected by the forged papers they had in their possession, had they succeeded in getting the countersign, on the night of their visit to Colonel Baird's camp. they could have marched a brigade of **Rebels into our**

forts, and captured our whole command without resistance; or if true, as they stated, they had inspected our
whole front, they could have given Bragg such information as might have led to the most appalling disasters to
Rosecrans' whole command.—A. B. V., Cor. Cin. Com.

> Our happy Government fain would they subvert,
> They sought its ruin and they felt its hurt.

STORY LXXI.

GATHERING BUTTERNUTS IN TENNESSEE.

On Tuesday, the 3d of March, 1863, General Steadman
ordered Colonel Bishop, of the 3d Minnesota, to take his
regiment, a section of the 4th Regular Battery, under
Lieutenant Stephenson, and 600 of Johnson's 1st East
Tennessee Cavalry, and proceed forthwith to Harpeth
River. Anticipating a fight, I went with the detachment.

As we passed through Nolinsville and Triune, the
few Butternut inhabitants gazed, with apparent envy, at
our well-clad soldiers. About nine o'clock at night we
reached the river; where the infantry bivouacked for
the night: the artillery planted their pieces in eligible
positions; while the cavalry crossed the river, and
commenced the search for Rebel gentry, who were supposed to be on short leave of absence to their homes.
Quite a number of *citizen* soldiers were thus picked up.

Major Tracy, of the cavalry, then proceeded with a
dozen men to the residence of General Starnes, and surrounded it, hoping to find the General at home: but the
bird had flown the day previous. The Major, however,

being a *searching* man, and full of inquiry, looked under the beds, and in the closets, then asked who was up stairs? "No one," was the reply, "but my brother, and he has never been in the army."

Major Tracy took a candle, went up, saw the young man, and asked him where the man had gone to who had been in the bed with him. The young man protested no one had been there, and Mrs. Starnes pledged her word, on the "*honor of a Southern lady*," that there was no one else in the house. But the Major turned down the sheets, and being a discerning man, discovered the imprint of another person having been in the bed: and from the distance they had lain apart, he felt sure it was not a woman.

So, telling Mrs. Starnes he hadn't much faith in the honor of a Southern woman, under such circumstances, he though he would take a peep through a dormant-window that projected from the roof, and there, sure enough, sat Major Starnes, a son of the Rebel General, in his shirt-tail, breeches and boots in hand, afraid to stir. It was a bitter cold night, and the poor fellow shook like an aspen leaf. He presented at once, a pitiable, yet ludicrous aspect. After taking him, and collecting some twenty or thirty horses, they returned to their headquarters, on this side of the river.—[ALF. BURNETT.]

STORY LXXII.

COLONEL BENJAMIN H. GRIERSON'S RAID.

IN pursuance of a plan for the destruction of all lines of communication between the Rebel Army of the West,

U

and that of General Bragg, in Middle Tennessee, Colonel Grierson, by order of General Grant, moved his forces, consisting of the 6th Illinois Cavalry, Lieutenant-Colonel Loomis; 7th Illinois Cavalry, Colonel Edward Prince, and the 2d Iowa Cavalry, Colonel Edward Hatch, from Lagrange, Tennessee, out on the Ripley road, and bivouacked for the night, on the plantation of Mr. Davis, five miles northwest of Ripley. This was on the 15th of April, 1863.

On the morning of the 18th of April, the command proceeded to Ripley. From thence, the 2d Iowa, marching on the left flank of the column, took a southeast course, crossing the Tallahatchie five miles northeast of New Albany. The main body proceeded due south, crossing the river two miles east of that point. Simultaneously, a battalion of the 7th Illinois, commanded by Major Graham, marched on the right flank of the column, and crossed at New Albany.

The Rebel General Chandler, then stationed with a body of troops at Senatobia, a few miles from New Albany, had his pickets on both sides of the river, to prevent our crossing. With these, all portions of Grierson's command had skirmishing, at times, till they were driven in. They attempted to fire the bridge at New Albany, but were prevented.

The 6th and 7th Iowa encamped about four miles south of New Albany; the 2d Iowa four miles east of the same place. Near midnight, this regiment was attacked by a considerable force of the enemy, which was promptly repulsed.

On the morning of the 19th, several movements were made by detachments, for the purpose of inducing the enemy, who were encamped in some force at King's

Bridge, under Major Chalmers, to believe our object to be to break up the different military organizations in that part of the country. The ruse succeeded, and the enemy were left in ignorance of the course taken by our forces.

Colonel Grierson, with the main force, at 9 o'clock, A. M., marched in a southerly direction; Colonel Hatch marching on the left flank, as before. The different detachments sent out, soon after joined the centre column, when the whole force proceeded to Pontotoc, where the advance encountered a small Rebel force, a portion of Captain Weatherill's command; which, after the exchange of a few shots, fled, and was pursued through the town by our cavalry. Their entire camp equipage was captured, and 400 bushels of salt, all of which was destroyed.

Colonel Grierson continued his march six miles south of Pontotoc, and encamped at eight o'clock, P. M., on the road leading to Houston.

Reveille was sounded on the morning of the 20th, at two o'clock; and at three o'clock, Major Tull, 2d Iowa, with about 175 of the best effective portion of the command, with one piece of flying artillery, and all prisoners and captured property, proceeded northerly, on his return to Lagrange, by order of Colonel Grierson, for the double purpose of relieving the command of all incumbrance, and inducing the enemy to believe he had retraced his steps; which the return of Major Tull would indicate. Major Tull sent a scout west, to cut the telegraph wires near Oxford. It should have been added, that a large Rebel mail was captured and destroyed at Pontotoc, several guerrillas killed and wounded, and a few captured.

After Major Tull's command had left, Colonel Grierson resumed his march southward, passed through Houston, and encamped about ten miles beyond.

About five o'clock, A. M., Colonel Hatch was ordered to take his command up the Columbus road, and destroy as much as possible of the Mobile and Ohio Railroad, attack Columbus, if the opposing force there was not too strong, and return to Lagrange, using his own discretion as to the route. In all of which, it was subsequently ascertained, he was entirely successful.

By this movement, the Rebel General Chalmers, who was on the lookout for Grierson, was completely deceived; and thus the main body of our cavalry got two or three days' start. The remaining forces (6th and 7th Illinois Cavalry) continued their march to Starkville, where another mail was captured and destroyed.

Four miles from Starkville, at Dismal Swamp, a halt was ordered, and half the command left the rest, and continued on southward about five miles, and after swimming bayous and wading through almost impassable swamps, reached one of the principal tanneries in the country; which was fired and entirely destroyed, together with a large stock of boots and shoes, saddles, bridles, &c., and several thousand dollars' worth of clothing.

This must have been a severe blow to the Rebel army, as every article was immediately needed, and had been packed for delivery with dispatch.

The command reunited on the 22d, and marched to within one mile of Louisville, Mississippi, a distance of twenty-seven miles, over an unpleasant route; the men, in many cases, having to swim their horses over streams, and lead them through blind marshes, many of the animals getting so deep in mire as rendered it impossible to extricate them, and they were left to perish. Frequently both horse and rider would go down together, the horse drowning, and the man barely escaping with his life.

Continuing on, with great perseverance, overcoming all obstacles, they crossed Pearl River Bridge on the next morning, driving away the Rebels, who were too late in their attempt to burn it, and arriving at Philadelphia, destroyed the mail, (as they did at every town they passed,) without doing any other damage. About two o'clock, P. M., on the 23d, the command took the road to Decatur, thence to Newton, on the Southern Railroad; and arrived at the latter place about daylight the next morning. Two trains of cars were there captured—one of twenty-five, and the other of thirteen—loaded with all kinds of commissary stores and warlike munitions; which, with the cars and locomotives, were destroyed.

Proceeding on, our troops fired the bridge about a mile east of Newton, and three heavy trestle-work bridges, further up the road, in the same direction; thus occupying themselves till reaching Nichol's plantation, seven miles west of War-trace, on the 25th. Here their course was changed to a more southerly one.

On reaching Raleigh, a halt was ordered for the night. Here a single scout was detailed to cut the telegraph wire on the Southern Railroad, between Lake Station and Jackson. Arriving within seven miles of the railroad, he came upon a regiment of Rebel cavalry, which had come from Brandon in search of Colonel Grierson's forces. The scout was closely questioned, and though the enemy was on the direct road to our own camp, but fourteen miles distant, he succeeded in misleading them, and returned with word of their approach.

Colonel Grierson, on learning that they were so near him, moved his command over Leaf River Bridge, which he destroyed, thus preventing the possibility of surprise in the rear. Proceeding to Westville, and crossing Pearl river, about ten miles from there, by ferrying the men and swimming the horses, the two battalions in advance, under Colonel Prince, made a rapid march to the railroad at Hazlehurst Station ; where our men captured and destroyed forty cars, four of which were loaded with shell and ammunition, the rest with quartermaster and commissary stores Another train escaped by leaving five minutes before the arrival of our troops.

Captain Forbes, Company B, 7th Illinois, was detached south of Starkville, with orders to proceed to Macon. Making a bold march to within a short distance of that place, he found the bridge had been destroyed, and the place was occupied by a considerable force of Rebels. He then moved to Newton, and from thence to Enterprise, nearly one hundred miles east of the main body of our forces.

On reaching Enterprise, Captain Forbes sent a flag of truce to Colonel Goodwin, commanding the Rebel forces there, demanding the surrender of the town. The Rebel Colonel requested an hour to reply, and Captain Forbes finding the Rebel force stronger than he had supposed, and having accomplished his object of diverting their attention—before the expiration of the hour, was on a rapid gallop to join Colonel Grierson, then more than a day's march in advance. Taking a westward course, he soon struck the route taken by the main force at Pearl River, which he soon joined by rapid marches.

Near Gallatin, our cavalry suddenly came upon a team hauling a 32-pounder, Parrott gun, destined for Port Gibson, which was captured and spiked.

About five miles east of Gallatin, Colonel Grierson detached a battalion to march immediately to the New Orleans, Jackson, and Great Northern Railroads at New Haven. They succeeded in destroying the railroad for some distance, burning several cars, water-tanks, and a considerable amount of other property, and cutting the telegraph wires, a very damaging work to Rebel interests.

The advance moved on Brook Haven, at daylight, on the 28th, so suddenly, as to surprise and capture two hundred Rebel prisoners. Some of them were found asleep in their quarters. A large number of muskets, packed ready for transportation, also, five hundred tents, at a camp of instruction, were destroyed.

The main body of our men, after leaving Gallatin, encountered Garland's cavalry, killing and capturing several, and routing the rest. Making a feint toward Port Gibson, and another toward Nashville, to deceive the enemy, they proceeded to Brook Haven, already occupied by our advance.

On the 30th ult, Colonel Grierson moved his force along the railroad, in a southerly direction, destroying all the bridges between Brook Haven and Bogue Chito Station. At the latter place fifteen freight cars were found standing on the track, partly loaded with army stores, which, with the depot, and railroad bridge were fired.

He then marched rapidly on to Summit, where twenty-eight more freight cars were destroyed. He then left the line of the railroad, for a point between Magnolia and Liberty, intending to reach the Clinton road. Information was received that a regiment of Rebel cavalry was moving towards Wassita. They were found at Wall's bridge, in Tickfaw.

Our cavalry immediately rushed in among them, killing eight or ten, and wounding many more, and completely routing the balance. Our loss was one killed and five wounded. Colonel Blackburne, of the 7th Illinois, who had been conspicuous for his bravery, during the entire raid, was among the latter.

He received a wound in the thigh, and slight ones in the head and breast. It was believed he would recover, but it was thought best to leave him at a house by the road side, where a surgeon and one man remained with him.

After dispersing the Rebels, our forces proceeded East a short way, when they changed their course, and went directly South. At Edwards' Bridge they found another cavalry regiment posted there to dispute their passage.

One battalion was sent to engage the enemy, while the main body went in the direction of Greensburg. At Edwards' Bridge the enemy could not be induced to fight, except in shirmishes, in which they lost several in killed and wounded, while not one of our men was hurt.

Thus far the appearance of our forces was a complete surprise to the Rebels wherever found. But at Oscia a deliberate plan had been laid for the capture of Grierson's command.

Hitherto the Rebels had evidently thought it was the intention of our forces to return to Lagrange, and had made every effort to intercept them on such return. But they had at last become convinced of Colonel Grierson's purpose to pursue his hazarous raid entirely through their country, and resolved, if possible, to stop his further advance.

In proceeding further South, he must needs cross several bridges, hence a regiment of cavalry was so posted as to flank Colonel Grierson's men, while a regiment of infantry was placed in his front to hold him in check until their cavalry could attack him in front and rear.

Seeing his danger, Colonel Grierson at once ordered a charge on the infantry, and dashing through their lines, in a few minutes left them far in the rear, without the loss of a man on his part; and so proceeded on to Greensburg, and thence to Clinton, crossing the Amite ten miles above.

On Big Sandy Creek a guerrilla Camp was attacked and 150 tents, camp equipage, and baggage destroyed, and several horses captured. Taking the Greensville Spring road, our forces then marched directly toward Baton Rouge.

About ten miles from the latter place they suddenly came upon Stewart's cavalry, who, after a short fight, retreated to the river, were surrounded and captured.

On Friday, May 1st, a courier arrived at Baton Rouge with the startling announcement, that a brigade of cavalry, from General Grant's army, having cut their way through the heart of the Rebel country, were within five miles of the city.

This information seemed at first almost incredible; but at four o'clock all doubt was removed, by Colonel Grierson and his heroes being escorted into the city by by Captain Godfrey's cavalry. At the picket lines they were met by Colonel Dudley and staff, who extended to them a hearty welcome. Spontaneously, as it were, the air rang with three cheers, loud enough to echo along the hills to Port Hudson.

The importance of this expedition can hardly be realized, without reflection on what it accomplished. In seventeen days the troops marched over eight hundred miles, fighting wherever they met opposition; killing and wounding many of the enemy; capturing more than one thousand men, and over twelve hundred horses; and, destroying more than four millions of dollars worth of property, and completely cutting off all communication with the strongholds of the enemy on two important railroads.

As an instance of the activity and perseverance of Colonel Grierson's command, it is stated that while in pursuit of a Rebel cavalry force, they traveled, thirty hours, seventy-five miles, fought four battles, skirmished considerably, forded a river, and all the time neither men nor horses had any thing to eat.

On the evening of the 6th of May, the Union citizens of New Orleans gave to Colonels Grierson and Prince a magnificent reception at the St. Charles Hotel; complimenting Colonel Grierson, by presenting him with a splendid war-horse, and Colonel Prince, by presenting him with a superb military saddle and bridle. Long before the appointed hour, the rotunda was filled to its utmost capacity. The speeches usual on such occasions were made; Colonel Grierson giving all the credit of his success to the brave men and officers under his command.

SKETCH OF COL. BENJAMIN H. GRIERSON.

COLONEL BENJAMIN H. GRIERSON is a native of Pennsylvania—was born in Pittsburg in July, 1827. Consequently, he is (July, 1864,) thirty-seven years of age. At a very early age he was removed to Trumbull county, Ohio, in which State he resided nearly fifteen years, and then removed to Jacksonville, Illinois, where he resided when the great Rebellion broke out.

He was in the produce business, and, to use his own words, "was also a musician, being able to play on any instrument, from a jewsharp to a hand-organ."

Shortly after hostilities commenced, he left for Cairo to join a company that had been raised in his town; but on arriving there he was called to the position of Aid to General Prentiss.

When the 6th Illinois Cavalry was organized, he was elected Major of that regiment, but remained on detached service as Aid to General Prentiss, with whom he served with distinction.

On the 28th of March, 1862, when Colonel Cavanaugh resigned, Major Grierson was unanimously elected by the officers to fill his place, and in December, 1862, he was ordered to command the 1st Brigade of Cavalry, consisting of the 6th and 7th Illinois, and 2d Iowa Regiments.

Colonel Grierson, with his command, had been engaged in all the cavalry skirmishes and raids of West Tennessee and Northern Mississippi, up to his memorable advent into Baton Rouge. In him were happily united to a good physical organization, sagacity and prudence, courage, tact, and indomitable energy, the natural precedents of glorious success.

INCIDENTS OF COL. GRIERSON'S RAID.

Although, in many instances, our troops passed themselves off for the rebel Van Dorn's, or Jackson's, cavalry, yet, whenever recognized by the country people, they were treated in the most respectful manner; and, on several occasions, the strongest demonstrations of Union feeling were voluntarily made.

Our men were frequently cheered, and invited to share hospitalities, in the name of the old flag—all showing that it is only necessary to once more establish the authority of the Government, to bring back to its allegiance the noble old State of Mississippi.

In many instances the inhabitants, along the different routes taken by our cavalry, when they found we were not as we had been described—namely, robbers and assassins, insulters of women and children, and everything else, base, and contemptible—bade us God speed, and acknowledged that they had been bitterly deceived. In every instance, private property was respected, unless found in the hands of guerrillas.

While several of our scouts were feeding their horses, at the stables of a wealthy planter of secession proclivities, the proprietor looking on, apparently deeply interested in the proceeding, suddenly exclaimed, "Well, boys, I can't say I have anything against you. I don't know but on the whole, I rather like you. You have not taken anything of mine, except a little corn for your horses, and that you are welcome to. I have heard of you all over the country. You are doing the boldest thing ever done. But you'll be trapped, though; you'll be trapped, mark me."

At another place, where our men thought it advisable to represent themselves as Jackson's cavalry, a whole company was graciously entertained, by a strong seces-sion lady, who insisted upon whipping a negro, because he did not bring the hoe-cakes fast enough.

On one occasion seven of Colonel Grierson's scouts stopped at the house of a wealthy planter, to feed their jaded horses. Upon ascertaining that he had been doing a little guerrilla business, upon his own account, our men encouraged him in the belief, that as they were the invincible Van Dorn cavalry, they would soon catch the Yankees. The secession gentleman heartily approved of what he supposed to be their intentions, and enjoined upon them the necessity of making as rapid marches as possible.

As our men had discovered two splendid carriage-horses in the planter's stable, they thought, under the circumstances, they would be justified in making an exchange, which they accordingly proceeded to do.

As they were taking the saddles from their own tired steeds, and placing them on the backs of the wealthy guerrilla's horses, the proprietor discovered them, and at once objected. He was met with the reply, that as he was anxious that the Yankees should be speedily overtaken, those after them should have good horses. "All right, gentleman," said the planter, "I will keep your animals until you return. I suppose you'll be back in two or three days, at the furthest. When you return, you'll find they have been well cared for."

Our soldiers were sometimes asked where they got their blue coats. They always replied, when traveling under the name of Van Dorn's cavalry, that they took them from the Yankees, at Holly Springs. This always excited great laughter among the secessionists. Our scouts, however, usually wore the regular secesh uni-forms.

V   16

A MULE CHARGE ON REBEL CAVALRY.

ON Thursday, April —, 1863, Lieutenant Cushing, of the United States Gunboat Commodore Barney, made a gallant reconnoissance, with seventy-five seamen, and a boat howitzer, from the Nansemond up to Chuckatuck village, about three miles distant from his vessel.

It appears that on the morning of that day, a citizen showed himself on the banks of the river, bearing a a white flag, when Acting Master Harris, of the Gunboat Stepping Stone, sent a boat to see what he wanted Upon the boat nearing the shore, it was treacherously fired into, and one man killed and others wounded.

Lieutenant Cushing organized his expedition to punish this treachery. His officers were Acting Ensign Hunter; Master's Mate Birtwisle, in charge of howiter, and Master's Mates Boardman and Aspinwall, in charge of seamen, acting as infantry; Lieutenant Cushing in command.

On reaching shore, the gallant young Lieutenant confiscated two mule-carts, one for a limber for his howitzer and the other for an ammunition wagon. Proceeding on, he drove in three different vidette parties of cavalry, and when he reached Chuckatuck, which contains one long street, he found quite a large body of the Nansemond cavalry drawn up, and preparing to charge on him.

Quickly unlimbering his howitzer, he threw in a charge of shrapnel, and gave the enemy its benefit, as they sounded the charge. The discharge of the howitzer frightened the mules in the carts, and they dashed up the street at full speed upon the advancing cavalry, the sailors in the carts cheering and yelling and firing as they went.

This novel charge threw the cavalry into disorder, and Lieutenant Cushing immediately rushed on with the rest of his force, killing three of the Rebels, and securing their horses, arms, and equipments, only losing one man on his side.

He destroyed a quantity of forage, meat, &c., and then retreated in order to his boats, the enemy being reinforced, and showing a disposition to cut him off. In his return, a sailor found one of the captured horses rather unmanageable, under nautical rule, and inclined not to mind the tiller-ropes or steerage-gear, as the jolly tar called the reins. Finding that the animal was determined to carry him back to the Rebel side, he brought him to an anchor, by drawing one of the holster pistols, and shooting him through the head. He then rejoined his companions, very well satisfied at having got clear of such a lubberly craft. The expedition was planned with great daring and successfully carried out.

STORY LXIV.

LIEUTENANT-COLONEL PHILLIPS' RAID IN MISSISSIPPI.

ABOUT the 9th of August, 1863, General Hurlbut, having ascertained that there was a large amount of railroad stock at Grenada, which the Rebels were endeavoring to get off south, by making temporary repairs to the railroad, with his usual energy and promptness, arranged an expedition to destroy it.

He sent a request to General Grant to make a diversion from the south to aid the enterprise. The expedition started from Lagrange, Tennessee, on the 13th of August, under command of Lieutenant-Colonel Phillips, of the 9th Illinois Mounted Infantry, and reached Grenada, on the Mississippi Central Railroad, on the 17th.

After driving General Skinner, with two thousand men, and three pieces of artillery, from the place, they destroyed fifty-seven locomotives, upward of four hundred cars, depot buildings, machine shops, blacksmith shops, and a large quantity of ordnance and commissary stores, beside capturing about fifty railroad men, and a number of other prisoners.

After Colonel Phillips had thoroughly accomplished his work, Colonel Winslow, from Grant's army, arrived with a force from below. Colonel Phillips's expedition returned in safety to Lagrange, on the 23d of August.

Lieutenant-Colonel Phillips and his gallant command were certainly entitled to much commendation, for patiently enduring the hardships of such a march, through Central Mississippi, in the middle of August, and so thoroughly crippling the remaining energy of the Rebellion in the Southwest.

MAJOR-GENERAL HOOKER.

JOSEPH HOOKER, of California, was twenty-ninth in a class of fifty members, graduating in 1837. Breveted for gallantry at the battles of Monterey, of the National Bridge, and of Chapultepec. In fighting the Rebels, his heroism has been too conspicuous to need any comment.

STORY LXXV.

"BILLY BRAY."

A spruce enrolling officer
    Of Salisbury, one day,
On visiting a country house
    Found all the males away.

So when the good old *lady*,
    Who answered to his call,
Had given their names and ages,
    He asked if that was all.

" O yes," replied the lady,
    " I have no more to say,
For sure we have none other,
    Excepting Billy Bray."

The officer was zealous
    That no one should escape,
Lest others should grow jealous,
    And get him in a scrape.

" Ay, ay," said he, " good woman,
    And where is Billy Bray?"
Quoth she "he's in the barrack,
    A working at his hay."

Then briskly to the barrack
    The officer he ran,
And looked about for Billy,
    But couldn't find his *man*.

Then to the house he hastened,
    And asked the worthy dame,
And got the age of Billy Bray,
    And straight enrolled his name.

And soon the drafting time it came,
  On the appointed day;
When high among the lucky names
  Stood that of Billy Bray.

But deep was the perplexity
  Which then and there befell,
For who he was, and where he was,
  No mortal wight could tell:

Till he who had enrolled him—
  The man in "blue and brass,"
Had looked about, and found him out,
  A snorting, live jackass!

And still, among those drafted ones,
  High on the list doth stand,
The petted name of "Billy Bray,"
  Of "O, my Maryland!"

STORY LXXVI.

SINKING OF THE CINCINNATI (Gunboat), AT VICKSBURG.

"On the 26th of May, 1863, it was determined to make an attack upon the rebel batteries to the north of Vicksburg, and opposite General Steele's column. The gunboat Cincinnati, Lieutenant Bache, was to co-operate and attempt to silence the water-batteries, previous to the assault from the land side. Accordingly, a little after eight, A. M., she commenced dropping down below Young's Point. When about two miles from Vicksburg, the famous gun, 'Whistling Dick,' in position just north of the town. opened upon her.

"At first the aim was too high, and the balls passed

over without doing any damage, but as the boat neared the batteries, it became more accurate, as the sound of the passing balls, growing sharper at every shot, plainly indicated.

"In order to attack the upper batteries it was necessary to drop below them, and round-to, with the head up stream. This position was a most unfortunate one, as it exposed the vessel to a raking fire, from one battery in front, and another from behind.

"The first shot which struck her, hit the iron plating, and did no material damage. But the captain had given orders to push up to within three hundred yards, and by the time she had reached that proximity, the shot hit her with fearful accuracy, generally passing directly through her port-holes.

"One battery, which fired from an elevation and at some distance, threw plunging shot, which went through her upper deck, and did great damage. Lieutenant Sokalski, of General Steele's staff, who had been sent to point out the position, to be taken in the assault, says that when Lieutenant Bache and two others beside himself were standing in the pilot-house, one of these plunging balls entered the port-hole of the pilot-house, passed through the thigh of the pilot, and then sheered down through the floor on to the gun-deck, at the same time breaking the wheel, and wounding another man through the hand and arm, with the splinters. Lifting the hatchway and rushing down the gun-deck, Lieutenant Sokalski found it filled with mangled and dead. It was a slaughter-pen. Blood and fragments of bodies, shot away, were scattered over the floor.

"It was discovered that one ball had passed through the boat below the water line, and that the boat was sinking. It was evident that to continue the fight longer would be to throw away the lives of the crew, and orders were given to start up the river as fast as possible. Lieutenant Starr, who, I was told, was second in command, went to the pilot-house and directed movements as best he could with a broken wheel and sinking craft. In the meantime she was riddled by shot after shot, and was fast sinking. For three-quarters of an hour she was toiling, crippled, up stream ; while the enemy, seeing her condition, redoubled the fury of the cannonading. More than fifty shot struck her before she reached the shore. But Lieutenant Bache refused to allow the colors to be lowered, and she sunk like the Cumberland, with the Stars and Stripes still waving."

MAJOR-GENERAL WM. T. SHERMAN.

WILLIAM T. SHERMAN, of Ohio, was sixth in the West Point class, of 1840, which numbered 42. He was sent with his company to California during the Mexican war, *via* Cape Horn, reaching there after the fighting was over, and thus saw no battle before that of Bull's Run, where he was distinguished.

He was Superintendent of the Louisiana State Military Institute when the Rebellion broke out; but eminently loyal as he was, he could not forbear to resign that position, and hasten to the service of his country, under the battle-flag of freedom. His heroism and generalship since then, are too well known to require special notice.

STORY LXXVII.

JOHN MORGAN'S RAID.

THE Rebel General John H. Morgan left Sparta, Tenn., on the 27th of June, 1863, with detachments from two brigades of cavalry, numbering, according to Captain Cunningham, of Morgan's staff, 2,028 effective men, with four pieces of artillery—two Parrot's and two howitzers, and crossed the Cumberland near Burkesville, on the 1st and 2d of July, in canoes and boats improvised for the occasion.

He had some difficulty in making the horses swim, but finally succeeded in getting all over by ten A. M. on the 2d. Colonel Dick Morgan then proceeded on a reconnoisance in force, having been told that Colonel Hobson's cavalry were about. He was met by Colonel Jacobs, with the 9th Kentucky cavalry, and repulsed after a gallant fight, yet claiming a victory. The loss was small on both sides.

Colonel Alston, Morgan's chief of staff, says that Colonel Johnston, after much difficulty, succeeded in crossing the river, and joined Morgan, with the 2d brigade (number of men not stated,) after dark. He reported having been much harassed by the enemy, but had succeeded in driving them back.

Captain Cunningham says, after driving back Jacob's cavalry, "our column marched on through Columbia, at which point it found the advance of Wolford's celebrated Kentucky cavalry, numbering 251 men, dispersed it, killing 7 and wounding 15 men; our loss, 2 killed and 2 wounded."

The facts in the case were as follows: the force he met at Columbia was a company of one hundred men, from the 1st Kentucky and 2d and 45th Ohio, commanded by Captain Carter, of Wolford's cavalry. Headed by this gallant officer they met and held in check an entire brigade of Morgan's men, for over three hours: and not till their brave commander had fallen, mortally wounded, and several others severely wounded, and six of the others slain, and ten or twelve wounded, did they think of retiring from the conflict. Captain Fishback fought them successfully for more than hour after the fall of Captain Carter, when, finding himself nearly surrounded, he withdrew his command, skillfully and successfully, and joined his regiment at Jamestown.

Colonel Wolford, then in command at Jamestown, having ascertained that Morgan's two brigades passed through Columbia that same night, July 3d, *en route* for Lebanon, sent dispatches to General Carter, and as soon as possible commenced pursuit, with about 1.200 men from the 1st Kentucky and 2d, 7th, and 45th Ohio regiments. Before reaching Lebanon, he was joined by the 2d East Tennessee, increasing his force to about 1,800 men, with two sections of Law's howitzer battery.

Arriving at the stockade at Green River Bridge, on the morning of the 4th of July, says Alston, "General Morgan sent in a flag of truce, and demanded the sur render; but Colonel Moore quietly remarked, 'if it was any other day he might consider the demand, but the 4th of July was a bad day to talk about surrender, and must therefore decline.' The colonel is a gallant man * * * and entitled to the highest credit for military skill. We would mark such a man in our army for promotion.

"The place was judiciously chosen, and skillfully defended," continues Alston, "and the result was that we were repulsed with severe loss, about 25 killed and 20 wounded. Among the killed, as usual, were our best men and officers, including Colonel Chenault, Major Brent, Captain Trible, Lieutenants Cowan, Ferguson, and another whose name I do not remember."

"Indeed," says Captain Cunningham, "this was the darkest day that ever shone upon our command; 11 commissioned officers were killed, and 9 wounded. After heavy slaughter upon both sides, our forces withdrew; loss, about 60 killed and wounded on each side."

Colonel Moore says, officially, "My position was strong, and his loss was over 50 killed, and over 200 wounded. I took no prisoners. My loss was 6 killed, 23 wounded, and one prisoner. The victory was complete. I fought with my fraction of a regiment of 200 men."

On Sunday morning, July 5th, General Morgan appeared before Lebanon with a force of 4,600 men, and demanded its immediate surrender, together with the troops, numbering about 325. Colonel Hanson commanding, refused to surrender, and Morgan immediately commenced the attack with his four pieces of artillery.

"After a fight of seven hours," says Alston, "General Morgan, finding the town could not be taken in any other way, ordered a charge to be made. Colonel Hanson still held out, in hopes of receiving reinforcements, and only surrendered, after we had fired the buildings in which he was posted. By this surrender we obtained a sufficient quantity of guns to arm all our men who were without them; also, a quantity of ammunition, of which we stood sorely in need.

"At the order to charge, Duke's regiment rushed forward, and poor Tommy Morgan, who was always in the lead, fell back, almost at the first volley, pierced through the heart. This was a crushing blow to General Morgan. Our men behaved badly here, breaking open stores, and plundering indiscriminately."

Morgan's victory at Lebanon was bought at the loss of fifty-six killed, and one hundred and forty-eight wounded. Our loss was, *in action*, three killed and sixteen wounded; *after action*, two men *murdered*, first sergeant, Joseph Slaughter, and private Samuel Ferguson; both killed on the way to Springfield.

While Alston was paroling the prisoners, at Lebanon, he was informed that a Federal force of two regiments of cavalry and a battery of artillery were approaching; he thereupon ordered the prisoners to Springfield, as he says, "upon the double-quick," where they arrived after dark, in a deluge of rain.

Alston, having been detained at Springfield, the next morning, two hours after the command had left, was himself made a prisoner, by our cavalry, on the Bardstown road. "My God!" says he, "how I hated it, no one can understand. The first thought, after my wife and children, was my fine mare, 'Fannie Johnson,' named after a pretty little cousin, of Richmond, Virginia. I said, 'poor Fannie, who will treat you as kindly as I have done?'"

The stubborn resistance Morgan met with at Columbia, Green River Bridge, and Lebanon, had retarded his march, and enabled a concentration of our forces at Lebanon, sufficient to begin the pursuit, with confident hope of success, should they overtake him. "Generals Hobson and Shakleford joined Wolford, near Springfield, and Hobson being the senior officer, took command of the whole force, increased by the 9th and 12th, and detachments of the 8th and 3d Kentucky cavalry. and one section of an Ohio battery, making Hobson's whole force nearly 8,000 men.

We were now twenty-four hours behind Morgan, and with our ammunition and ambulance train, making a column of three miles in length. As we looked along our line of jaded horses, and thought of his fresh ones, being gathered along his line of march, we could hardly be hopeful of success in the pursuit, unless General Judah should head him in front, or General Boyle at Louisville.

We pursued, however, with great energy, and, until our provisions were exhausted, we gained upon the enemy. He exhausted the supplies of the people before us; and hence the delay at Lebanon Junction, in order to get rations for a further pursuit.

This enabled him to reach the Ohio river, at Brandenburg. on the 7th of July; where, as Cunningham says, "Captain Sam Taylor, (of the old Rough and Ready family,) had succeeded in capturing two fine steamers." With these Morgan crossed his forces over to the Indiana shore, not, however, without stout resistance from the Home Guards, with one piece of artillery.

The crossing, owing in part to this opposition, occupied them from eight o'clock, A. M., of the 8th, till seven, A. M., of the 9th; after this was effected, Morgan took the precaution to burn one of the steamers—the other was released. Our forces arriving soon after, found it necessary to send for another; and then it took until daylight the next morning to get all our forces over; thus giving the enemy again twenty-four hours advance.

W

On the 9th, Morgan arrived at Corydon, where the militia, in small force, gallantly resisted his advance, killing and wounding several, and detaining him for some three hours. Cunningham says—" fighting near there 4,500 State militia. and capturing 3,400 of them, and dispersing the remainder!"

With this exception. Morgan met with but little hindrance in all his raid through Indiana and Ohio, till he attempted to recross the Ohio at Buffington Island. This was not owing to any lack of patriotism among the people, but to the utter surprise and panic caused by his sudden appearance along their highways. The militia was concentrated at the large towns and cities, and Morgan, informed by his scouts and sympathizers, had only to avoid those places and pursue his course.

Whatever his original object and prospects may have been, not having met with the promised reception, his purpose now, probably was, to get out of the State, if possible, knowing that his pursuers would allow him but little time for ulterior exploits.

The people, through fear, even fed and watered his troops, without delay; and thus enabled him to outmarch us, upon the fresh horses stolen, from the country for five miles on each side of his line of march. The country thus stripped of horses inevitably prevented us from keeping equal pace with him.

But there never was a more enthusiastic reception of troops than we received, all through Indiana and Ohio; hundreds, yes, thousands of people flocking with provisions to aid us in overtaking the invader; while thousands of beautiful young ladies and enthusiastic matrons and children, handed us water and bread as we passed their doors.   It was one grand cheering procession, urging us forward and enlivening our march,

We gathered a few horses, also, by order of the General, giving receipts for them; and some may have been pressed by the soldiers without leaving any; yet, notwithstanding all our efforts to keep up the command, more than five hundred men were left on the line of march from the exhaustion of their horses.

General Hobson declared his intention to overtake and fight the enemy with five hundred men, should all the rest give out upon the road.

Cunningham (although a great liar and Rebel scamp, occasionally told some truth,) says: "From Corydon we moved on without a halt, through Salisbury and Palmyra to Salem, at which point, telegraphing with our operator, we first learned the stations and numbers of the enemy aroused for the hunt—discovered that Indianapolis was running over with them—that New Albany contained 10,000; that 3,000 had just arrived at Mitchel; and, in fact, that 25,000 men were armed and ready to meet the 'bloody invader.'"

At Salem they captured 500 Home Guard, and destroyed the railroad bridge and track, sent a scout to the Ohio and Mississippi road, near Seymour, to burn two bridges and a depot, and destroy the track for two miles, which was done in an incredible short time.

From Salem they passed on to Lexington, destroying in the night the depot and track at Vienna. From Lexington they passed on north to the Ohio and Mississippi Railroad, near Vernon, where they "had a skirmish with General Manson's infantry force, as a feint, while the main force moved round the town to Dupont, where squads were sent out to cut the various railroads entering at Vernon.

"Not much brighter," says Cunningham, "were the bonfires and illuminations in celebration of the Vicksburg victory, by the Yankees, than our counter illuminations around Vernon. Many old ladies were aroused from their slumbers to rejoice over the brilliant victories recently achieved. Surmises were various and many. One old lady knew that the city of Richmond was on fire; another, that Jeff. Davis had been killed; a third, that the Army of Virginia had been used up. Not one knew that General John H. Morgan was within two hundred miles of them."

From Vernon they proceeded to Versailles, where Cunningham says they captured 500 militia. "Captain P., a Presbyterian Chaplain, imitating his commander's demeanor, rode boldly up to the company, and inquired for the captain. Being informed that there was a dispute as to who should lead them, he volunteered his services, was soon elected Captain, and when the advance-guard of Morgan's men had passed, ordered them into the road, and surrendered them to Morgan."

"Crestfallen, indeed, were the Yanks; but General Morgan treated them kindly, returning to them their guns, advised them to go home, and not come hunting such game again; as they had every thing to lose and nothing to gain by it."

From Versailles they moved on to Harrison, Ohio, where they burnt a fine bridge, and passed in the night around Cincinnati, between that city and Hamilton, and at daybreak on the 14th were eighteen miles east of Cincinnati. Near Camp Dennison, they captured and burnt a train of cars.

"From the 14th to the 19th, every hill-side contained an enemy, and every ravine a blockade. Dispirited and worn down, they reached the river, at three, A. M., on the 19th, at a ford above Pomeroy, called Portland, at Buffington Island, and commenced crossing."

At Louisville, Kentucky, General Judah had embarked his command on a fleet of steamers, which was increased at Cincinnati, accompanied by the Gunboats Moose and Springfield, Lieutenant Le Roy Fitch commanding, and proceeded up the Ohio, and landed at Portsmouth on the 16th, at four, P. M., and in an hour were in pursuit of Morgan, who was thought to be but little in advance. But he led them on, through Webster, Porter, Centreville, and so on, to Pomeroy.

The advance consisted of the advance guard, General Judah, escort and staff, one section of Henshaw's battery, and the section belonging to the 5th Indiana Cavalry. The 5th Indiana Cavalry, 14th Illinois, part of 11th Kentucky, and 8th and 9th Michigan, all cavalry, composed the main body. Hobson's, Shackleford's, and Wolford's commands were several miles to the left. John Morgan was in the valley below.

Here it was that a fight ensued, which opened rather inauspiciously. Here also the gallant Major McCook received his death-wound, and here also A. A. G. Keyes, of General Judah's staff was captured.

After a momentary check, and some disorder, the gallant 5th Indiana Cavalry, under Colonel Butler, and the no less gallant 14th Illinois, under Colonel Capron, under cover of the fire of a gun of Henshaw's battery, and two guns of the 5th Indiana Cavalry, dashed forward, and quickly changed the aspect of affairs; and Hobson arriving, charged on the enemy's centre and flank, and the gunboats also opening fire, they found

17

themselves unable to endure it, and broke in wild disorder.

General Shackleford and Colonel Wolford, pressing forward to the scene of battle, were met by 500 Rebels under Dick Morgan and Ward, who attempted to cut through our lines and escape. Our line of battle was soon formed, expecting Morgan's whole force to meet it in front.

General Shackleford ordered a charge, which being made, the enemy fled, leaving several killed and wounded behind. A flag of truce was then sent into the woods, when the Rebs surrendered, and marched out without further loss of life.

"Seeing that the enemy had every advantage of position," says Cunningham, "an overwhelming force of infantry and cavalry, and that we were becoming completely environed in the meshes of the net set for us, the command was ordered to move up the river, at double quick;   *   *   *   and was moved rapidly off the field, leaving three companies of dismounted men, and perhaps 200 sick and wounded in the enemy's possession. Our cannon were undoubtedly captured at the river."

In fact Dick Morgan, Basil Duke, and Colonel Ward, with their commands were captured, numbering over seven hundred men, and as many horses.

Morgan, with the residue of his command, fled in a parallel direction with the Ohio River, keeping out behind the hills, to avoid the gunboats, not approaching the river till he reached Bealville, a distance of about fourteen miles, when, supposing he had outstripped the gunboats, he rode up, with a bold front and demanded of the citizens assistance in crossing.

Under threats they ostensibly complied, yet causing all possible delay; so that by the time 300 of the command were embarked, occupying all the flats and scows that were furnished, the gunboats appeared in sight, yet did not arrive in time to prevent their escape across the river. Some attempted to ford, but were compelled to swim or drown—the latter alternative being the fate of a few.

The inevitable Cunningham says: "My poor mare being too weak to carry me, turned over, and commenced going down: encumbered by clothes, saber, and pistols, I made but poor progress in the turbid stream. But the recollections of home, of a bright-eyed maiden in the sunny South, the pressing need of soldiers, and an inherent love of life, actuated me to continue swimming. * * * But I hear something behind me snorting! I feel it passing! Thank God I am saved! A riderless horse dashes by; I grasp his tail—onward he bears me—and the shore is reached!"— Farewell, Cunningham.

Lieutenant Fitch reports to Secretary Wells of the Navy, after the Buffington affair, "I followed further up the river, and met another portion of Morgan's force fording, about fourteen miles above, and shelled, and drove most of them back. Several were killed, fifteen to thirty wounded, and twenty horses captured."

Morgan fell back, out of reach of the cannon, and drew up his force, seeming to wait a land attack. Judah and Shackleford were a mile or two in the rear, moving up rapidly; our boys on the gunboats were about to land, to attack the Rebels, when two steamers loaded with infantry, appeared in sight, coming down from the direction of Parkersburg, and they, landing above town, succeeded in getting in Morgan's rear.

Shackleford and Judah coming up, the combined force commenced the attack, completely surprising the Rebels, who had not anticipated the nearness of Hobson's and and Judah's forces; nor were they aware of the reinforcements by the steamers.

General Shackleford's report to General Burnside says: "We chased John Morgan over fifty miles to-day, (July 20th.) After heavy skirmishing for six or seven miles, between the enemy and the 45th Ohio, (Colonel Carter) of Colonel Wolford's brigade, which was in advance of the enemy, we succeeded in bringing him to a stand, about three o'clock, P. M., when a fight ensued, which lasted an hour, when the Rebels fled, taking refuge upon a high bluff. I sent a flag of truce demanding an immediate and unconditional surrender of Morgan and his command.

"The flag was received by Colonel Coleman and other officers, who came down and asked a private interview. They asked an hour for consultation among the officers. I granted them forty minutes, in which time the command, except Morgan, who deserted, taking with him a small squad, surrendered.

"It was my understanding that Morgan himself surrendered; and learned it was the understanding of his officers and men.

"The number of killed and wounded is inconsiderable. The number of prisoners is between 1000 and 1500, including a large number of Colonels, Majors, and line officers. I captured between 600 and 700 prisoners yesterday. I think I will capture Morgan himself to-morrow."

But Morgan with the remnant of his band continued their flight, but being hotly pursued, had but little time for mischief. His raid being converted into a flight, we must pass rapidly also in our sketch, as to notice the innumerable particulars and incidents would prove tedious.

On Saturday morning, the 25th, he was at Antrim, Guernsey County, and reached Cadiz, Harrison County, at eight o'clock. At noon he neared Winterville, four miles from Steubenville, and being headed off by the militia, he moved northward, in the direction of the Cleveland and Pittsburg Railroad; but his ultimate purpose seemed to be to cross the Ohio River near Wellsville.

Major Rue, by order of General Burnside, left Cincinnati at midnight on the 23d, with about 400 men, chiefly composed of those who had given out in the chase through Southern Indiana and Ohio, and proceeded by cars to Steubenville. The men had been refreshed by rest, and had fresh horses.

On the evening of the 24th, they arrived at Bellair; and from thence proceeded to Shanghai. Morgan was then at Richmond, eleven miles west of Steubenville, closely pursued by Major Way, 7th Michigan, of General Shackleford's command. Major Rue unloaded his men and moved forward to Knoxville, Jefferson County, on the direct road to New Lisbon, Columbiana County. He pushed rapidly forward, and on Sunday came to a point within four or five miles of New Lisbon. Morgan having turned eastward, was advancing along the Beaver Creek road, toward the river at Smith's Ferry, near the State line. The road on which Major Rue was advancing, was nearly at right angles with that on which Morgan was advancing.

When almost in sight of the road, Major Rue saw a

cloud of dust ahead, and knew that Morgan was coming. The Rebels descried him almost at the same moment, and a race ensued between them to reach first the inter- section of the roads. The Major was doomed to expe- rience the mortification of seeing Morgan pass the point ahead of him, and thought he had escaped.

But the Major had a guide who knew the country like a book. It was ascertained that by taking a diago- nal road, there was yet a chance of cutting off the bold Kentucky raider. Leaving thirty men to guard the road where Morgan, as he thought, had passed him, the Major and the rest of the command put spurs to their horses. It was a tremendous charge. The distance was a mile and a half. His horses comparatively fresh— Morgan's jaded. It was more exciting than a steeple- chase; and this time the Major, to his intense gratifica- tion, struck the Beaver Creek road a "leetle ahead."

Some twenty men, who first reached the road with Major Rue, formed across it, the others coming speedily up. The Rebel saw they were caught, and checked up. Major Rue fully expected a fight. But a white flag came forward, and with it a demand to surrender.

Major Rue replied, that he couldn't see it, and that if Morgan didn't surrender immediately, and uncondition- ally, he would open fire on him. It soon appeared that Morgan had made a sort of *quasi* surrender to James Burbick, a militia Captain, *who was his prisoner*, who, it was pretended, had paroled Morgan and his officers. This proceeding being very properly ignored by Major Rue, who considered the surrender as made to him, he advanced and was met by Morgan, who quietly re- marked: "You have beat me this time;" and expressed gratification that he had been taken by a Kentuckian.

The surrender took place about two o'clock Sunday, P. M., and in about three-quarters of an hour General Shackleford came up and took charge of the prisoners.

Impelled onward by the impetuosity of Major Rue, we passed Major Way with one of Wolford's regiments, on a different road, West Steubenville, on Saturday evening.

On Sunday morning, about eight o'clock, he brought Morgan to a stand, near Salineville, where he fought, defeated, and utterly routed him—killed from 20 to 30, wounded about 50, and took 200 prisoners, 150 stands of arms, 150 horses, with but little loss on his part; and subsequently captured 55 more of the Rebels. It was after this discomfiture that Morgan encountered Major Rue's command, and was captured near New Lisbon, as before stated.

General Shackleford immediately telegraphed as follows:

"HEADQUARTERS UNITED STATES FORCES.
"In the field three miles south of New Lisbon,
July 26, 1863.

"To Colonel LEWIS RICHMOND, A. A. G.:

"By the Blessing of Almighty God, I have succeeded in capturing John H. Morgan, Colonel Duke, and the balance of the command, amounting to about 400 prisoners.

"J. M. SHACKLEFORD,
"Brigadier-General Commanding."

The prisoners were then forwarded by railway to Cincinnati, as those previously taken, had been, by river, on the returning boats. Morgan, Duke, and their staff-officers, with 13 privates, numbering 28, were sent to Columbus for safe keeping, by order of the War

Department, where they arrived on the 30th of July, and were conducted to the Penitentiary, and turned over by General Mason to the Warden, and placed in close quarters, not only as prisoners of war, but as hostages for Colonel Straight and his officers immured in the Libby Prison at Richmond. Fifty-two more of Morgan's officers, including Colonel Duke, were transferred to the Penitentiary on the 1st of August from Johnson's Island, where they were at first sent. The 13 privates were transferred to Camp Chase, where were some 1,300 of their comrades. A large number were also sent to Indianapolis.

The costs and damages occasioned by the Morgan raid, in Ohio alone, as stated by Governor Tod in his Message to the Legtslature, (January 4, 1863,) were—pay of militia, $250,000; damages by the enemy, $495,000; by our own troops, $152,000; being an ag-aggregate of $897,000, exclusive of subsistence and transportation assumed by the General Government.

> To-day. O freedom's children come,
>   And shout with one accord,
> In praise of Burnside and our boys,
>   And Hobbs and Shackleford ;
> For Morgan, bandit chief. is caged,
>   Though like a hare in fright,
> Through sombre woods. from cliff to cliff,
>   He fled both day and night !
>
> So shout. while he and Basil Duke,
>   Within the dreary shades
> Of prison walls, are musing on
>   The gain of making raids.
> Through proud Ohio's rich domains,
>   Where men are brave and true,
> And women love the dear old flag,
>   Of red, and white and blue !

Bring forth the rusty guns, and let
  A joyful noise be made :
Lay by the implements of toil—
  The anvil, ax, and spade :
Heed not the silver-tasselled corn,
  Heed not the new-mown hay,
Come all, and lift your voices loud,
  In songs and shouts to-day.—HATTIE GERMAN.

STORY LXXVIII.

SIEGE AND CAPITULATION OF VICKSBURG.

INCLUDING THE CHIEF PRELIMINARY OPERATIONS.

IN December, 1862, General W. T. Sherman, with a strong force of infantry, on steam transports and some gunboats, entered the mouths of the Yazoo river, on the 28th, and landing the infantry five miles above Vicksburg, the defences of which, both natural and artificial, were then but little known, commenced an assault with a view to the capture of that place. The attempt being unsuccessful, and the loss considerable, he retired up the river to Arkansas Post; which by a most brilliant combined naval and military attack was captured, with nearly 8,000 prisoners, on the 11th of January, 1863. Whatever credit General McClernand may be entitled to, for this result, it is certain that *General Sherman commanded in person*, the attacking land forces, which, with the gunboats Louisville, De Kalb, Cincinnati, and Lexington, and some light-draughts, soon silenced the fort, and compelled its unconditional surrender.

The expedition next moved down to Milliken's Bend on the 17th of January, and there disembarked. General Grant taking command in person, and feeling satis-

X

fied that Vicksburg could only be turned from the south side, set to work enlarging the canal, which had been previously located by General Williams, across the peninsula, on the Louisiana side of the river; hoping to make a channel which would pass transports for moving the army, and carrying supplies to the new base of operations below. In this he was frustrated by heavy rains and high water.

A new route was next explored and judged practicable, through certain bayous communicating with Tensas river. This, with the aid of dredge boats, was so improved that one small steamer and several barges were taken through; but the river falling rapidly, and the roads becoming passable between Milliken's Bend and New Carthage, near the middle of April, made this route impracticable and unnecessary.

Soon after commencing the first canal, the General caused a channel to be cut from the Mississippi river into Lake Providence, which it was thought might afford a passage, by its connection with Bayou Baxter and Bayou Macon, for transports, through Tensas, Wachita, and Red rivers, to the Mississippi below.

Another attempted route was by way of Yazoo Pass, Coldwater, and Tallahatchie rivers into the Yazoo, in the hope of obtaining a foothold on high land above Haines's Bluff; but it was found that a sufficient number of boats of the right class for conveying a sufficient force, could not be had; beside which, it was found that while our troops were opening one end of the route, the enemy were obstructing the other, thus gaining time to fortify Fort Pemberton, at Greenwood, so that our gunboats were unable to silence their batteries; so the project was abandoned.

Another expedition was attempted by Steele's Bayou, Black Bayou, Deer Creek, Rolling Fork, and Sunflower, to the Yazoo, with the same general objects in view, but failed of success, from want of sufficient knowledge of the route. These failures were considered by the General as probably Providential, in driving him ulti- mately, to a line of operations, which proved eminently successful.

The waters fast falling, and the roads beginning to be passable, about the middle of April, the land forces took up the line of march for New Carthage, via Rich- mond; the 13th Army Corps moving first, commanded by General McClernand, and the 17th under General McPherson, soon following. At the same time, prepa- rations were being made for running transports down past the Vicksburg batteries, with Admiral Porter's gunboat fleet.

On the night of the 16th of April, Admiral Porter's fleet, and the transports Silver Wave, Forest Queen, and Henry Clay, ran the Vicksburg batteries. The boilers of the transports were protected as well as possible, with bales of hay and cotton.

More or less commissary stores were put on each. All three of these boats were struck more or less frequently while passing the batteries, and the Henry Clay, by the explosion of shell, or by other means, was set on fire, and entirely consumed. The other two boats were not seriously disabled. No one on board of either was hurt.

Six more boats were then prepared in like manner, for running the batteries, viz.: Tigress, Anglo-Saxon, Cheeseman, Empire City, Horizonia, and Moderator. These left Milliken's Bend on the night of the 22d of

April, and five of them got by, but in a somewhat damaged condition.

The Tigress received a shot in her hull, below the water line, and sunk on the Louisiana shore, soon after passing the last of the batteries. The crews of these steamers, with the exception of the Forest Queen and Silver Wave, were composed of volunteers from the army.

Upon the call for volunteers for this dangerous enterprise, officers and men presented themselves by hundreds, anxious to undertake the trip.

Twelve barges, loaded with forage and rations, were sent down in tow of the last six boats, and half of them got through in a condition to be used, and five of the transports were soon put in running order, and the remainder were in a condition to be used as barges, in moving troops.

The 13th Army Corps having got through to the Mississippi, as much of it as the barges would carry were embarked and conveyed to the front of Grand Gulf on the 29th of April. The plan was for the navy to silence the guns of the enemy, and the troops to land under cover of the gunboats, and carry the place by storm. But this was found impracticable, after five hours bombardment, from the fact of the enemy's guns being too elevated, and the fortifications too strong to be taken from the water side.

It was therefore determined to again run the gauntlet of the batteries, and turn the enemy's position by effecting a landing below. Orders were at once given for the troops to debark at Hard Times, on the Louisiana shore, and to march down to a point opposite Bruinsburg, between Grand Gulf and Rodney.

At dark the gunboats again engaged the batteries' and all the transports ran by, with but little injury. The work of ferrying the troops across to Bruinsburg, was commenced at daybreak in the morning, both gunboats and transports being used. As soon as the 13th Corps were crossed, three days' rations were given them, and they started at once on the road to Port Gibson. The 17th Corps crossed over, received their rations and followed, as speedily as possible. The 15th Corps, under General Sherman, had remained at Milliken's Bend, with orders to make a demonstration on Haines' Bluff, making as large a show as possible, in order to prevent any heavy reinforcements being sent from Vicksburg to the assistance of the Grand Gulf forces. This ruse was executed with most admirable success. •

At two o'clock, on the 1st of May, the advance of the enemy was met eight miles from Bruinsburg, and compelled to fall back; and from position to position they were driven, with considerable loss, all day, toward Port Gibson, where it was thought they would make another stand; but in the morning it was found they had retreated.

Port Gibson taken, Grand Gulf was evacuated by the enemy; and General Grant, in person, with a small cavalry escort, went there and made arrangements for changing his base of supplies to that place.

General Sherman's Corps having come up, the army moved rapidly on, though upon different roads, from victory to victory, including in brilliant succession, Champion's Hill, or Baker's Creek, Raymond, Jackson, and Black River Bridge, where the entire garrison and seventeen pieces of artillery were captured.

General Sherman, by the morning of the 18th of

May, had crossed the Black River, at Bridgeport, above, by means of pontoons, and was ready to march on Walnut Hills. McClernand and McPherson built floating bridges during the night, and were ready for crossing their commands by eight o'clock, A. M., of the 18th.

Sherman marched at an early hour, taking the Bridgeport and Vicksburg road, turning to the right when within three and a half miles of Vicksburg, to get possession of the Walnut Hills and the Yazoo River, which he successfully accomplished before night.

McPherson crossed the Black River above the Jackson Road, and came into the same road with Sherman, but in his rear. He arrived at night-fall with his advance to where Sherman turned to the right.

McClernand moved by the Jackson and Vicksburg road to Mount Albans, and there turned to the left, to get into Baldwin's Ferry Road. By this disposition, the three army corps covered all the ground their numbers would admit of, and by the morning of the 19th, the investment of Vicksburg was made as complete as could be, by the forces at General Grant's command.

During the day there was continuous skirmishing, and, relying upon the demoralization of the enemy, in consequence of their late repeated defeats, a general assault was ordered at two, P. M., in hopes of being able to carry their works.

The 15th, Sherman's Corps, from having arrived in front of the works on the 18th, to get a good position, were enabled to make a vigorous assault. The 13th and 17th Corps succeeded no further than to gain advanced positions, covered from the fire of the enemy. The 20th and 21st of May were spent in perfecting communications with the army supplies, which, it may well be supposed, were beginning to be much needed, after marching and fighting for twenty days, on an average of about five days' rations drawn from the Commissary Department.

On the 21st, the General, having completed his arrangements for drawing supplies of every description, determined to make another effort to carry Vicksburg by assault. Orders were accordingly given for a general assault on the whole line, to commence at ten o'clock, A. M., on the 22d.

Promptly, at the appointed time, the three army corps, then in front of the enemy's works, commenced the assault. General Grant had taken a commanding position near McPherson's front, from which he could see all the advancing columns from that corps, and a part of each of Sherman's and McClernand's.

A portion of the commands of each, succeeded in planting their flags on the outer slopes of the enemy's bastions, and maintaining them there till night. Each corps had many more men than could possibly be used in the assault, over such unfavorable ground as intervened between them and the enemy.

The assault was gallant in the extreme, on the part of all the troops; but the enemy's position was too strong, both naturally and artificially, to be taken in that way. At every point assaulted, and at all of them at the same time, the enemy was able to show all the force his works could cover.

The assault failed, with much loss on our side, but without weakening the confidence of our troops in their ability to ultimately succeed.

No troops succeeded in entering any of the enemy's works, with the exception of Sergeant Griffith, of the

21st Iowa, and some eleven privates of the same regiment, none of whom returned except the Sergeant, and possibly one of the privates.

After this failure, General Grant determined on prosecuting a regular siege. The troops being now fully aware of the necessity of it, worked diligently and cheerfully, and the work progressed rapidly and satisfactorily, until the 3d of July, when all was about ready for a final assault.

Of this state of readiness on our part, the Rebels were not ignorant; and dreading the consequences, and anticipating the result of an assault, General Pemberton, on the afternoon of the 3d of July, sent a letter, under a flag of truce, to General Grant proposing an armistice, and the appointment of commissioners to arrange terms of capitulation. The result was the surrender of the city and garrison of Vicksburg, at ten o'clock, A. M., July 4th, 1863, on the following terms:—

The entire garrison, officers and men, were to be paroled, not to take up arms against the United States, until exchanged by the proper authorities; officers and men, each to be furnished with a parole, signed by himself; officers to be allowed their side-arms, and private baggage; and the field, staff, and cavalry officers, one horse each; the rank and file to be allowed all their clothing, but no other property: rations from their own stores, sufficient to last them beyond our lines; the necessary cooking utensils for preparing their food; and thirty wagons to transport such articles as could not be carried.

These terms were considered by General Grant, as more favorable to the government than an unconditional surrender, as it saved us the transportation of the prisoners to the North; which at that time would have been very difficult, owing to the limited amount of river transportation on hand, and the expenses of subsisting them.

Our army was thus left free to operate against Johnston, who was threatening it from the direction of Jackson; and our river transportation was ready to be used for the movement of troops to any point the exigency of the service might require.

However expedient the arrangement may have been, it failed to receive the hearty approval of the country, from the general lack of confidence that the Rebels would observe it on their part in good faith. That they did not, has been subsequently abundantly shown; the Rebel government itself sanctioning the wholesale violation of the parole.

STORY LXXIX.

CAPITULATION OF PORT HUDSON.

On the morning of the 7th of July, 1863, a salute was fired from both the upper and lower fleets, immediately on the reception of the news from Vicksburg, and the bands of the different regiments struck up national and patriotic airs. The wildest enthusiasm prevailed among the soldiers all day; and the proximity of the contending forces, enabled the Rebels in Port Hudson to hear the cheering, without enlightening them as to the cause.

At several points on the lines, the Rebels and our troops were so near together that conversations could be held, and were carried on, without danger to either party.

18

Toward evening, on the 7th, the curiosity of the Rebels to learn what was going on, became so great, that one of their officers called out to a Union officer, asking, "What are you making all that noise about?" The answer was, "We have taken Vicksburg."

The Rebel officer said he did not believe it, and on being asked what would convince him of its truth, he replied, "Nothing but a copy of the dispatch, or some reliable authority."

The Union officer then told him he would procure a copy of General Grant's official dispatch, and pass it over the parapet to him. The Rebel said if he would do so, and vouch for its genuineness, on his honor as a gentleman, and a soldier, he would be convinced.

The Union officer at once procured a copy of the dispatch, and taking it to the enemy's breastworks, gave it to the officer with whom he had been conversing, and at the same time assured him, on the honor of a soldier, that the dispatch was genuine, and that he had copied it with his own hand.

The Rebel having read it, said he was satisfied of its truthfulness, and that he thought it useless for Port Hudson longer to attempt to hold out. Things remained in the same position as previous to the interview, until two o'clock the next morning, when a parley was sounded from the Rebel works, and an officer came out, with a dispatch from the Rebel General Gardner, asking on what terms a surrender would be accepted.

As soon as the message could be conveyed to General Banks, an answer was returned, in effect, that only an unconditional surrender would be accepted.

General Gardner accepted the terms, and asked a few hours to make the necessary arrangements. He was strong-hold.

The Rebels were all drawn up in line of battle, numbering about four thousand men fit for duty, with their arms stacked in front of them, and surrendered; and being in a suffering condition for want of food, were promptly fed from the commissariat of our army.

In addition to the number aforesaid, there were about fifteen hundred sick and wounded men—about five hundred of the latter. Their wounds were, generally, very severe—in the head, by the bullets of our sharpshooters.

Our batteries had done a great deal of damage, having destroyed an immense amount of stores. The Rebel sick had suffered terribly, from their almost total destitution of medical stores.

The United States flag was run up at nine o'clock, on Thursday morning, the 9th of July, and was saluted by the Hartford as she passed. There was a good supply of ammunition in the fort, all of which fell into our hands. This was the fifth day after the surrender of Vicksburg.

There had been much toil, privation, and suffering on both sides; but the justice of our cause had inspired our troops with a determined, persevering energy, and indomitable bravery, that could not fail, under skillful and courageous leaders, of triumphant success and ultimate victory.

"And conquer we must, for our cause it is just,
And this be our motto, in 'God is our trust;'
And the Star-spangled Banner in triumph shall wave
O'er the land of the FREE, and the home of the BRAVE."

STORY LXXX.

MIDNIGHT CHARGE OF THE MULE BRIGADE UP LOOKOUT VALLEY.

WHILE General Hooker's army was moving up Lookout Valley, from some unknown cause a stampede among the mules occurred, which is worth relating, as it was an incident that afforded much merriment at the expense of the Rebels. It was in the dead of the night, when both armies were resting from the fatigues of the previous day, and the sentinel's tread was the only sound that disturbed the universal quiet.

Rushing from the wagons, to the number of about thirty, the mules made for the enemy's lines like frightened sheep. The drivers were awakened by the noise just in time to witness the disappearance of the animals through our advanced pickets. The enemy's pickets were not caught napping.

Hearing the mule brigade tearing across the valley, they mistook them for Yankee cavalry, discharged their muskets at the supposed "Yanks," and fell back upon a battalion, stationed a little in the rear of them, with the cry that the enemy were upon them. The battalion taking the alarm, sprang to arms, only in time to hear the sound of the frightened mules, whose race was not checked by the volley from the pickets.

They retreated, also, a short distance, to a point where a whole Rebel brigade had stacked their arms, and were calmly dreaming of home and battle scenes. In rushed the battalion, more dead than alive from fright, with the exclamation—"Hooker has surprised us! his cavalry is upon us!" The valiant sons of Mars did not wait to gather up their blankets or guns, but made the fastest pedestrian time on record back to the main force; leaving upon the field, for the mule brigade, over one thousand stand of arms, among which, were three hundred new Enfield rifles, blankets, small arms, knapsacks, &c.

Meantime our teamsters had given the alarm, and a force was sent out for the recovery of the mules, and in a few hours, the expedition, inaugurated by the mules, returned to our lines with the valuable spoils. This is no fancy sketch; its correctness is vouched for by a member of General Thomas' staff, who was present when the expedition returned.

It will be recollected that in his report of Hooker's victory, General Thomas stated that 1,500 stands of arms were captured. Readers were, no doubt, generally at a loss to discover by what process more arms were taken than prisoners. In the midnight charge of the mule brigade, they may find a solution of the problem. Through its aid a large amount of valuable stores and arms were secured, and General Hooker was enabled to push his advance much nearer the point of ground contended for. All will agree that the charge of the mule brigade is worthy of a place in history.

STORY LXXXI.

STORY OF GENERAL SIGEL.

On the return of General Fremont's army from Southwestern Missouri, Sigel commanded the Division that came by Lebanon to Rolla. A few miles north of Leba-

Y

non the army encamped for the night, on the farm of a man who was in sympathy with the Rebellion, and his fence-rails were all burned for fire-wood, and his farm stripped of whatever was useful and necessary to subsist the troops and horses of the train.

In the morning the farmer came with a large bill of damages, and asked for payment. The Quartermaster came to General Sigel to know what should be done about it. Colonel Warmoth was present, and the General asked him whether the man was a loyal citizen. The Colonel replied that he was a conditional Union man at first, but that he had afterward sympathized with the Rebellion.

Turning to the Quartermaster-General, Sigel then replied—"Mr. Quartermaster, then you *sympathize* with the Government." It is hardly necessary to add, that the Secesh farmer did not obtain what he came for.

STORY LXXXII.

GENERAL ORDER—A HEROINE.

Headquarters, District of Central Missouri, }
Jefferson City, August 9th, 1863. }

GENERAL ORDERS NO. 42.

On the night of the 6th instant, a party of bush-whackers, some three in number, visited the house of a Mr. Schwarltz, about twelve miles from Jefferson City, Cole County, and on demanding admittance, were refused by Miss Schwarltz, a young lady of fifteen. They replied that they would come in, at the same time trying to break down the door.

While this was going on, the other inmates of the

house, viz., Mr. Schwarltz, John Wise, Captain Golden, Government horse-dealer, and a young man in his employ, all left, taking with them (as they supposed) all the arms and ammunition; but in their hasty retreat they left behind a revolver, which Miss Schwarltz appropriated to her own use.

She went to the door, and on opening it, presented the pistol to the leader of the gang, telling them to "come on, if they wanted to, and that some of them would fall, or she would." They threatened to kill her if she did not leave the door. She replied, "the first one who takes one step toward this door, dies, for this is the home of my parents, and my brothers and sisters; and I am able, and shall defend it." Seeing that she was determined in her purpose, after holding a consultation together, they left.

Here is an instance of true courage, in a young girl of fifteen years of age, who, after all the inmates of the house, even her father, had fled, leaving her alone to her fate, with a courage worthy a Joan of Arc, boldly defended her native home, against three blood-thirsty, cowardly ruffians; and by her coolness and heroic daring, succeeded in turning them from their hellish designs.

It is with feelings of no ordinary pride and pleasure, that the Commanding General announces this fact to the citizens and soldiers in his district. On the other hand, those miserable cowards, who deserted this brave girl in the hour of danger, flying from the house, leaving her to her fate, are unworthy the name of men, deserve the scorn and contempt of the community at large, and their society should be shunned by every one who has the least spark of honor or bravery within him.

By order of Brigadier-General BROWN.

J. BAINSFORD, A. A. G.

STORY LXXXIII.

GENERAL HOWARD—AN INCIDENT.

An unrecorded incident of the midnight fight between Hooker's and Longstreet's forces, in Lookout Valley, on the night of the 30th of October, 1863, is related by C. D. Brigham, correspondent of the *New York Tribune*, as follows:—

"A short time subsequent to this magnificent charge on the enemy in their breastworks, by General Geary's brigade, General Howard, taking with him a small escort of cavalry, started for that part of the field where General Geary was supposed to be. He had not gone far, when he came up with a body of infantry. 'What cavalry is that?' was the hail. 'All right,' responded General Howard, at the same time calling out, 'What men are these?' 'Longstreet's,' was the reply. 'All right—come here,' said General Howard. The men approached. 'Have we whipped those fellows?' asked the General, in a manner to keep up the deception. 'No, d——n them, they were too much for us, and drove us from our rifle-pits, like devils. We're whipped, ourselves.' By this time the Rebels had gathered nearer. 'Lay down your arms!' demanded General H., in a stern voice. The men surrendered.

"Taking his prisoners in charge, General H. proceeded on his way. He had not gone far, before another party of Rebel infantry called out, 'What cavalry is that?' 'All right,' was the response, again, of General Howard, as he proceeded. On approaching the position occupied by Geary, that officer had observed the advancing horsemen, and infantry, as he supposed the prisoners to be, and taking them to be Rebels, he had ordered his guns to be loaded with canister, and in a moment more would have given the intrepid Howard and his little force the benefit of it.

"But the General who had successfully deceived the enemy, found a way to make himself known to his friends, and so escaped a reception of that kind."

STORY LXXXIV.

EXECUTION OF REUBEN STOUT ON JOHNSON'S ISLAND.

REUBEN STOUT, Company K, 60th Indiana, convicted of desertion, and the murder of SOLOMON HOFFMAN, on the 14th of March, 1863, at Madison, Carroll County, Indiana, was shot on Friday, October —, 1863.

The exection was on the Bay shore, in front of the prison yard. The Hoffman Battalion was formed in a hollow square, open on the bay side, where the prisoner was seated on his coffin. Colonel Pierson and staff were within the square. The execution party was in command of Lieutenant McElroy, Provost Marshal. The orders and sentence were read by Lieutenant Bailey, Post Adjutant.

Portions of the prisoner's statement, as herewith given, were then read by the Chaplain, it being too lengthy to be read entire. Prayer was offered in English by the Chaplain, and also by Rev. M. Miller, pastor of the German Church in Sandusky, in the German language.

After the services the cap was placed over the eyes of the prisoner, by E. M. Keith, the Hospital Steward, and the command given to fire by the Provost Marshal. The prisoner fell immediately, seven balls taking effect, there being eight of the execution party, one having a blank cartridge. Dr. Woodbridge, Surgeon of the Post, went up and examined the prisoner, and pronounced him dead.

The battalion under the command of Major Scoville, marched past the body, the band playing the dead march. When past the body, they march to the parade ground at a quick step. The remains of the prisoner were decently laid out, and buried in the prison grave-yard on the island.

Stout left a statement, which was published in the Sandusky papers, from which we extract the following:—

"I staid with my company and regiment, until November 26th, 1862, when we got a furlough to go home, the regiment having been captured at Crane River, Kentucky, and paroled as prisoners of war. We were sent to Indianapolis to be exchanged and draw arms again. All the men of the regiment got furloughs for a few days to go home to their friends.

"I went home and staid out my time, and then started to go to my regiment. I went as far as Lafayette, my wife and her sister going as far as Dayton, Indiana. I took sick at Lafayette, and stayed there about five days. My father-in-law then took me home to his house to stay till I got well.

"After I had been there about two weeks, I was advised by various persons not to go back to the army. They said this was only an 'Abolition war,' and ad-

vised me to stay at home, and they would protect me.
I was induced to go to a meeting of the so-called
'Knights of the Golden Circle,' and was made a mem-
ber of that organization.

"The obligation of the order bound us to do all we
could against the war—to resist a draft, if one should
be made, and likewise to resist and oppose all con-
fiscation, or emancipation measures, in every possible
way. We were sworn to stand by each other in all
measures of resistance. We were pledged to do all we
could to prevent another man or dollar going from the
State for the further prosecution of the war. I met
with this secret meeting several times, and entered into
their views and plans.

"I was led by the evil counsels of this traitorous
organization, to stay away from my post of duty in the
army, for which I am truly sorry. I am sorry that I
ever lifted my hand against the life of my fellow-man.
I would affectionately, and earnestly urge all in the
service of their country, not to do as I have done; but
to be faithful to their obligations as soldiers, avoiding
all disloyal counsels and obligations."

STORY LXXXV.

COLONEL LONG'S RAID IN BRAGG'S REAR.

THE battle of Chattanooga was fought and won
without the aid of cavalry on our side; the ridge being
so steep as to render their use in front impracticable.
But the indefatigable Grant did not allow the cavalry
to remain idle.

On the afternoon of Tuesday, the 24th of November, 1863, Colonel Long, with one battalion of the 1st Ohio, 3d Ohio, and 4th Michigan Cavalry, and 17th Indiana, and 98 Illinois Mounted Infantry, quietly crossed Sherman's pontoons, and while the enemy's attention was attracted by Sherman's batteries started for Bragg's rear, and a little after dark were three miles in the rear of his right, where they came upon, and captured, eleven wagons laden with forage; and then moved on six miles further, when they stopped and fed; after which they moved on to Altamont, and destroyed the railroad and telegraph, and captured two couriers with important dispatches from Joe Johnson to Bragg.

Early on the next morning, having heard of a train of supplies belonging to Cheatham, *en route* from Long-street to Bragg's army, Colonel Seidell, of the 3d Ohio, supported by the rest of the command, started to capture it.

After a rapid ride of ten miles, they came up with, and captured the train which proved to be a very valuable one, consisting of eighty wagons laden with Quartermaster's stores, and Paymaster's chest, containing eighty thousand dollars in Rebel currency, and five hundred in gold and silver. The guard, horses, and mules were also all captured.

Retracing their steps, they approached Cleveland, in the suburbs of which, they took six teams, and soon after three well-laden Quartermasters' wagons. The whole command then entered Cleveland, to the surprise and joy of the citizens, and consternation of the 24th Rebel Cavalry; who were not long in putting a safe distance between themselves and the "Yanks."

At Cleveland large supplies of wheat and flour were

captured, and the factory for making percussion caps and shells was destroyed. Wednesday night was spent in Cleveland, and on Thursday morning a detachment was sent to Charleston, where a sharp fight occurred, with the loss to us of private Kasson, 3d Ohio. The 98th Illinois gave it to them with their "Spencers," while the 3d Ohio charged their works, taking eight prisoners; the enemy opening on them with a battery on the opposite side of Chickamauga River. They returned on the Dalton and Kingston Railroad, destroyed it for twelve miles, and rejoined the command at Cleveland.

At four o'clock, A. M., on the 26th, the pickets were attacked, and at five the command was in line, and fought briskly two hours, and then fell back on the Harrison road, as the enemy appeared in force with artillery.

They arrived in Chattanooga, at eight o'clock, P. M., on the 26th, with three hundred and sixty-five prisoners, four hundred mules, and four Rebel flags; one of which belonged to the celebrated Buckner Guards, and was inscribed "victory or death."

The Union citizens of Cleveland, presented the 3d Ohio with a fine flag; and seemed anxious to testify their good will in every way. Every thing they could do for the boys, during their short stay, was cheerfully done.

This raid was one of the best, and most successful of the war, and its execution could not have been entrusted to worthier hands. They proved themselves a veteran force, and rendered signal service to the army, at a critical time.

STORY LXXXVI.

QUEER ADVENTURE AND NARROW ESCAPE.

LIEUTENANT McINTIRE of the 9th Illinois Cavalry, relates that just as the fight near Summerville, West Tennessee, commenced, he arrived on the ground with a dispatch from General Grierson to Colonel Prince.

Finding himself surrounded and unable to escape, he sprang from his horse and crawled under a house; but fearing that this might not be a safe place, he crept to a cotton gin a short distance off.

In the gin he found a large heap of cotton-seed. Jumping into the heap he covered himself with the seed, so as leave only his head out, over which he pulled a basket.

Here the Lieutenant was feeling comparatively safe, an officer of the 7th sprang in the door, with a dozen Rebels at his heels. The officer ran up stairs and hid under some loose boards in the floor. The Rebels put a guard around the house and began a vigorous search.

Up stairs and down they went, several times, and every hiding place but the right one was examined. They knew that the officer was there, in some place, and they were determined to have him.

Presently the heap of cotton-seed caught their attention, and forthwith they commenced plunging their sabers into it. The heap was probed in all directions, but providentially without touching the Lieutenant's body.

At last, one of the Rebs, exasperated beyond endurance, at their ill-success, vented his anger on the basket over the Lieutenant's head, by striking it a furious blow with his sword.

Had the Lieutenant not kept a vigorous hold to the handle, the basket would have been knocked a rod. Just then some occurrence outside caused them to hurry away, and both officers escaped.

------◄◆◆►------

STORY LXXXVII.

ESCAPE OF DR. RUCKER FROM A REBEL PRISON AND HIS SUBSEQUENT ADVENTURES AND FINAL SAFETY.

Dr. William T. Rucker, a well-known Union leader of West Virginia, who was captured at the surrender of Summerville, in Nicholas county, Va., in July, 1862, arrived in Washington in November. 1863, having escaped from the Rebel Penitentiary in Pittsylvania, Va. The story of his treatment and escape is full of interesting and instructive incident.

The Doctor was first sent, with other prisoners, to Sulphur Springs, where he was put in irons and otherwise harshly treated. He was afterward sent to Lynchburg, where, being well known, his active loyalty induced even greater severity. He was put in double irons, with the cuffs firmly riveted about his arms and legs.

In August he was sent to Richmond, and closely confined in Castle Thunder, with a special guard over him, to prevent his escape. While at Richmond he saw two Union prisoners shot at Libby, and one at Castle Thunder, on the most trivial provocations.

Governor Letcher represented to the Rebel Secretary of War, that Rucker was a notorious character, guilty of treason to the State of Virginia, and, therefore, he should of right be surrendered to the State authorities for trial. After considerable correspondence on the subject, the Confederate authorities consented, and turned over the prisoner to be tried for crimes alleged to have been committed against the State of Virginia. He was accordingly taken from the prison at Richmond, sent to Allegheny county, and confined in a jail to await his trial.

Ten separate indictments were brought against him —one for murder, one for treason, one for arson, three for horse-stealing, one for wagon-stealing, and one for bridge-burning. Dr. Rucker believes that he escaped being indicted for several other crimes, simply because they did not occur to the minds of the Grand Jury.

On the charge of murder, the prisoner pleaded a change of venue, which was sustained, and the case was sent to Botetourt county. On all the other charges he pleaded *alien enemy*, but being a citizen of Western Virginia, he was held to be a citizen of Virginia, and hence the plea was disallowed. The trial was several times continued, and often deferred, though the prisoner vigorously urged a trial, knowing that the sooner his case was brought to a crisis, the better it would be for him. He was forced to employ four different counsel at $2,000 each, and these were threatened with mob-violence if once they appeared in the defence.

When nearly a year had passed in a fruitless effort to procure a trial, during which time Dr. Rucker was held in close confinement, the United States Government determined to hold one Dr. Greene, an Assistant-Surgeon in the Rebel army as a hostage for his return.

In June, 1863, he was removed to the prison in Pitt-

sylvania, the strongest and most secure prison in the
State.   It was now evident to his friends that escape
was impossible, and he was given over as lost: friends
were not allowed to visit him, but bitter enemies had
full privilege to taunt and insult him through the
prison bars.   The Union people were permitted to send
him provisions but not to see him.   The Rebels told
him that the Confederate Government would starve the
Union prisoners, until the Yankee Government would
consent to their terms of exchange, and leave such men
as himself, Colonel Straight, and officers of negro regiments in their hands to be properly punished.

By careful observation, Dr. Rucker ascertained that
the jailor's son, not twenty months old, at times had the
key to the debtor's room, which was directly opposite
his cell, to play with; he at once determined to secure
the key and effect his escape.   At a favorable moment
he bribed the child with chestnuts and fruits, and thus
gained possession of the much coveted key.

On the night of the 18th of October, 1863, soon after
dark, he carefully turned the key, slid back the bolts,
and almost in a moment was free.   He passed out of
the village of Pittsylvania on the Raleigh road, having
determined to reach the Union troops on the North
Carolina coast.   When a short distance on the road he
discovered that he had left behind papers that would
betray his route through North Carolina, he changed
his course, retraced his steps through the village, traveled all night as rapidly as possible, (having secured
a horse not far from the village.) and was at daylight
in a town far to the northward, where he was received
by a trusty friend and concealed till the 27th.

During this time he was visited by many old acquaintances, who gave him proper assistance, and among other things, a blooded horse, valued at $1,000. provided especially for the occasion. On the night of the 27th, with this animal he traveled sixty-five miles. During the next day he slept soundly at the house of a loyal friend, his horse being concealed in a corn-shuck pen. Early at night he resumed his journey, and at two o'clock next morning passed through Covington. Allegheny county. In this village he called at the house of a supposed friend, to make some inquiry, and immediately proceeded on his way.

When a few miles from Covington he found his strength so rapidly failing, that he determined to stop in a thicket near the road and rest. Soon after daylight, judging from the noise and confusion along the road, he believed himself betrayed by his Covington friend, and afterward learned that the wife of the gentleman, of whom he made inquiry, had published the fact of his passage through the village. He determined to abandon his horse and equipments, and flee to the mountains. He remained two days and nights in the Alleghenies without food, and only once found water.

On the evening of the 31st of October, pressed with hunger, and perishing with cold, he descended to the foot of the mountains. When night set in, a heavy rain commenced falling, and the night was dark and stormy. It was a question of life or death: scouts thirsting for his blood were on every side, and every road: twice they had passed close to his retreat in the mountains, and he knew not what moment he might fall into their hands. He, however, determined to come out into the valley, and seek relief. The first house he passed he knew to be the residence of a notorious Rebel.

As he was passing a narrow ravine near this house, he suddenly heard a soft and low whistle; he instantly stood still, as if pierced to the heart, and transformed to stone. While deliberating what to do, the sound was repeated. It might be an enemy signaling to a comrade, or it might perchance be a friend. He seized his pistol and demanded, "Who's there?" A voice replied ——. The Doctor thought he recognized both the name, and the voice to be those of a faithful negro boy, the property of the Rebel owner of the house near by. The negro inquired. "Are you Dr. Rucker?" "No," said the Doctor, "what do you know about Dr. Rucker?—come closer." The negro half frightened, yet still confident, said, "Your voice sounds mighty like de doctor's." He stepped forward, and there was a mutual recognition, and short greetings.

The loyal negro had come out to save his friend. He told him a guard was stationed on every road, and that he was completely surrounded: the scouts had been at his master's house, the night before, and he overheard in their conversation that they were after Dr. Rucker, and expected to catch him on the road near by. He had determined to save him if possible, and for that purpose had watched for him in the ravine, where he had provided some bread and meat. This the famished fugitive eagerly consumed, and then followed his faithful guide, who piloted him round three sets of pickets, and left him safe with a friend, several miles beyond. Thence he made his way across Green Briar River, and was piloted to a concealed fortification, erected by the Union men and conscripts, who were well armed, and determined to defend themselves till death.

Dr. Rucker remained in this fortress two days, and

GALLANTRY OF LIEUTENANT MILNE.

I MUST not forget to mention the gallantry of a young officer in the engagement at Lafourche, Louisiana. Sergeant Henry Milne, of the 4th Wisconsin, was recently promoted to a first lieutenancy in the 1st Louisiana Native Guard, (Heavy Artillery,) and detailed as assistant superintendent of Negro labor.

Riding through Lafourche one day, he gave information of the approach of the enemy to Colonel Stickney, of the 17th Massachusetts, the commanding officer of our forces, and informed him that he could successfully manage the field-piece which stood before them. Although an entire stranger, in the emergency, he was appointed chief of artillery. He dismounted, and immediately commenced drilling the artillerists.

When the enemy's cavalry appeared, he loaded with shell, trained the gun and fired. He killed two men, dismounted twelve, and killed two horses. At closer range he used only canister. The enemy charged upon the battery, but he cried, "Steady, boys,"—and took good aim.

The contest had now become so close, that a Rebel soldier had his hand clasped tight around the throat of an infantry captain, one of whose soldiers repulsed his impudence by thrusting his bayonet entirely through the Rebel's heart.

Another ran up to Lieutenant Milne, placed his hand upon the gun and shouted, "Surrender!" "Never!" was the answer. "Hand me a shot, boys," said the Lieutenant. "Don't you fire that again!" screamed the Rebel. Lieutenant Milne, with the strength of a giant, hurled the ball at his antagonist, who fell dead at his feet. Rallying again, to the task before him, he loaded and fired with lightning-like rapidity, until the enemy were repulsed, and the victory won. His faithful horse lay dead under his gun, but eighteen dead butternuts bore him company. General Emory publicly announced his determination to promote the young hero, the gallant Lieutenant Milne.

STORY LXXXIX.

JOHN MORGAN'S RAID AGAIN.
INCIDENTS FROM THE NEWSPAPERS.

NEAR Corydon, Indiana, a minister, named Glenn, who owned the finest house in that section, fired upon the Rebels. He was dragged into the house by his wife, who closed the doors. The Rebels burst open the door, wounded him through both thighs, set fire to the house, and left Glenn to perish in the flames.

His wife and other ladies in the house, dragged him out to an orchard, and thus saved him from being roasted alive. Near Maukport, they also killed Garrett

Hunt, and just above the town, they murdered Wm. Frahee.

The story runs that Morgan captured Wash. De Pauw, one of the wealthiest men of Southern Indiana, and said to him, "Sir, do you consider your flouring-mill worth $2,000?" Mr. De Pauw said he thought it was worth that. "Then," said the robber chief, "you can save it for the $2,000." Mr. De Pauw paid the money. "Now," proceeded Morgan, "do you think you woollen-mill is worth $3,000?" Mr. De Pauw admitted that it was probably worth more than that. "Well," said the Rebel, "you can have it for $3,000." And Mr. De Pauw took it. So they levied $5,000 on him.

Near Corydon, William Heth, keeper of the toll-gate, fired on the Rebels. They shot him dead and burned his house. They also burned a fine stone-mill in the neighborhood; and killed Caleb Thomas and Jeremiah Nance.

Lieutenant Adams, of Morgan's band, with a squad, after burning a bridge north of Salem, went to a Quaker farmer's house, hard by, and called for some milk. The Friend demurely accompanied the Lieutenant to the spring-house, and told him to help himself and men. While drinking the milk, the following conversation occurred:

Lieutenant Adams. "You're a Quaker, ain't you?"

Friend, (*very soberly.*) "Yea."

Lieutenant Adams. "Then you're an abolitionist?"

Friend. "Yea."

Lieutenant Adams, (*fiercely.*) "A staunch Union man?"

Friend, (*emphatically.*) "Yea."

Lieutenant Adams, (after a pause.) "Got any Butternuts around here?"

Friend. "Yea."

Lieutenant Adams. "Then, why don't you hang them? We have a way of choking such people down our way.

At Salem, after burning the depot, Morgan announced his intention to burn all the mills and factories in the town, and issued orders to that effect. He afterwards reconsidered these orders, and told the owners of such property, that he would spare it upon the payment of $1,000 for each mill and factory.

These levies upon the citizens were responded to, and the money paid over to the free-booter chief. This alone saved the town from a conflagration, which the location of the mills would have rendered inevitable.

When Morgan took Colonel Craven, of Ripley, he behaved roughly at first. He asked where the Colonel lived. "At Osgood," was the answer. "What, that little town on the railroad?" "Yes," said the Colonel. "Well," said Morgan, "I have just sent sixty men up there to burn the town. "Burn and be d——d," said the Colonel, "it isn't much of a town, any how." Morgan laughed heartily, at this answer, and said: "I like the way you talk, old fellow," and released him, with the injunction to follow till the rear-guard had got past.

At Dupont, Ia., the great John himself did not exhibit that chivalry, which in some quarters has been claimed for him. He selected for his headquarters the residence of Mr. Samuel Stout. The family of Mr. Stout had retired, but were ordered to vacate their beds; this done, they were soon occupied by Morgan and his staff. Mrs. Stout and her daughters were ordered to prepare breakfast for the crowd, and have it ready precisely at four o'clock. Mr. Stout was told to have every thing in the best manner, and under penalty of death to awaken his guests precisely at four.

After partaking of a bountiful repast. Morgan ordered Stout to set out immediately, with his advance guard, as guide. Stout asked the privilege of taking a bite himself, before starting: but was informed that his present well-being required immediate and prompt action.

He was at once placed on an old. sharp-backed horse, without a saddle, and started on a long trot. After travelling twelve miles, Mr. Stout informed his captors that his knowledge of the roads extended no further. He was permitted to dismount, a sorer, if not a wiser man, and find his way home on foot as best he could.

Till now. in all his troubles and trials, one pleasing sensation would occasionally flit across the bewildered brain of Mr. Stout—Morgan had promised to reward him liberally ; but his visions of green-backs and gold eagles were not realized. The renowned chief had forgotten his promise.

One of the Rebels, says a correspondent of the *Commercial*, very cordially invited me to make a visit at his house, "when this cruel war is over." (My house was honored with thirty or forty Rebel guests.) I gave it as my opinion, that his chances for getting home, to receive company. were rather slim.

He replied. saying. he supposed I would be pleased to hear that he and his comrades were all killed or captured. I assured him he was correct in his supposition. "I like your honesty." was the Rebel's reply.

One of them expressed great disgust at "Northern sympathizers:" said he, "if they sympathize with the South, why don't the d——d cowardly traitors come and fight for us?" Upon the whole, I think some good will result from Morgan's raid through Indiana and Ohio.

Like a sudden clap of thunder, came Morgan among us, and passed off to the east like a meteor, leaving the natives gazing after him in stupefied horror, rubbing their eyes, and wondering whether it was all the dream of a nightmare, or a reality. Quite a number of men and boys followed in Morgan train, keeping a safe distance behind, however, hoping to recover their stolen horses.

One old Pennsylvania Dutchman, who resides in this neighborhood, (East Sycamore, Hamilton County, O.,) by some means, lost but one of his horses; he mounted the other, and hastily pursued the flying Secesh. When near Batavia, he mingled a little too close with them, as may be proved from the fact that they took the horse he rode, with saddle and bridle. It is told that he gave vent to his injured feelings by saying to the 'Reb,' who took his horse, "that is my horse, I wish, him good luck. I wish he preak your neck." "What's that?" thundered Secesh. "I wish my horse good luck. I wish he preak your G—t t—m neck," repeated the candid German, with the additional expletive.

Morgan knew, before he crossed the river, who his friends were, and who had arms. Upon entering Corydon, Ia., he showed a list (and so at Salem,) of every citizen who had a Henry rifle, or other improved arm, and immediately sent patrols to bring them in.

Where the K. G. C.'s were the thickest, there was full

information in his possession, of all he wished to know; but when he got what he wanted, he treated his tools as badly as enemies, and bade them good-bye, by taking the horses with which they had followed to guide him.

On his way through Butler County, Morgan rested a few minutes at the house of a peace Democrat. John, in conversation, learned that his host had eight horses, and generously proposed to divide, taking four himself. The old man had to accede, and then asked advice, as to how to save the other four.

The guerrilla chief told him that his rear-guard would be along in about ten hours, (calculating that Hobson would be along in that time,) and that he must cheer for Vallandigham and Jeff. Davis, to save his horseflesh.

At the expected time, Hobson's men came along, and Mr. Butternut came out, cheering lustily, as directed. Hobson doesn't see the joke, but takes off the remaining four horses. It was very wicked of Morgan to cheat and deceive an old admirer.

In taking all the horses one gentleman had, there was one, a great favorite, which he begged might be spared, offering to pay over the full price for him. "How much do you value him at?" the gentleman was asked. "Two hundred dollars," was the reply. "Produce it then, and you may keep your horse." No sooner was the money placed in the impudent rascal's hands, than he pocketed it, and led off the horse.

George T——, Jr., living between New Haven and Harrison, met Hobson's men, the morning after Morgan's forces went through, and believing them some of Morgan's men, hurrahed for John Morgan, and told them he was and had been a Morgan man. A Union soldier called him to his side, and clubbed him with his carbine, knocking his infernal butternut head nearly off.

STORY XC.

HOW JOHN MORGAN GOT 300 HORSES.

JOHN MORGAN, during his celebrated raid through Indiana, took occasion to visit a little town, hard by, with 350 of his guerrillas. while the main body was marching on.

Dashing suddenly into the little "burgh," he found about 300 home-guards, each having a good horse tied to the fences; the men standing about in groups, awaiting orders from their aged captain, who appeared to be on the shady side of sixty.

The hoosier boys looked at the men with astonishment, while the captain went up to one of the party and said:—

"Whose company is this?"

"Wolford's cavalry," said the Reb.

"What? Kentucky boys? We're glad to see you, boys. Where's Wolford?"

"There he sits," said a ragged, rough Reb., pointing to Morgan, who was sitting sideways on his horse.

The captain walked up to Wolford (as he and all thought), and saluted him:—

"Captain. how are you?"

"Bully; how are you? What are you going to do with all these men and horses?" said Morgan. looking about.

"Well, you see that the d——d horse-thieving John Morgan is in this part of the country, with a passel of cut-throats and thieves; and between you and I, if he comes up this way, Captain, we'll give him the best we've got in the shop."

"He's hard to catch; we've been after him for fourteen days, and can't see him at all," said Morgan, good-humoredly.

"Ef our hosses would stand fire, we'd be all right."

"Won't they stand?"

"No, Captain Wolford, 'spose while you're restin' here, you and your company put your saddles on our hosses, and go through a little evolution or two, by way of a lesson to our boys? I'm told you're a hoss on the drill."

And the only man Morgan is afraid of, Wolford (as it were), alighted, and ordered his "boys" to dismount, as he wanted to show the hoosier boys how to give Morgan a warm reception, should he chance to pay them a visit.

This delighted the hoosier boys, so that they went to work, and assisted the men to tie their old, weary, worn-out bones to the fences, and place their saddles upon the backs of their fresh horses, which was soon done, and the men were in their saddles, drawn up in line, and ready for the word.

The boys were highly elated at the idea of having their "pet horses" trained for them by Wolford and his men, and more so, to think that they would stand fire, ever afterward.

The old Captain advanced, and walking up to Wolford (as he thought), said, "Captain, are you all right now?" Wolford rode up one side of the column, and down the other, when he moved to the front, took off his hat, paused, and said, "Now, Captain, I'm ready. If you and your gallant men wish to witness an evolution, which you, perhaps, have never seen, form a line on each side of the road, and watch us closely, as we pass."

The captain did as he was directed. A lot of ladies were present on the occasion, and all was silent as a maiden's sigh.

"Are you ready?"

"All right, Wolford," shouted the captain.

"*Forward!*" shouted Morgan, as the whole column rushed through the crowd, with lightning speed, amid the shouts and huzzas of all present—some leading a horse or two, as they went, leaving their frail tenements of horseflesh tied to the fences, to be provided for by the citizens.

It soon became whispered about, that it was John Morgan and his gang; and there was not a man in the town who would "own up" that he was gulled out of his horse. The company disbanded that night, though the captain, at last advices, still held the horses as prisoners of war, awaiting an exchange.

STORY XCI.

CAPTAIN ANDERSON'S RAID.

EARLY in January, 1864, Captain J. M. Anderson, of the 30th Ohio Infantry, who had been detailed as general recruiting officer for colored troops in Louisiana, applied to Major-General McPherson, of the 17th Army Corps, at Vicksburg, for a company of men to make an excursion into the Tensas country, in Louisiana, for negro recruits.

Aware of the difficulties and dangers of the undertaking, the General declined giving him the force

2 A

desired, being fearful of their being captured: whereupon the Captain, nothing daunted, procured six negro recruits in Vicksburg, armed them with muskets, and accompanied by W. P. Crockett, (son of the old hero, David Crockett,) as guide, and three Northern gentlemen, set out for Waterproof, Louisiana, ninety miles down the river.

With this small, but indomitable party, with but six muskets and two pistols for their entire armament, he landed at Waterproof, by night, and as a side operation, captured a Rebel Lieutenant, a Surgeon, and two privates, who were attempting to cross the river into Mississippi.

The captives confessed that they were of the party that had lately fired into the Steamer Welcome, at that place. They were consequently kept under a guard of two men, and delivered to the proper authority, as prisoners of war. on the Captain's return.

Immediately impressing, from the nearest plantation, a sufficient number of mules to mount his party, the Captain pushed on into the country, for Tensas River, thirty-five miles distant. A short distance out he discovered, and gave chase to, three Rebel officers, but without success, as the speed of their horses soon distanced his mules.

Continuing on, he gave notice to the negroes on his route, that he should cross the Tensas River the coming night. for a train of mules and contrabands, and return on the following morning, at which time he notified them to be ready mounted, and return with him.

Riding his mules to the extent of their speed, and changing them three times on the journey, he reached the Tensas River, at Kirk's Ferry, crossed on flat boats, and went five miles beyond, to the plantation of Captain King, who was absent in the Confederate army.

Without delay, he divested the place of all the able-bodied negroes, mules, horses, and wagons, and with those who flocked to him, on the way, safely recrossed the river at sunset, and visited the plantation of Colonel Hall, friend and confederate of General Harrison, whose 400 cavalry were encamped within four miles. From Colonel Hall, he took his pistols, shot-gun—all his able-bodied negro men, with mules and horses sufficient to mount them.

As was afterward learned, a courier got information from the negroes of his intended movements, escaped across the river, and informed the Rebels that the Yankees would recross the Tensas, by daylight in the morning, at the upper crossing. Whereupon, a force of thirty cavalry was sent thither, and lay in ambush till the following morning, to intercept the Captain and his party.

Meanwhile the raiders had pushed on, capturing mules, horses, pistols, shot-guns, and negroes, and by a forced march, reached Waterproof, at daylight the next morning, (about thirty hours from the time he had left there,) with a train of over a hundred horses and mules, many wagons, and three hundred and fifty negroes. Here he encamped, and gathered forage, and provisions for the party.

About eight o'clock, three negroes arrived on horseback, announcing that the Rebel cavalry were only five miles in their rear, cautiously advancing, for fear of finding a gunboat; but none was at hand for the Captain's protection. He accordingly sent messengers immediately down the river road, to seek one, and send it up, saddled up, and hastened down the river, where, about ten miles below, a gunboat came to his protection, and conveyed the train to Vidalia, opposite Natchez, where the Steamboat Diligent was chartered, and took the entire party and train, including mules, horses, and negroes, to Vicksburg.

STORY XCII.

THRILLING INCIDENT AT FORT DONELSON.

SOME six or eight years previous to the commencemen of the war, a citizen of Massachusetts being unjustly suspected of a crime, suffered the loss of friends, business, and reputation, which, being unable or unwilling to bear up against, he determined on changing his location.

Accordingly, having so disposed his property that it could be easily managed by his wife, he suddenly disappeared, leaving her a comfortable home and the care of two boys of the ages of ten and twelve years.

The first fear that he had sought a violent death, was partly dispelled by the orderly arrangement of his affairs, and the discovery that a daguerreotype of the family-group was missing from the parlor-table. Not much effort was made to trace the fugitive.

When, afterward, facts were developed which established his innocence of the crime charged, it was found impossible to communicate with him; and, as the publication of the story in several widely circulated papers failed to recall him, he was generally supposed to be dead.

At the outbreak of the war, his eldest son, who had become a young man, was induced by a friend, a Captain in a Western regiment, to enlist in his company. He carried himself well through campaigns in Missouri and Tennessee, and after the capture of Fort Donelson, was rewarded with a First Lieutenant's commission. At the battle of Murfreesboro he was wounded in the left arm, but so slightly that he was still able to take care of a squad of wounded prisoners.

While performing this duty, he became aware that one of them, a middle-aged man, with a full, heavy beard, was looking at him with fixed attention. The day after the fight, as the officer was passing, the soldier gave the military salute, and said: "A word with you, if you please, sir. You remind me of an old friend. Are you from New England?"

"I am."

" From Massachusetts?"

" Yes."

" And your name?"

The young Lieutenant told his name, and how he came to serve in a Western regiment.

" I thought so," said the soldier, and turning away, he was silent. Although his curiosity was much excited by the soldier's manner, the officer forbore to question him and withdrew. But, in the afternoon, he took occasion to renew the conversation, and expressed the interest awakened in him by the incident of the morning.

" I knew your father," said the prisoner; " is he well?"

" We have not seen him for years," said the Lieutenant; "we think he is dead.

Then followed such an explanation of the circumstances of his disappearance as the young man could give. He had never known the precise nature of the charges against his father, but was able to make it quite clear that his innocence was established.

"I knew your mother, also," continued the soldier; "I was in love with her when she married your father."

"I have a letter from her, dated ten days ago," said the Lieutenant. "My brother is a nine months' man in New Orleans."

After a little desultory conversation, the soldier took from under his coat a leathern wallet, and disclosed a daguerreotype case. The hasp was gone, and the corners were rounded by wear.

"Will you oblige me," he said, "by looking at this, alone, in your tent?"

Agitated, almost beyond control, the young officer took the case, and hurried away. He had seen the picture before. It represented a man and a woman sitting side by side, with a boy at the knee of each.

The romantic story moved the commander of the division to grant the young man a furlough, and both father and son reached home in a few days after. The reader is left to imagine the sequel.

STORY XCIII.

GENERAL NELSON AT PITTSBURG LANDING.

It was nearly sunset when Nelson, at the head of his troops, landed on the west bank of the river, in the midst of the conflict. The landing and shore of the river, up and down, were covered with demoralized and beaten soldiers, whom no appeals or efforts could rally.

Nelson with difficulty forced his way through the crowd, shaming them for their cowardice as he passed—rode upon a knoll overlooking his disembarking men, and cried out in stentorian tones: "Colonel A., have you your regiment formed?" "In a moment, General," was the reply. "Be quick; time is precious; moments are golden." "I am ready, now, General." "Forward—march!" was the command, and the gallant 6th Ohio was led quickly to the field.

That night Nelson asked Captain Guynne, of the Tyler, "to send him a bottle of wine, and a box of cigars; for to-morrow I will show you a man-of-war fight."

During the night Buell came up, and crossed the river, and by daylight next morning, our forces attacked Beauregard, and then was fought the desperate battle of Shiloh. Up till 12 M. we had gained no decided advantage; in fact, the desperate courage of the enemy had caused us to fall back.

General Buell now came to the front, and held a hasty consultation with his Generals. They decided to charge the Rebels, and drive them back. Nelson rode rapidly to the head of his column, his gigantic figure conspicuous to the enemy in front, and in a voice that rang like a trumpet over the clangor of battle, called for four of his finest regiments in succession—the 24th Ohio; 36th Indiana; 17th Kentucky; and 6th Ohio.

"Trail arms—forward—double-quick time—march!" —and away with thundering cheers, went those gallant boys. The brave Captain, now Brigadier-General Terrell, who alone was left untouched of all his battery, mounted his horse, and with wild huzzas, rode with Nelson upon the foe.

It was the decisive moment: it was like Wellington's "Up, guards, and at them!" The enemy broke, and their retreat commenced. "That was the happiest moment of my life," said the officer, my informant, "when Nelson called my regiment to make that grand charge."

Let the country mourn the sad fate of General Nelson; he was a loyal Kentuckian; fought gallantly the battles of his country; earned all his distinction by gallant deeds. All his faults were those of a commander anxious to secure the highest efficiency of his troops, by the most rigid discipline of his officers, and in this severe duty he at last lost his life.

SKETCH OF GENERAL NELSON.

MAJOR-GENERAL WILLIAM NELSON was a native of Maysville, Mason County, Kentucky. He entered the Naval School, at Annapolis, at the age of fifteen, and graduating, was appointed a Midshipman in the United States Navy, January 28th, 1840. He was first attached to the Sloop-of-war Yorktown, in commission for the Pacific, and soon after joined the Pacific squadron, under Commodore T. Ap Catesby Jones. In 1845, he was commissioned as passed Midshipman, and ordered to the Frigate Raritan, forty-four guns, attached to the Home Squadron, under Commodore David Conner.

In 1847, he was made Acting Master of the Steamer Scourge, a three gun vessel in the Home Squadron, then commanded by Commodore Perry. During the Mexican war, he commanded a navy battery at the siege of Vera Cruz, and won a high reputation as an artillerist.

Subsequently he commanded the Steamer Michigan, a one-gun vessel, running up and down the lakes. Shortly after his appointment, he was transferred to the flag ship of Commodore Morgan, the Independence, a fifty-four-gun razeed ship of the line, of the Mediterranean squadron. He was afterward transferred to the Cumberland, a forty-four-gun frigate, and at length returned home in the Mississippi, of ten guns, Captain Long, which brought over Kossuth. In April, 1855, he was commissioned Lieutenant, and put in command of the Store Ship Fredonia, of four guns, attached to the Pacific squadron.

He returned home in 1857, and went in 1858 in the Niagara, to return to Africa the negroes taken from the Steamer Echo. He was next ordered on the St. Louis, a war sloop of twenty guns, Commander Ogden, of the Home Squadron, where he remained until May, 1860, when he was ordered home, and at the commencement of 1861, was reported in the Navy Register as being on ordnance duty at the Washington Navy Yard.

At the commencement of the Rebellion he was detached from the Navy Department, and placed on special duty in the War Department. In the spring of 1861, he was detailed to command the Ohio River fleet of gunboats.

While on the Ohio River, in consideration of his extensive acquaintance with the people of Kentucky, and his large relationship in that State, he was considered the person, during the ill health of General Anderson, to be sent into Kentucky, to sound the loyal sentiment there, and strengthen it.

In April he went thither, and began the formation of a camp, and the recruiting of troops, at a point between Garrardsville and Danville, which was named "Camp Dick Robinson." He afterward formed a camp at Washington. Mason County, and others at other points, and was highly successful in raising and organizing troops.

He was next engaged in pursuit of the Rebels in the mountainous regions of Eastern Kentucky, defeating them on several occasions. He also fought and whipped Humphrey Marshall repeatedly. He afterward was appointed to command the 2d Division of General Buell's army, advancing with him through Kentucky and Tennessee, acting as Major-General, though commissioned as a Brigadier.

He participated in the battle of Shiloh, at Pittsburg Landing, where his bravery was conspicuous. He commanded in person at the battle of Richmond, Kentucky, was wounded, and being partially recovered, returned to Louisville, and took command of the forces there; having been, in the interim, made Major-General of volunteers.

He was a man about forty years of age, of massive, fine *physique*, of commanding presence, and imperious manners, which last resulted in his death. on the morning of the 29th of September, at the Galt House, in Louisville, at the hands of Brigadier-General J. C. Davis, who shot him with a pistol in the abdomen. His death ensued in half an hour.

STORY XCIV.

FORAGING EXPLOIT.

AFTER the battle and capture of Mission Ridge, General Palmer pushed his division forward in the direction of Graysville, and after securing a large number of arms and provisions, encamped on the north side of Chickamauga, and three-fourths of a mile from Graysville.

Major D. W. Norton and Lieutenant J. W. Shaw, of the General's staff, were in want of forage for their horses, and crossed the river, with an orderly, on a midnight forage. Arriving at Graysville, they reconnoitered the houses in search of corn, looked in through a window, and discovered seven Rebels asleep before the fire, with their guns stacked. Entering very quietly, they removed the guns, and then awakened the Rebels; who, springing up, asked—

"How far back is the enemy?"

"If you mean the Yankees," replied the Major, "they are not very far."

Rebel. "What do you mean?"

Major. "I mean that you are our prisoners."

The Rebels started for the place where they had deposited their guns: when the Major and Lieutenant drew their revolvers, and ordered them to lie down; informing them that they had the house surrounded, and would stand guard till morning, when they would be sent in.

The Rebels obeyed the order, and prepared to finish their nap. Leaving them to sleep, the officers went out, dispatched the orderly for reinforcements, entered other houses, where they secured more in a similar manner, and when the guard arrived, turned over nineteen Rebel prisoners, that they had taken by their sharp strategy, among whom were four commissioned officers.

Other houses were searched, in which Rebels were found, and at one o'clock the officers returned to General Palmer's camp, with about one hundred prisoners. The exploit was a daring one, and highly pleased "Old Pap," as the boys of the 14th Corps style their popular commander.

STORY XCV.

CLINTON WATERS, THE SCOUT.

CLINTON WATERS, a member of the 17th Indiana regiment, probably performed as much scouting as any man in the Army of the Cumberland.

Just before the entry of our army into Chattanooga, Colonel Wilder, with his command, was on the north side of the river, awaiting the development of the enemy's movements, which were such as to excite suspicion.

Waters was selected for the duty of obtaining information, and permitted to take his own course. An opportunity soon presented itself. The following day our soldiers were bathing in the river, on the north side. The Rebels came down the southern bank, stripped themselves, and plunged in.

A few minutes later the soldiers of the two armies were mingling together in the river, cracking their jokes and enjoying themselves to their hearts' content. Gradually Waters made his way to the south bank, and by freely expressing his joy at the kind reception given by the Yankees, excited no suspicion. Arriving at the bank, he leisurely put himself into a suit of Rebel uniform, and made his way up through the town.

After mingling with the men, he learned the exact state of affairs, and turned toward the river. As he passed the guards, he observed that they eyed him sus- piciously, and having learned all that was of importance, he reached the river, plunged boldly in, swam across, and soon after presented himself at the Colonel's head- quarters, with the information that the town had been evacuated by Bragg, and that but four regiments of cavalry, and a small force of infantry remained.

Waters soon exchanged his Rebel suit for his own dry clothes, but did not return the stolen wardrobe.

A subsequent exploit is also worthy of record, show- ing, as it does, the happy faculty he possessed to improve the opportunities offered. On the day of Wilder's fight with Pegram, at Rock Springs, Georgia, Waters was captured while carrying a message. He was sent to Richmond, imprisoned, but bribed a Rebel with a gold watch he had concealed. to permit him to act as nurse. Shortly after, an order came for the exchange of some of the prisoners, and, being under charge as a spy, he was determined to escape.

Providing himself with a pair of crutches on the day of the exchange, he bandaged his legs, scratched his face, applied court-plaster, and otherwise assumed the appearance of a wounded prisoner.

The inmates of his hospital were ordered out, and, assuming the name of a deceased comrade, he succeeded in gaining an exchange, and in due course of time arrived North. He subsequently raised a company for the 123d Indiana, of which he became Captain.

2 B

STORY XCVI.

TORPEDO EXPLOSION.

On the 4th of August, 1863, an expedition left Fortress Monroe, under the direction of Major-General Foster, accompanied by the turreted iron-clad Sagamon, and gunboats Commodore Barney and Cohasset, and proceeded up James river. When within seven miles of Fort Darling, at a point called Dutch Gap, a torpedo was exploded under the bow of the Commodore Barney, by a lock strongly connected with the shore.

The explosion was terrific. It lifted the gun-boat's bow ten feet out of the water, and threw large quantities of water high into the air, which, falling on deck, washed overboard fifteen of the crew. Among them was Lieutenant Cushing, Commander of the Barney. Two sailors were drowned, and the rest were saved. Major-General Foster was on board when the explosion took place.

The enemy then opened on them from the shore with 12-pound field-pieces. The Barney was penetrated by fifteen shots, besides a great number of musket-balls, but not a man was injured except the Paymaster, who was slightly wounded by splinters.

The gunboat Cohasset received five 12-pound shots, one of which passed through her pilot-house, instantly killing her commander, Acting-Master Cox, striking him in the back. The object of the reconnoisance being effected, the fleet returned. The Barney went to Newport News for repairs.

STORY XCVII.

HOW A GUERRILLA CAME TO GRIEF.

In the fall of 1862, Samuel A. High, a notorious West Virginia guerrilla, who had long been a terror to the loyal people of Hampshire and adjoining counties, for some unknown reason, surrendered himself to the authorities; who, from motives equally inexplicable, knowing him to be a murderer and highway robber, set him at liberty; after which, he engaged in kidnapping Union men.

On Saturday night, late in October, Mr. John N. Spencer, of Mill Creek, was laying in the woods, as all loyal men in that region then had to do. The night being rainy, Mr. Spencer became wet and cold, and went to his house and made a fire, when High, and nine or ten other, who seemed to have been waiting for him, rushed from the woods into the house, and seized Spencer, and started off with him in search of another loyal man, near by on the way.

High and one of his comrades got up a dispute, as to who should shoot Spencer, but coming to a brother-in-law of High's, High and two others stopped to take care of Spencer, and sent the others on.

They went into the house, High and the guards set their guns down, and all gathered around the fire. Spencer, in the mean time, not feeling quite easy after the dispute above alluded to, under the pretence of being too warm, slipped his chair back until he could reach High's gun, in which he succeeded, and in a moment the notorious High was a corpse before him.

Spencer, taking advantage of the consternation of High's two accomplices, made his escape, taking with him High's gun, a hunting rifle. The guards, meantime, broke and ran after their comrades.

Spencer immediately started for New Creek Station, where he arrived in safety with his prize-the gun. He was greeted as the hero of the times, all rejoicing that High's race was run.

STORY XCVIII.

ESCAPE OF LIEUTENANT RAYNOR, OF OHIO, AND OTHERS, FROM RICHMOND.

Mr. Murphy, learning that his wife was in deep distress at his imprisonment, determined to effect his escape, and in concert with Lieutenant Raynor, and Captain Hurd, devised a plan.

They observed that the surgeons were permitted to pass in and out without obstructions, they being distinguished by a bit of red ribbon; and as the sentinels were changed every two hours, they could pass by the guard as surgeons, provided they could get the necessary badge.

Tearing a bit of red flannel from one of their shirts, and putting it on his coat, Lieutenant Raynor passed out without difficulty, and by a previous arrangement, he made a purchase of a pocket compass, and a map of Virginia. Mr. Murphy and Captain Hurd passed out on the next relief, by the same means, and met Lieutenant Raynor on the corner of a neighboring street. This was about eight o'clock.

Their plan was to strike a northeast direction from Richmond, and crossing the Rappahannock, to reach the Potomac, where they expected to reach our fleet. This they successfully accomplished, after great priva tion and suffering, extending through several days, of which the following is a brief narrative:

After going half a mile beyond the city limits, they struck the Union turnpike, which they followed out. Owing to the darkness, they successively ran upon a toll-gate, guarded by soldiers, and a breast-work with cannon, from which they retreated, and succeeded in turning, unperceived, through neighboring fields. They met country wagons, all of which they avoided.

After travelling fifteen miles, as daylight dawned they went to sleep in the woods. At nine o'clock in the morning they resumed their march, keeping in the woods, however. as long as daylight lasted. They eat during the day their only food, a sandwich each, which they had brought with them.

The second night they crossed the Chickahominy river on a mill-dam, and continued their march till day-light, when they reached a large plantation, and nearly encountered a number of negroes going to their work. They succeeded in avoiding them, and continued their journey during the day, crossing the Pamunkey river by means of a raft, which they constructed.

They then built a fire in the woods and made a good meal of roasted corn and potatoes, both of which they had secured in fields on ·their route. During their whole route, the roads frequently took them out of their course; in which case they would abandon them, and guided by their compass would go across the country till they struck another road which suited their destination. Generally, they slept during the day, doing most of their travelling by night, and of course at times suffering terribly from hunger, thirst and insects. On Saturday they succeeded in crossing the bridge over the Mattapony river, without attracting observation.

Their map, of course, was of but little use to them as regarded the details of the country through which they were travelling, and they were at a loss to determine where they were. On one of the roads they came to a country store, on which they discovered by moonlight a notice posted, which they tore off and took with them to the woods.

On lighting a piece of candle, they discovered it to be a notice to the creditors of the late General Garnet, who was killed in Western Virginia, to present their claims at Bowling Green, in Carolina county. This saved them the risk of making personal enquiries as to where they were, which they had determined to do the next morning.

On that night they met a negro in the woods, but they passed by each other without salutation. They were assisted too, by the inspection of a guide-board, and at this point a negro came suddenly upon them unawares, but in a seeming fright ran away. Fearing that he might give the alarm, they ran for a long distance, that they might be beyond the danger of pursuit.

On Wednesday morning, about two o'clock, they reached the Rappahannock where they fortunately found a small boat. Mr. Murphy took off his shoes in passing through a small village near the river, that he might avoid making any noise, and in getting into the boat he accidentally left his shoes on the river bank. This was the occasion of much subsequent suffering, as he had to perform the remainder of the journey barefooted, by which his feet became terribly bruised and swollen.

Having crossed the Rappahannock they started for the Potomac, and had travelled but a short distance when they found themselves upon the margin of a deep swamp, through which they were compelled to wade in mud knee-deep for half a mile. They continued on their course until they came in sight of the Potomac.

They encountered a party of negroes unexpectedly, and were compelled to speak or be subjects of suspicion. They enquired for a boat to carry them across the river, announcing themselves to be Confederate officers, obtained a boat and found one of our vessels, which took them on board, thus ending their perilous and fatiguing journey, their bold, hazardous, and successful adventure from gloomy prison walls to liberty and life.

STORY XCIX.

HOW A BLOCKADE RUNNER WAS CAUGHT.

THE following account of the manner in which a blockade runner was caught, is extracted from an English Magazine, and was probably written by an Englishman; who, with several others, was anxious for a safe passage from Nassau to Dixie.

Finding a steamer about to sail, he inquired of the Captain, "When do you start?" The commander's voice sunk to a whisper, as he told me that at sunset every landsman must come on board, taking boat at some secluded jetty to avoid prying eyes; and using all reasonable caution, since Nassau teamed with Northern spies.

Half an hour after sunset he was to hoist a signal, which was to be replied to; and then the pilot would come off, and the steamer would stand out to sea. "After dark," muttered Pritchard, with an oath, "we may hope to get past that Yankee thief that hangs about the island. The Governor bade her keep at the distance of one marine league, but she's always sneaking in— now for coal, now for bread, now because her engine is out of order; and the United States consul communicates with her every day. I tell you, shipmate, there isn't one of us that isn't dogged up and down by rascals in Federal hire. See there! that mulatto hound has been after me these four days," pointing to a dark-complexioned fellow, in the dress of a stevedore, who, on seeing himself observed, as he stood under the geranium hedge, lay down with well-feigned nonchalance, and lit his pipe.

I found a good deal of quiet bustle and suppressed excitement on board the Bonnybell. The fires were bunked up, the swarthy faces and red shirts of the engineer and his gang, were visible at the hatch of their Cyclopean den, getting a breath of the cool breeze before starting. Some brass guns, that had been hidden under fruit-baskets, hen-coops, and tarpaulins, were visible enough now: and beside them lay piled little heaps of round shot. The crew bustled to and fro, and the Captain was so busy, that he could but return a brief word and a nod to my greeting. The sky grew darker, and surrounding objects dimmer, every instant.

Before long the passengers arrived. Several Southern gentlemen, a few ladies and children, all making their way back from Europe, to their homes in Carolina and Virginia, by this dangerous route; and all in danger of imprisonment at least, if captured.

By the uncertain light, I could see that most of them were pale and nervous: but they talked in an undertone among themselves, and did not appear anxious to converse with strangers.

"Get up steam!" By this time the hoarse roar of the escaping vapor grew loud and menacing, there was a fresh bustle on deck, and I heard the Captain give orders to stand by for slipping from the moorings, and to hoist the signal, as we only waited for the pilot.

"There they are, sleek and right—three red lights, and a green one," murmured a tall Virginian, at my elbow; and looking up, I saw the colored lamps glimmer from the mast head. Instantly, they were answered by a similar signal from some window on shore.

"We'll soon see the pilot now," said Pritchard, rubbing his hands in a cheery manner; "the signal's made and repeated. In ten minutes our man will be with us. Helloa!—boat ahoy!—what d'ye want?"

"Bonneybell ahoy!" was the rejoinder, in a shrill, harsh voice, cautiously lowered for the occasion,— "pilot wants to come on board."

There was a stir, and a start of surprise, among those on deck; and as a rope was thrown down to the boatmen, Captain Pritchard bent over the side, exclaiming:

"You're uncommon quick, my hearty. If you've come from shore since the lights were hoisted, you must be own cousin to the flying Dutchman. Are you sure you're our pilot?"

"I'm the pilot engaged by Colonel Jeremy Carter, of Spottsylvania, if that'll do," answered a very tall, bony, black-haired man, as he actively ascended the side. "Zack Foster's my name, and I know every inch about Charleston where I was raised."

While the Captain—reassured by the mention of Colonel Carter's name—gave hasty orders to cast off the cable and go ahead, I, in common with the rest of the passengers, and the unoccupied portion of the crew, looked with much interest at the new-comer. The latter was about forty years of age, long and lean of figure, with a hardy, sun-burned face. There was no mistaking the resolute air and daring of the man. His mouth was as firm as iron, though a little dry humor seemed to lurk about his lips, and I hardly liked the expression of his half-shut eyes, which had a lazy cunning in their dark glance. Still, though dressed in a black suit of shore-going clothes, and a swallow-tailed coat, of antiquated cut, there was something about Mr. Zack Foster that spoke the thorough-bred seaman.

He took no share in the proceedings, for his duty did not begin till we were clear of Nassau Roadstead; but yet he seemed impatient for the start, gnawing viciously at his quid, and drumming on the taffrail, with a finger that seemed as hard and brown as bronze.

It was an anxious time, when the Bonnybell, under a full head of steam, went darting out of the bay, her lookout straining their eyes to pierce the mist, and give warning to the helmsman of vessels ahead; while Pritchard walked to and fro, too fidgetty and eager to endure conversation, listening every instant for some sound that was to indicate that the Federal cruizer had taken the alarm. But on we went without check or hindrance, and all drew our breath more freely, as the lights of the town, began one by one to vanish, as if the sea had swallowed them, and the dark head-lands faded away into obscurity.

The American gunboat was neither seen nor felt; a circumstance which I did not the less regret, because I perceived, not only by the display of the cannon alluded to, but by the resolute demeanor of several of the crew, who stood grouped about a couple of uncovered arm-chests, that our pigmy foe would not have found an entirely unresisting prize.

One slight circumstance, hardly, as I thought worth mentioning, did occur before we had run half a mile to seaward. There came a long, faint hail, from so great a distance as to be hardly distinguishable, even by a sailor's practiced ear, but which was announced to be addressed to us.

"Some boat, perhaps, with a message for a passenger. The lubbers deserve rope's-ending for being so late— can I lie-to safely, do you think?" said Pritchard to the pilot, irresolutely, and giving the word, "Slacken speed." What the pilot answered I know not. I only caught the concluding phrase—

"Yankee tricks; so Cap you'd best look sharp about you."

So Pritchard thought. He gave the word to go at full speed, and we heard no more about the matter.

The run was speedy and pleasant, over a dimpling summer sea, with no boisterous behavior on Neptune's part, to make even the lady passengers uneasy. We saw several vessels, but none of a hostile character; and the voyage was as agreeable and safe hitherto, as any yachting excursion in holiday waters. We were all disposed to be pleased, and the pilot, although a saturnine and morose personage, viewed through this rose-colored haze of satisfaction and hope, became a popular man on board,

Captain Pritchard pronounced him worth his weight in gold; for if there were no gales, or rough seas to thwart our purpose, fogs were rather frequent, and here the pilot's intimate acquaintance with the rocks, shoals, and islets—many of which were not noted down in the chart—more than once saved the Bonnybell from an ugly thump upon some hidden obstacle.

For an American, Zack Foster was singularly silent; yet there was something elephantine about his high forehead and narrow dark eyes, which suggested shrewdness, rather than vanity. He did his work, answered when spoken to, but seldom addressed any one.

"Land-ho!" sung out the look-out man at the mast-head, and Pritchard and the pilot, who were pouring together over the map, close to the binnacle, looked up, while the passengers edged nearer to hear the news. Pritchard lifted his telescope, while Foster went aloft for a better view!

"LAND-HO!"

"Edisto Island, as I said, Cap!" hailed the pilot; "and beyond it is the Carolina coast. We're close to home, gentlemen and ladies."

There was a cheer from the little group gathered near the helm, but directly afterward came two shrill cries of "sail ho!"

"Uncle Sam's breakers. We must put out a few miles yet, Cap.," said the pilot, as he leisurely descended the rope ladder. There were many good glasses on board, and we all gazed eagerly through them, and with beating hearts we recognised the port-holes, the grinning

cannon, the "star-spangled flags," and warlike display
of the Federal blockading squadron."

The steamer was put about, and we stood further out,
until shore and ships were alike lost to view. The dis-
appointment of the passengers, who had been granted a
mere glimpse of the land, that to them was home, was
considerable; but none could doubt the prudence of de-
laying our entrance into Charleston harbor until night
should assist us in eluding the hostile war vessels.

There was no going to bed on the Bonnybell that
night; we all kept to the deck, gazing eagerly out over
the sparkling and phosphorescent sea, glimmering and
glancing with St. Elmo's fires. There was a pale young
moon—a mere sickle of silver—in the sky; and objects
were so faintly discernible, that the utmost caution was
necessary.

The second mate took the helm, while the first mate
superintended the almost constant heaving of the lead,
and the captain and pilot stood on the forecastle, noting
the replies of the sailor, chaunted, as they were, in a
shrill monotone, in accordance with old custom.

"Ten fathoms, sheer! By the deep, nine! By the
mark, seven!" called out the leadsman from the chains.

"Water allers does shoal here, Cap. I know the
channel, though, as well as I know my parlor ashore,
at Nantucket—at Savannah, I mean," said the pilot,
with some confusion.

"By the mark, five!" was the next call.

Captain Pritchard here grew uneasy. He did not
pretend to equal the pilot in local knowledge, but he
was too good a seaman not to take alarm at the abrupt
lessening of the depth of water. He gave orders to
reduce the speed, and we moved but slowly on, the lead
going as before.
2 C

"Are you sure, Mr. Foster, you're not mistaken? It seems to me the water shoals at the rate of a fathom for every hundred yards traversed. We may have missed the Swash, left Moultrie to leeward, and got into the net-work of sand banks, near. Hilloa! what's that ahead of us? Boats, as I'm a sinner!"

At the same moment the pilot thrust his hand rapidly into the breast of his coat, drew out something, and flung it on the deck, where it instantly began to sputter and hiss, and directly afterward, the livid glare of a blue-light flashed through the darkness, showing funnel and rigging, the pale faces of the passengers, the narrow channel of fretted water, and the sandy islets on either bow.

Nor was this all, for by the ghastly light we could distinguish two dark objects on the foamy sea ahead of us—boats full of men pulling swiftly, but noiselessly toward us, and no doubt with muffled oars.

"By the mark, two!—shoal water—we're aground!" cried an ill-boding voice, that of the sailor in the chains; and the Bonnybell came suddenly to a check, throwing most of the landsmen from their feet, while the ominous scrooping of the keel told that the steamer was aground.

A loud clamor instantly arose—many voices shouting at once, in tones of inquiry, dismay, or command; and even above this turmoil arose the hurrah of those who manned the boats, and who now came dashing up, pulling and cheering like madmen.

"Treachery! treachery!" cried several of the passengers and crew, pointing to where the pilot stood beside the blue-light, that his own perfidious hand had kindled; while already the man-of-war's men, for such we could not doubt them to be, began to scramble on board.

"The Yankee blood-hounds sure enough; but you shall not live to share the prize-money!" exclaimed Pritchard, snatching up a hand-spike, and aiming a blow at Mr. Zack Foster, that would have been a lethal stroke had not that astute person swerved aside, receiving the weapon on his left shoulder.

Our men set up a faint cheer, and a shot was fired, luckily without effect. But resistance would have been madness, so thickly did the American sailors crowd up our gangway, their pistols and cutlasses ready for the fray; while among them were nine or ten marines, well-armed with musket and bayonet, and who drove the Bonnybell's crew below hatches without any serious show of fighting.

The Federal Lieutenant in command, to do him justice, seemed anxious that no needless violence should be used, while proclaiming the vessel a prize to the boats of the United States war-brig Dacotah, he yet restrained the fury of that precious guide, Mr. Zack Foster, who had recovered from the effect of his knock-down blow, drawn a bowie-knife, and rushed upon Pritchard, who was struggling in the hands of his captors.

"Gently, sir," said the Lieutenant; "gently Quartermaster Fitch. These caged birds are under Uncle Sam's protection, and I cannot allow any ill-usage of my prisoners. Do you hear me, sir?"

"Quartermaster!" exclaimed poor Captain Pritchard, as his wrists were thrust into the handcuffs. "You don't mean that double-dyed villain, that Judas of a pilot, is a Yankee petty officer after all? I wish I'd only guessed the truth a few hours back, and—if I swung for it—I'd have chucked the spy overboard as I would a mangy puppy."

The Lieutenant made no answer, but ordered the Captain and mates sent below, and proceeded at once to seize the steamer's papers, to place the passengers under arrest, and to take steps to get the Bonnybell off the sand-bank.

He then compelled the ngineer to set the machinery at work, and we ran down, under the skillful pilotage of Mr. Fitch, to Edisto Island, in which anchorage we came to our moorings under the guns of the Dacotah, and within a short distance of several other vessels of the blockading squadron.

STORY C.

ESCAPE FROM LIBBY PRISON.

EARLY in December, 1863, the Union officers confined in Libby Prison conceived the idea of effecting their escape; and after the matter had been seriously discussed by a few of them, they undertook to tunnel out, by commencing operations in the cellar, near a chimney; the cellar being under the hospital, and used as a receptacle of straw, thrown from the beds when changed, and for other refuse matter.

Those who were in the secret improvised a rope, and by removing a few stones from the chimney, nightly let working parties down into the cellar, who from thence prosecuted their projected excavation, hiding the dirt under the straw, after tramping it down, so as not to attract observation.

As the work progressed, a spittoon from the officer's room with a string attached was used for hauling the dirt out, as filled by the digger, and returned empty by similar means.

After digging several feet with fingers, knives and chisels, the workers were stopped by piles driven in the ground, at least a foot in diameter. Undismayed, however, by this obstacle, such knives as were to be had were put in requisition, and after a tedious and laborious operation, a passage was effected through them, and then in a few moments the tunnels reached the sewer.

But here, the stench of the sewers, and the flow of filthy water, proved an insurmountable obstacle to men whom neither earth nor wood could check, and the project in that direction was necessarily abandoned.

Communicating their failure to others, a party of seventeen, after viewing the premises and surroundings, concluded to tunnel under Carey street, on the opposite side of which was a carriage house, under which they proposed to emerge. There was a high fence around it, the guard being on the outside of it. The prisoners then commenced digging on the other side of the chimney, but were soon stopped by a stone wall three feet thick. Knives were again called into requisition, by the diligent use of which, nineteen days and nights upon the mortar, enabling them to remove the stones, a passage through the wall was effected, and excavation resumed on the other side.

After digging some days it was thought the point must be nearly reached for coming out : and to test the matter, Captain Gallagher, of the 2d Ohio regiment, under pretence of having a box in the carriage house, for which he wished to search, (that place being the receptacle for goods sent the prisoners from the North,) was permitted to go, under guard, to the carriage house; and in passing paced the distance as well as he could, without exciting suspicion, and concluded that the street was about fifty feet in width.

On the 6th or 7th of February, concluding they had gone far enough, the workers commenced digging upward, when hearing the guards talking above them, they found that they were yet a few feet outside the fence. A small hole was made up through the surface of the ground by the falling in of a stone, the noise of which was heard by a sentinel, who asking his comrade what it meant, they after listening awhile concluded it was rats, and proceeded on their beats. The hole was stopped with an old pair of pantaloons filled with straw, and supported by boards brought from the prison.

The tunnel was then continued six or seven feet further, and feeling assured that there was no further impediment to their emerging into daylight, the working party informed others in the prison that there was a way open for escape. One hundred and nine of them decided to make the attempt. Others, fearing the consequences of recapture, declined.

On the evening of the 9th of February, about half-past eight o'clock, the prisoners started out, Colonel Rose, of New York, leading the van. Before going out they had divided themselves into squads of two, three, and four, and each squad was to take a different route, after getting out, and to push for the Union lines.

The aperture was so narrow, that but one man could go out at a time, and each squad carried provisions with them in a haversack. Colonel W. P. Kendrick, of West Tennessee, Captain D. J. Jones, of the 1st Kentucky Cavalry, and Lieutenant R. Y. Bradford, of the 2d West

Tennessee, were to go out last, and from a window could see the fugitives walk out at a gate at the other end of the inclosure, and walk fearlessly away.

The street-lamps were extinguished between one and two o'clock, when the exit was more safely accomplished. At half past two, Captain Jones, Colonel Kendrick, and Lieutenant Bradford passed out in the order named; and as Colonel K. emerged from the hole, he heard the guard within a few feet of him, sing out "Post No. 7, half past two, in the morning, and all's well!" Once out, they proceeded up the street, keeping in the shade of the buildings, and passed eastwardly through the city.

The route through which Colonel Kendrick, and those of his party passed, and the hardships they endured, it will be necessary to state but briefly: Keeping the York River road to the left, and moving toward the Chickahominy River, they passed through Bear Swamp, and crossed the road leading to Bottom Bridge.

Sometimes they waded through mud and water, almost up to their necks, keeping the Bottom Bridge road to the left. While passing through the swamp near the Chickahominy, Colonel Kendrick sprained his ancle and fell; and while lying there, he looked up and saw in a direct line with them, a swamp bridge and parties passing over it with muskets.

They therefore moved further south, and passing through more of the swamp, reached the Chickahominy, about four miles below Bottom Bridge. Here was a difficulty. The river, though but twenty feet wide, was very deep, and the refugees much fatigued. Chancing, however, to look up, Lieutenant Bradford saw that two trees on opposite sides of the river, had fallen so that their branches were interlocked across the stream; when, by going up one tree and down the other, the fugitives soon reached the east bank of the Chickahominy.

They subsequently learned from a friendly negro, that if they had crossed the bridge they had seen, they would assuredly have been recaptured; for Captain Turner, the keeper of the Libby prison, had been out and posted guards there, and had alarmed the inhabitants, and organized them as a vigilance committee to capture the escaped prisoners.

After crossing over this natural bridge, they laid down on the ground and slept until sunrise on the morning of the 11th, when they continued on their way, as near eastwardly as they could. Having eaten nothing up to this time, they were almost famished; for, as should have been stated, Lieutenant Bradford, who had charge of the haversack for this squad, had been compelled to leave it in the tunnel, from the narrowness of the passage. About noon they met some negroes, who informed them as to where the Rebel pickets were, and also gave them some food.

By advice of the negroes, they remained in the woods until night, when the negroes furnished them a supper, after which they proceeded on their way, having been first directed how to avoid the Rebel pickets.

At one point they met a negro woman, who told them that her mistress was a Secesh woman, and that she had a son in the Rebel army. The party, however, being exceedingly hungry, determined to secure some food. This they did by boldly approaching the house, and informing the mistress that they were fugitives from Norfolk, who had been driven out by Butler, when the Secesh sympathies of the woman were at once aroused; and she ministered to their necessities, and started them on their way, with instructions how to avoid the Yankee soldiers, who occasionally scouted in that vicinity

This information was exceedingly valuable to the refugees, as by it they discovered the position of the Union forces. When about fifteen miles from Williamsburg they came upon the main road, and found the tracks of a large party of cavalry. A piece of paper found by Captain Jones, satisfied him that they were Union cavalry; but his companions were suspicious, and avoided the road, and moved on to the "burnt ordinary" where they awaited the return of the cavalry, and from behind a fence corner, where they were secreted, the fugitives saw the flag of the Union, supported by a squadron of cavalry, which proved to be a detachment of Colonel Spear's 11th Pennsylvania regiment, sent out for the purpose of picking up escaped prisoners, as Colonel Straight had ere this, with a number of other fugitive officers, reached Yorktown.

The party rode into Williamsburg with the cavalry; where they were quartered for the night, and where they found eleven others who had escaped safely, and where they were furnished by Colonel Spear and his command with clothing and other necessaries.

At all points along the route, the fugitives were enthusiastically received by the negroes, and there was no lack of white people who sympathized with them and helped them on their way.

Of the one hundred and nine who left the prison, Rebel authorities subsequently claimed to have recaptured forty-three, and sixty are known to have arrived within our lines in safety; leaving but six unaccounted for; most of whom it was hoped would yet come in, as the Rebel scouts had given up the pursuit.

Colonel Straight of the 51st Indiana Volunteers, and Captain II. B. Chamberlain of the 97th New York Volunteers, after leaving the prison took a northeasterly course, and halted at four o'clock, on the morning of the 10th of February, in a dense wood close by the Chickahominy swamps, and remained the next day. At dark they started again on their journey, crossing the Chickahominy on a fallen tree, and got into a dense thicket, and accomplished only five miles. The third night they started again, steering for the Pamunkey River. The detours they had to make to keep under cover of the woods, and traversing swamps, took them till daylight to reach midway between the Chickahominy and Pamunkey. Next night they reached the Pamunkey ten miles above the White House. The river was up—deep, dangerous and cold—swimming it impracticable.

After four day's delay a negro took them across in a boat—another negro piloted them down the river, fifteen miles, they reached York River, got across in a skiff, reached Yorktown on the 21st and Fortress Monroe the 24th of February.

the long roll for the 32d Michigan, was the subject and centre of attraction.

At Chickamauga he had served as "marker," carrying the guidon, by means of which the lines are formed —a duty similar to that of the surveyor's flag-man, who flutters a red signal along the metes and bounds.

On the Sunday of the battle—the little fellow's occupation gone, he picked up a gun that had slipped from some dying hand, provided himself with ammunition, and began putting in the periods, quite on his own account; blazing away close to the ground, like a fire-fly in the grass.

Late in the waning day, the waif, left almost alone in the whirl of the battle, a Rebel Colonel dashed up, and looking down at him, ordered him to surrender. "Surrender!" he shouted. The word was scarcely out of his mouth, when Johnny brought his piece to "order," and as his hand slipped down to the hammer, he pressed it back, swung his gun up to the position of "charge bayonet," and as the officer raised his sabre to strike it aside, the glancing barrel lifted into range, and the proud Colonel fell dead from his horse.

A few swift moments ticked on by musket-shots, and the tiny gunner was swooped up and borne away captive by the Rebels. Soldiers bigger, but not better were taken with him, only to be swept back again, by a surge of Federal troops, and the prisoner of thirty minutes was John Clem, "of ours" again, and General Rosecrans made him a Sergeant, and the stripes of rank covered him all over, like a mouse in harness; and the daughter of Mr. Secretary Chase presented him a silver medal, appropriately inscribed, which he worthily wears, a royal order of honor, upon his left breast; and all men conspire to spoil him, but since few ladies can get at him here, perhaps he may be saved.

But, what about last night? Well, like Flora McFlimsey, the Sergeant had "nothing to wear;" the clothing in the wardrobe of loyal livery was not at all like Desdemona's handkerchief, "too little," but like the garments of the man who roamed over a baker's oven, "a world too wide," and so Miss Babcock, of the Sanitary Commission, suggested to a friend, that a uniform for the little Orderly would be acceptable.

Mr. Waite, and other gentlemen of the "Sherman House," order it; Messrs. A. D. Titsworth & Co., made it; Chaplain Raymond brought it; Miss Babcock presented it; and Johnny put it on. Chaplain Raymond, of the 51st Illinois, by the by, a most earnest and efficient officer, accompanied the gift with exceedingly appropriate suggestions and advice.

This morning we happened at the headquarters just as the belted and armed Sergeant was booted and spurred, and ready to ride. Resplendent in his elegant uniform, rigged cap-a-pie, modest, frank, with a clear eye and a manly face, he looked more like a fancy picture than a living thing.

Now he is in his thirteenth year, yet he would be no monster if called but nine. Think of a sixty-three pound Sergeant—fancy a handful of a hero, and then read the "Arabian Nights," and believe them! Long live the little Orderly!

www.ingramcontent.com/pod-product-compliance
Lightning Source LLC
Chambersburg PA
CBHW020938030726
47496CB00005B/1248